AMEX:NLN

Coming in 2006 from

PRESS

Why waste your time reading blogs of boring people? An imprisoned dictator has so much more to say.

Finally! A collegiate edition of sophomoric jokes. Didactic and scholarly analysis included... FREE!

Also coming this fall,

Favorite Cartoons of the 21st Century
A brand new collection of cartoons from the next generation of cartoonists.

National Lampoon's Not Fit For Print
All the stuff that's too vile and too tasteless for us to publish anywhere else. Guaranteed to offend.

A brand new collection of True Facts
Funny-but-true. Absurd-but-true. Disturbing-but-true. They're all here.

togatv.com

dotcom

On The Cover... Nicole Bennett
Photography by... Jeremy Montemagni

Published by National Lampoon Press

National Lampoon, Inc. • 8228 Sunset Boulevard • Los Angeles • California • 90046 • USA • AMEX:NLN

NATIONAL LAMPOON, NATIONAL LAMPOON PRESS and colophon are trademarks of National Lampoon

The magazine rack / edited by Jay Naughton and MoDMaN
foreword by Pete Cummin. -- 1st ed.

p. cm.

ISBN 0-977871-800 - $17.95

Book Design and Production by
JK NAUGHTON

Art direction by
MoDMaN

PRINTED IN THE UNITED STATES OF AMERICA

1   3   5   7   9   10   8   6   4   2

JUNE 2006

WWW.NATIONALLAMPOON.COM

pg. 33

pg. 105

THING. WE...MUST...CON-VERT...THEM. GET...THE ...SANDWICHES...READY.

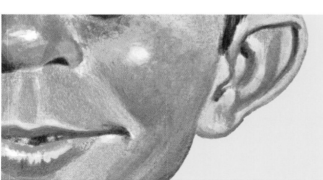

pg. 53

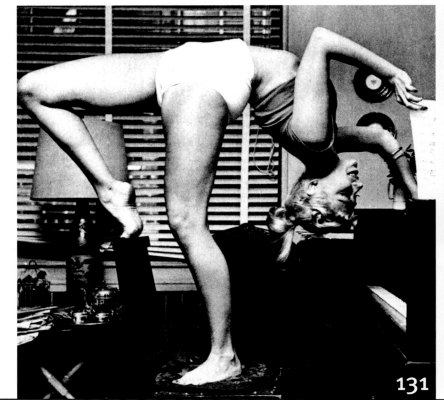

131

125

pg. 177

pg. 191

MAGAZINES ARE FUN.

The magazine parody is an art form long rooted in National Lampoon's history. For it was the success of *Harvard Lampoon's* 1969 parody of Time magazine that first convinced publisher Matty Simmons to put his faith in three of those *Lampooners* – Henry Beard, Doug Kenney and Rob Hoffman – and launch the National Lampoon in April of 1970.

Even before the magazine's first issue, the editors knew that if they knew one thing, they knew three. One, as a magazine, National Lampoon had the unique ability to mimic other magazines completely, from their writing and artwork right down to graphics and layout. Two, since everyone was familiar with these other publications, making fun of them would be as easy as standing on a chair at Thanksgiving and mocking your Uncle Harold's cough. Three, if done correctly, parody can be cruel AND fun.

> **"The second most important paper product in any bathroom is toilet paper. The first is a good magazine."**
> – William Randolph Hearst*

For 35 years now, every publication from Playboy to Ladies' Home Journal has had a bull's-eye on its cover, courtesy of National Lampoon. This book includes 23 parodies, published between 1971 and 2004, in either the magazine or, more recently on the National Lampoon website.

The parodies are divided into five sections: News, Kids, Men's, Women's and Special Interest. Introducing each section is a quote* from legendary publishing tycoon and former Harvard Lampoon editor, William Randolph Hearst. Also, before each parody you'll find a brief description of the magazine being parodied and a quote* referring to it from a well-known public figure.

Why the important quotes from important people? I'm not even going to answer that. Let's just say, as a society, magazines help bind us (ha! ha! a little publishing humor) and, as Benjamin Franklin once said, "If millions of people are familiar with your subject, then thousands will get the reference and hundreds will get the joke. This is parody gold. Now where are my damn eye glasses?"*

One last note, please remember that a lot of this material was created by guys who went to Harvard, so if you don't find yourself laughing, chances are, it's your fault.

[signature]

* Please, it's parody. To actually get real quotes from these people would have required real work which defeats the purpose of publishing a compilation book in the first place.

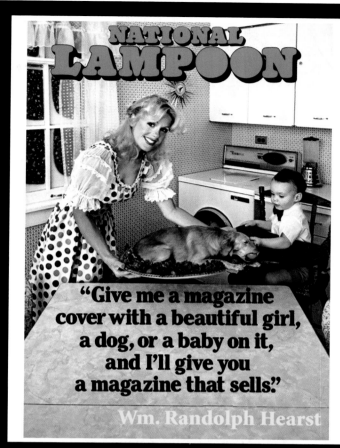

"Give me a magazine cover with a beautiful girl, a dog, or a baby on it, and I'll give you a magazine that sells."

Wm. Randolph Hearst

Our Annual Swimsuit Issue

APRIL 1983 · THE HUMOR ... OR ADULTS · $2.00

Swimwear supermodel Christie Brinkley on location, in front of a backdrop in Manhattan

"News is what I say it is. Unless it is a parody of news, and then it is what someone claims I said it was, so as to get a laugh at my expense. I should buy those persons and turn them into tiki lamps."

– William Randolph Hearst.

NEWS

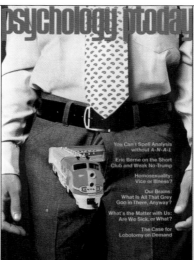

CONSUMER REPORTS

Consumer Reports began publishing in 1936, courtesy of the Consumers Union, a non-profit group featuring "unbiased" test results of cars, appliances and assorted brand-name products. Unsullied by advertising, *Consumer Reports* still enjoys a spotless reputation, thanks to a unique grading system of red dots, black dots and half-dots that help us differentiate the Rolls Royces from the Yugos.

This parody first appeared June 2004 on NationalLampoon.com.

"I have a bone to pick with *Consumer Reports*. Last year they rated my erection capabilities an ●. This is only true if I've been drinking heavily. Usually, I'm an ◒ and on some mornings, especially if I really need to pee, I'm as high as an ◓."

– Bob Dole, 1996 Republican Presidential Nominee and Viagra pitchman, 1998.

Consumed Reports

FLU OR ANTHRAX

WEAPONS of MASS DESTRUCTION

BEST IF USED ON OR BEFORE NOV. 04

Suitcase Nukes

perfect for summer travel

Botulism Toxin A-6

The contemporary terrorist has long asked: "Can't I have my weapons of mass destruction without all that messy...well, destruction?"

It's just this concern addressed by Botulism Toxin A-6, $72.95 per test tube, by Johnson & Johnson. Biological weapons akin to Botulism are quickly becoming the choice of the insurrectionist Gen-Y'rs across the globe—our CR testers found plenty of reasons why.

The Test

Three strains of botulism currently exist: food-borne botulism, wound botulism and rare and pricey boutique toxin infant botulism, which only grow in the intestines of the innocent. All three forms of botulism are extremely fatal and not to be trifled with—so the joy of Toxin A-6, which successfully cultivates all three strains in one ultra-light test tube container, was the talk of the CR offices for a week.

▶ Chemical Agent CX-Phosgene-D

▶ Happy Sunshine Thermonuclear Device

The Results

Our eager testing unit took A-6 for a test drive at a local mall food court, waiting to get mouthed off by some teenagers. When two test subjects presented themselves—informing us that our lab coats looked "gay" and were "for fags"—our team gave each of their Arby's roast beef sandwiches a liberal A-6 dousing while CR Tester Phillips distracted the pair with improv rap. CR is pleased to report the almost immediate appearance of double vision, blurred vision, drooping eyelids, slurred speech, difficulty swallowing, dry mouth, and muscle weakness. Other botulism symptoms such as lethargy, poor muscle tone and constipation were difficult to measure, given the test subjects and the fact that they were eating at Arby's. Nonetheless, CR feels confident in making Botulism Toxin A-6 a Consumed Reports Best Buy. Deadly to the last drop.

Fendi Mother/Daughter Handbag Detonation Kit

Terrorism might be off-limits for the fairer sex in Afghanistan. But in progressive America, many determined women have sent a message to police and international authorities: "Hey, we're just as capable of sprinting thirty pounds of explosive ordinance into a crowded subway as a man—and we can still look good doing it."

Fendi responds with the Fendi Mother/Daughter Handbag Detonation Kit line of ready-made dirty bombs for only $1,400 each, perfect for the working mother on the go juggling the kids' soccer practice with sending a message to Congress etched in the blood of massively detonated innocents. Now moms can combine both activities through this classic, hand-sewn handbag/children's backpack combo, embalzoned with all the hottest toy brands your little one's been dying to get their hands on.

Each combo is packed with a generous key-charge of Composition B and just a whisper of cesium isotope 12, enabling this briefcase bomb to spread radioactive material to a blast radius usually reserved for the big-league terrorist players.

The Test

Consumed Reports tested this product in-house during a Bring Your Daughter To Work day, detonating twelve office floors and spreading clouds of radiation that poisoned, scorched and sterilized any remaining survivors. A timely summer breeze then carried the carnage to our neighboring office for a further 180-person body count, with nearly 60 more reporting critically injuries and radioactive bowel implosion. That's not just impressive—at only $1,400 per combo, that's value.

Ratings

weapons of mass destruction

- ◉ excellent
- ◕ very good
- ○ good
- ◑ fair
- ● poor

	WEAPON	PRICE	SCORE	DESTRUCTION			EASE OF TRANSPORT	
				Avg Deaths Caused	Panic Score	Collateral Damage	Size	Launch Capability
❶	CX-Phosgene D	$1500	▭	◉	◕	◉	◉	◉
❷	Botulism Toxin A-6	$73	▭	◕	◉	◕	◉	●
❸	HFTSD Nuclear Weapon	$14M	▭	◉	◉	◉	◉	●
❹	Fendi Mother/Daughter Kit	$1400	▭	◕	◕	○	◉	◕
❺	x-130 Grenade Helmet	$28	▭	◉	◑	◕	◉	○
❻	Boeing 757	$850,000	▭	◕	◕	○	●	◕

Product Review

The Results

Fendi's Mother/Daughter Handbag Detonation Kit is an inspiring lesson to terrorists that you don't have to exclude your family from the things you feel passionate about. What's left of our CR testing team immediately went home after the assessment and spent a little quality time with the kids—mixing homemade nitroglycerin, rigging deadly traps in the back yard and filling up bottles with gasoline and schrapnel

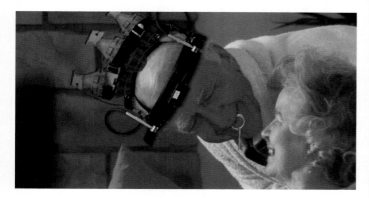

X-130 Grenade Helmet

You've seen them on the news and on the runway. It's a trend of these modern times that ask you to not only do your job, but look good doing it. But recent trends have emphasized fashion over function (100% Cotton High-Density Explosive Polar Fleece Pullovers, $28 by Old Navy being the latest example). Today's terrorist is more and more letting manufacturers know: "When I strap 24 lbs of high-grade Petrolan B explosive to my chest and run onto a Tel Aviv bus, making a stylish fashion statement isn't my primary concern."

This winter's release of x-130 Grenade Helmets, $28 by Bombardier, responds to this need: it's ugly. It's odd-looking. And it's effective. Fitted with three MarkII-A1 fragmentation grenades with M10A3 fuses, the x-130 makes up for its ungainly appearance with a lightweight aluminum alloy casing and a combined blast of over 3000 potentially lethal serrated cast iron fragments upon explosion. Best of all, the x-130 is custom-made for the tinkerer. The manual helpfully suggests doubling the destructive power of the Grenade Helmet by putting ball bearings in one's mouth or duct taping aerosol spray cans to the thighs. "You're only limited by your creativity," says one Bombardier representative.

The Test

Using our testing subjects in Baghdad, immediate results were highly favorable. Upon receiving their models, the Bathist militants were impressed with their lightweight design and non-chafing chin straps. One tester noted "It is unbelievably light. Do I even have it on? Ha ha." He then shoveled a handful of ball bearings into his mouth and paused to look in the rearview mirror of our humvee.

"Duh I luh sihlly ih thih? I huhp I duhn luh sihlly," he worried. We gave him several compliments until his spirits rose and, smiling broadly, he happily sprinted into a US motorcade.

The Results

These helmets made quite a stir—first from soldiers doubled over with laughter, then from survivors cursing the names of Saddam Hussein and Bombardier when the helmet exploded, killing 6 soldiers and injuring 34. While some flaws were apparent—designed for one-time-only use, the x-130 is predictably light on extras such as handy pockets or pouches—the x-130 is nonetheless a definitive statement of utility over style. A Consumed Reports Best Buy.

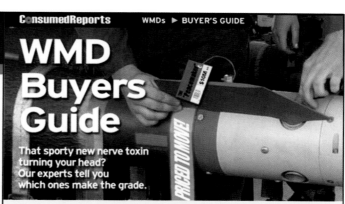

WMD Buyers Guide

That sporty new nerve toxin turning your head? Our experts tell you which ones make the grade.

"Never rush into any weapons purchase," explains Professor Steven Mancuso of the University of Michigan. "Conventional, WMD, or otherwise. In the game of large-scale population slaughter, timing is half the battle." (The other half, of course, is murdering people.)

Professor Mancuso offers these tips for the discerning buyer:

Keep Your Eye on the Market

The smart weapons buyer always has an eye on the status of a product's real value as opposed to its indexed price. Remain educated on radioactive half-lives and the latest advances in missile propulsion. When at pay-at-purchase retailers, never pay more than fair market value for black market nerve toxins and "missing" Soviet warheads.

Forget About Banks

The best source for financing your mass destructive needs has never been conventional lenders. Who needs the hassle of credit checks, interest rates, or actually paying the money back? You're better off seeking "charitable organizations" interested in your political cause.

Consumed Reports Best Bets include: Al-Haramain Islamic Foundation in Saudi Arabia, the Palestinian Liberation Organiz-ation in the West Bank, and the National Right to Life Committee in Washington, DC.

When in Doubt, Read the Newspaper

Knowing how to read the up-to-date events of violent geopolitical discourse can help the informed consumer know the best available options available in the global arms markets.

When a strain of anthrax is found in mailers to government officials, the commodity value of wholesale anthrax goes down as law enforcement and security agencies actively search for sources and suspects, instantly creating a buyer's market as inventory becomes priced to move.

When bartering for better prices, make sure weapons are pointed away from you.

Gun shows are breeding grounds for militia groups, where a Lynyrd Skynyrd compliment can go a long way.

Keep an eye out for garage sales. Often owners will be happy to get rid of it all.

Consumed Reports

Reader MAIL

With Consumed Reports'
Acclaimed Weapons
Correspondent &
International Terorrorist
**ABDELKARIM
MOHAMED AL-NASSER**

THIS WEEK'S TOPIC:
WEAPONS CONCEALMENT

Any true connoisseur of weapons of mass destruction is naturally a big fan of Saddam Hussein. As with any of the all-time greats, of course, they eventually lose the spark that made us watch out for them as young rookies with something to prove. Saddam's empire was decimated by a regimen of international sanctions, bombings, and two major wars. But whatever his downfall, no one could deny: more than any other dictator in his field, that man could hide a weapon.

This month I'll be responding to your letters about proper weapons concealment techniques, and sharing the Consumed Reports test results of several exciting new products that might help you conceal them. Also, my regular readers should note that the Pose Your Favorite Goat With Your Favorite Weapons photo contest is still running. Some of the entries I've seen so far have been truly heartwarming. Don't forget to send yours in soon—contest ends July 20th!

Dear Abdelkarim Mohamed Al-Nasser,

Longtime reader, first-time writer! I am a twenty something despot of a fledgling rogue nation not yet on the radar screen of international terror. I followed your advice in the December 2003 issue about using the bodies of my citizens as camoflauge for my weapons to distract peacekeeping forces. Sadly, however, the population of Blujikistan is still quite small. Between the famine, riots, and my secret police, I find I am quickly running out of bodies. What can I do?

Ibrahim Al-Mughassil

Dear Ibrahim,

I asked around the CS offices, and it turns out you're in luck. DDC Plastics has a very affordable line of products with the start-up rogue nation in mind. Our Consumed Reports testers tell me their new line of Armament Amigo Civilian Human Shield Dummies (1,500 p/half-dozen) will be on sale this fall, and they're worth keeping an eye out for.

Each dummy is individually contoured in high grade vinyl and can be affixed via a sophisticated 7-point Velcro locking system to the exteriors of missile silos, biological weapons labs, or nearly any other recognized military target as set out by the Geneva Accords. Each doll also has fully poseable hands with five distinct points of articulation, allowing you to pose them amusingly during peacetime.

After a three week test period, our statistical analysis showed the Amigo to be nearly indistinguishable from living humans when viewed in satellite photos or from stealth recon planes. As weapon accessories go, the Armament Amigo offers a certain style and flair to military defense that is sorely lacking in the current market, while its function provides a peace of mind that should bolster your confidence while boosting your credibility in the international community. Thanks for writing, and good luck with the famine!

Dear Abdelkarim Mohamed Al-Nasser,

After months of tedious negotiation with Russian dissidents, I finally procured a warhead with the proper specs to meet even the highest standards of international threat constitution. Now I find that mere days after my chemical warfare program has come to fruition, I have UN weapons inspectors requesting entrance into my country. My advisors assure me the stockpiles of Chloropicrin will be safe in the Imperial Palace's backyard shed, but I remain unconvinced. How can I ensure that my stockpile of illegal neurotoxins, infectious hemorrhagic agents and nuclear warheads is safe from prying eyes?

Muhammad Atef

Dear Muhammad,

Your answer may come in the of the form of the new Pediatric Warden Model False-Bottomed Children's Hospital, $846,000, the latest in Cabot Construction's line of WMD storage accessories. Manufacturer statistics showed a 79% success rate in deceiving assistants to United Nations weapons inspector Hans Blix as a genuine radiology center, despite its function of housing up to 7,000 cubic liters of the most ungodly weaponry imaginable in a dry, climate controllable subterranean storage facility. These numbers average a full 33% above those of commonly used alternatives, like the garage, or a solitary shed in the woods. This is also an 11% improvement over its Series A predecessor, which did not come licensed for surgical operations in Canada.

The Pediatric Warden is tough to beat, though if you find yourself strapped for the finances to obtain it, there are still several avenues available to you. My readers are always sending me inventive and cost-effective methods of weapons concealment. Sandra-Mae Finch from Arkansas, for instance, got rid of nosy police poking into her chemical weapons stockpiles on her compound. Her solution? Decorate flowers and an adorable snout (right). As Sandra-Mae proves, you needn't always break the bank to obtain firstrate camouflage for your illegal weapons stockpiles. Sandra-Mae is still, of course, a painted whore in the lands of the Great Satan—though I hope you'll agree that when we slay every American with the sword between our hands through the spirit of the Great Prophet Muhammad Bin-'Abdallah, it would be wise to torture her first for her con-

cealment secrets, many of which are admittedly precious.

Once again it would seem I am out space. Next month I will be answering your questions about U.S. Embassies abroad: should we still be attacking them, or is it too five minutes ago? I look forward to your letters. Until next month, this is Abdelkarim, telling you not to smite any infidels I wouldn't smite.

END

TRUE CRIME

True Crime magazine was founded in 1924. Its factual tales of real murders helped to expose society's filthy underbelly for what it truly was: quality entertainment. Throughout the 30's and 40's the 'true crime' genre continued to flourish with its detective stories and pulp fiction paperbacks, before eventually declining in the 1950's. However, thanks to the power of television, shows like *America's Most Wanted, Unsolved Mysteries* and *CSI: Anywhere* remind us once again that other people's heartbreaking tragedy can be fun stuff.

This parody first appeared in the September 1975 issue of National Lampoon.

"When I was ten, my friends used to stare at the African tribeswomen pictured in *National Geographic*. 'Not me,' I'd say. 'It takes my mother's skirt and a *True Crime* story about a grisly unsolved murder in the Northwest to get my soldier at attention.'"

– J. Edgar Hoover, Director, FBI, 1968.

BUXOM MOM OF 5 UNMASKED AS LAUNDROMAT OVERLOADER!

Citizen's Arrest

THE MAGAZINE OF AMERICA'S 218,000,000 CRIME FIGHTERS WITHOUT GUNS

AUGUST 1975   50¢

Bee-line
Biscuit Co.

Leonard Bryson, President

The Case of the Brazen Blonde:
She Opened Her Boss' Mail— and Wound Up in Jail!

"I'LL NEVER CATCH ME ALIVE!"
CAN A CITIZEN ARREST HIMSELF?

HOW TO MAKE A "POST NO BILLS" PINCH STICK

"MY OWN MONGOLOID BABY —A LITTERBUG!"

"I'LL NEVER TAKE ME ALIVE!"
*The citizen who arrested himself—
and escaped!* p. 38

COLLARING FIDO & FRIENDS
*Alert citizen sends licenseless
mutts to the doghouse!* p. 39

**THE CASE OF THE JAYWALKING
GERIATRIC**
*Our senior citizens aren't immune
to Citizen's Arrest!* p. 41

Citizen's Arrest
MAGAZINE
"Official Journal of America's 218,000,000 Crimefighters Without Guns"

AUGUST 1975

THIS MONTH:

CITIZEN'S ARREST is published by 21ST CENTURY COMMUNICATIONS CORP., 635 Madison Ave., New York, N.Y. 10022. © Copyright 1975. All letters and manuscripts, solicited or unsolicited, may be used as evidence in civil and/or criminal proceedings against the author. Sending unsolicited material with inadequate return postage constitutes interstate littering, and violators will be prosecuted. The publisher is immune to arrest for negligence in the loss of manuscripts, photographs, etc., unless sender provides proof of transmission in the form of a postal receipt. Readers are urged to be alert for unauthorized reproductions of material in CITIZEN'S ARREST and are warned that failure to report same may constitute a violation of the law.

LETTERS

Dear Sir:

I'm fed up to here (my right forefinger is resting on my adam's apple) with all this so-called "no-fault" nonsense. Everything is somebody's fault, and people who are at fault should be arrested, by vigilant U.S. citizens where necessary, and prosecuted to the fullest extent of the law.

Vernon T. Purtell
Chaise Lounge, Mich.

Vernon—You're right as rain! And for openers, how's about turning yourself over to the nearest citizen for violating Sec. 1156 of the Michigan Civil Code in that you did "counsel noncompliance to a valid statute of the State of Michigan," namely, their recently enacted no-fault law!—Managing Editor. (We regret that Editor Bill Gwathmey will be unable to answer this month's letters as he is currently under office arrest for creating an unsanitary condition in his wastebasket.)

Dear Editor,

My pet collie has been intercepting my newspaper and transporting it across my property line for several years. It suddenly occurred to me that this might constitute harboring a felon or some sort of accessory charge on my part. Of course, the paper is delivered by hand and not mail, but I'm still worried.
Todd C. Bettner
Cabstand, Ill.

Todd—Sounds to me like you're mighty close to a minor infraction. The collie is clearly "seizing or causing to be seized a thing of value" and is wide open to literally hundreds of counts of "transporting stolen goods" to boot. Since he hasn't yet been charged, you're off the hook on "assisting a fugitive," but judging from your postmark you have "had reason to believe a misdemeanor had occurred" for nearly a week now, and if you're still feeding him and providing him with "an abode or other domicile, temporary or permanent," you're in hot water. While you're at it, trace back that chain of delivery. If it's the usual case of a kid on a bicycle, you probably have littering violations and numerous counts of operating a vehicle for a commercial purpose without a license right under your nose. It'll go easier with you if you do your duty pronto.—Managing Editor

Dear Editor,

Congrats on "Loose Lips Get Pink Slips" (C/A, Dec. 1974) and plain talk on citizen apprehension of would-be hijackers in airport waiting rooms. I have Xeroxed this article and distributed it to the entire staff of my local laundry and drycleaning chain.
Milton C. Sweetfoot, Jr.

Milton—Reproducing all or part of a copyrighted article without written consent is an offense. We only hope one of your laundry employees reads this and takes the step that will force you to "come clean."—Managing Editor

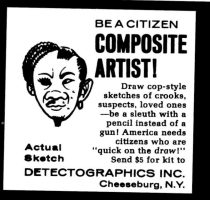

Chamber of Horrors: An ordinary living room is transformed into a one-way ticket up the river during a party. Clockwise from top: painting affixed to wall with nonregulation hanging materials threatens lives and limbs of partygoers; failure to inspect identification of possible underage guest leaves host open to alcoholic beverage violation; bulbs of excess wattage over maximum ratings constitute negligent maintenance of a hazardous condition; overloaded ashtray, even without mishap, is in contravention of fire codes— spilling of ashtray subjects guests to civil endangerment, and as hostess rushes to kitchen for rag to clean up mess, she compounds the infraction by leaving the scene of an accident; host good-naturedly claps guest on back— gesture could be construed as 15th degree assault if recipient takes it amiss; host has prepared hors d'oeuvres and served same, but he lacks food service inspection certificate and washrooms do not have clearly posted signs instructing host and hostess to wash hands before leaving room; presence of unleashed pet in room is breach of sanitary regulation—if his shots and treatments aren't up-to-date, the offense is a great deal more serious. In addition, host, in giving directions to his house, indicated route which included legally closed road; front and back doors of house are not accredited egresses; and gasoline in cars of guests in driveway exceeds amount which may be stored in residential area without a permit.

CHAMBER OF HORRORS:

HE BEGGED HER TO SLEEP ON A CRIME!

Her honeymoon suite was about to become a hotbed of evil—would Jody win her race against shame?

Vinnie: He broke the law just for kicks.

A True Case History from the Files of <u>Citizen's Arrest</u> Magazine

Jody: Her horrified scream came too late.

"**L**et's hit the hay!" Vinnie's suddenly husky voice jarred Jody's reverie as she perched demurely on the edge of the bed in their little honeymoon cabin. He was already starting to loosen his white-on-white silk tie.

"Ship!" A curse escaped Vinnie's lips. "Dropped a mommafumpin' cufflink under the copstruckin' bed!" He bent to retrieve the ornament while Jody's nervous fingers fiddled with the latch of her cosmetic case. The hair on his naked back was like black tumbleweed, Jody thought, an unwelcome shiver of near repugnance passing through her. Love should be in her heart on this magic wedding night, Jody knew. But what she felt was more like panic. Panic—and fear. Maybe her girl friends back in Cannonsburg, Pa. had been right, whispering about Vinnie. Jody had laughed off their warnings as mere jealous carping at her catch. But now . . . well, maybe he was a "torpedo," maybe Italian boys from South Philadelphia were as rough as her girl friends hinted. And cruel. And insatiable.

A dull ripping sound startled Jody. Vinnie uncoiled from his crouch. Held aloft in triumph was the cufflink. But something in his other hand caught her eye.

"What's that?" she asked. Her level tone took Vinnie aback, forcing a sheepish smile in place of the usual leer. "Just this," he answered. He flipped a little square patch of fabric into her lap. "Stupid gobdan thingamajig you find on every mattress—you know, that dumb fuppin' thing that says—"

But Jody's voice was a hacksaw of rage ripping across his words.

"—That says 'Do Not Remove Under Penalty of Law.' You . . . you fool! You idiot! You just removed the tag from that mattress in direct disobedience of United States Government regulations! You destroyed legal proof that this article has been made in compliance with an act of the District of Columbia approved July 3, 1926; Kansas approved March, 1923; Minnesota approved April 24, 1929; New Jersey revised statutes 26:10, 60 to 18, Louisiana Act 467 of 1948 and Massachusetts General Law, Section 270, Chapter 941!"

"Huh?" Vinnie was half-listening, picking his nose. "Mattress tag . . . Massachusetts . . . wadda funk you talkin', c'mon, hon, in the sack, in the sack, an' I mean *now*!"

"No, Vinnie." Jody's coolness surprised even herself. "Not now, not ever. I may have married a criminal—well, everyone makes mistakes. But I'm not going to sleep with one, and not on a bed that is in blatant violation of a Federal statute of United States law!"

Vinnie slumped against the headboard, thunderstruck. "Aw, come on, hon, I know you're nervous on your weddin' night an' all, but let's not make a futtin' federal case outta some crappy piece of paper I tore off da bed!"

"That is just what I *am* making out of it, Vinnie—a federal case. Vincent Impagliaroni, I hereby make a Citizen's Arrest on a charge that you did willfully and unlawfully remove a mattress tag certifying that said mattress was made by the manufacturer in accordance with the law, and that the materials in said article were described thereon in accordance with the law! It's all over, Vinnie. Get your things."

There. She had mustered from somewhere the courage to bring it off. Relief flooded her being.

"No, no, Vinnie. Leave the jar of Vaseline. You won't need that where *you're* going. That reminds me. I'll call the officer in charge and ask if they have a honeymoon suite . . . at the Crowbar Hotel."

THE END

Crime struck this honeymoon cottage at 11:45 P.M. X marks location of bed.

LIFE

Since 1936, LIFE magazine has depicted American culture through the lens of the photographer. Founded by Time and Forbes founder Henry R. Luce, LIFE's photo spreads cover everything from the Fort Peck Dam on the Columbia River to circus elephants in Manhattan. Published weekly, LIFE was forced to go monthly in 1972; its Rockwellian portraits seemingly outdated in America's new landscape of sex, drugs, rock-and-roll and a whole lot of television.

This parody first appeared in the April 1979 issue of National Lampoon.

"Life? Life is hard. You get out what you put into it; and in your case, I'm seeing a lot of marijuana and hippie sex."

— President Richard Nixon, 1972, regarding his views on life, not LIFE the magazine which was the question we had specifically asked him.

LITE

April 1979/$1.50

That Crazy Jogging Fad

Blockbusters!
Successful Movies Make Big Money

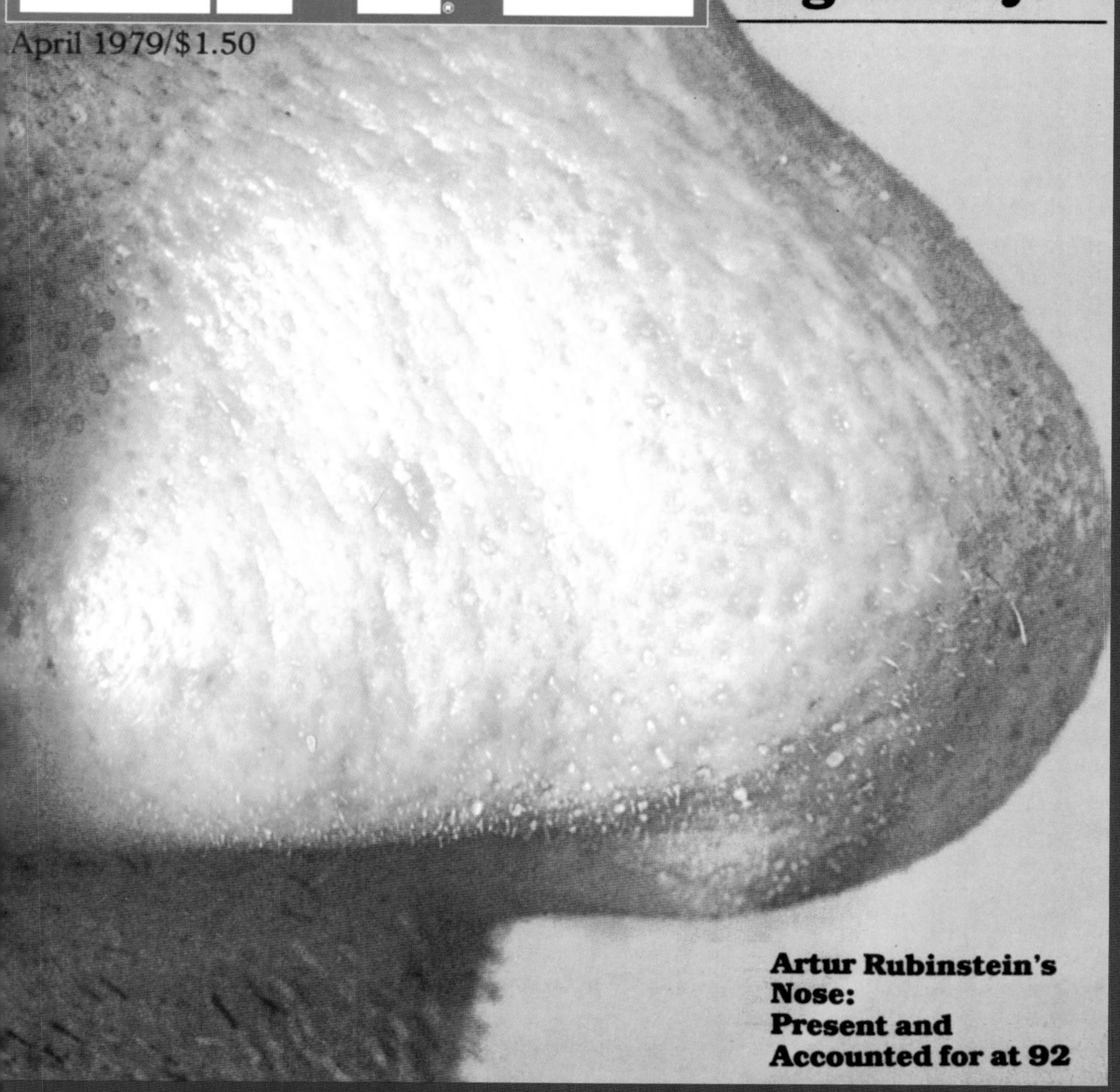

Artur Rubinstein's Nose: Present and Accounted for at 92

April 1979   Volume 1, Number 1

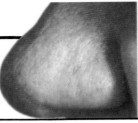

Cover: Artur Rubinstein's nose, by John Barrett

LITE is published whenever the editors get together and have a four-hour working lunch at 21 or the Four Seasons. Articles are chosen on how well they fit the demographic range of the magazine. The readership of LITE ranges from 3 to 112, earning an income of 17 cents to 125 billion dollars a year. Our average reader is alive, lives at home, and likes to look at color pictures on any subject, as long as they are pretty. Any resemblance to photojournalism magazines, past or present, is a moot point.

The Treasures of Grant's Tomb

Ivy wreath, probably a funeral offering. Some of the ivy leaves remain intact after 94 years. The inscription reads "R.I.P."

President Grant. He was carefully embalmed, and his coffin weighs more than three hundred pounds.

Indian Head penny, a small coin of the period. Possibly it was dropped by one of the workmen employed in building the tomb. It is made out of copper and bears an engraving of an Indian.

For more than a year the treasures of Grant's Tomb, on loan from the U.S. government, have been touring Egypt, where they have attracted record crowds in Cairo, Alexandria, and Thebes. Ulysses S. Grant, who was a president of the United States, died in 1885, and his elaborate tomb was erected on the shore of the Hudson River in North America. Sealed inside were a wide range of ceremonial and everyday objects typifying life in America's nineteenth century.

America's Enduring Love Affair With White Bread

Although Sunday dinner at the Hendersons in Leonia, it's served plain or fancy, the Henderson family always

Tom Rozjniak, a salesman for a chemical company, prefers his white bread untoasted, even though it's harder to spread a hard pat of butter on when it's soft.

Wherever America eats, you'll see plenty of white bread, whether it's a formal dinner or a late-night snack. "Pass the white bread" is as familiar a phrase as "pass the salt" or "can I have more water, please."

We will always have a tradition of home-baked white bread, but it is the mass-produced loaves that have made us famous, the perfectly-sliced loaves in their colorful, shiny packages that taste precisely the same, whether they're sold in Kennebunkport, Maine, or Seattle, Washington.

New Jersey, usually features turkey and mashed potatoes, no one ever slights the white bread. Whether comes back for more.

Nancy Jeffries and her granddaughter Melissa, of Denver, Colorado, wouldn't dream of having their sandwiches on anything but white bread.

Engineer Bruce Configlia pauses for a lunch break high atop Alaska's Mt. Whitney Hydroelectric Plant. He prefers white bread "at least half of the time."

Our Majestic Cow

Milk, meat, and natural beauty come together in this all-purpose beast

Blueball, Buttercup Farm's prize-winning heifer, pauses thoughtfully before her daily date with the milking machines.

They move or sit still with a purposeful majesty, cast against the natural splendor of high, rugged mountains, tall trees, deep-flowing rivers, and perennially green grazing land. Here in this one remarkable animal is a source of both meat and dairy products, as well as valuable by-products. Nutritionists and conservationists both agree that the cow is perhaps our most important beast.

Today's dairy farmer feeds his cows a balanced diet to ensure even better dairy products for us all.

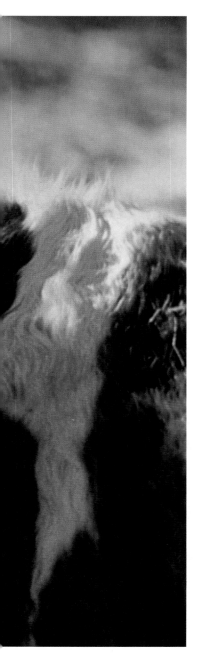

Untroubled by the towering beauty of Mt. Shasta, a grazing herd of cows present a picture of contentment.

JUST ONE MORE PICTURE, PLEASE

Caught in a casual moment at the end of a long day filled with audiences, prayers, and meditation, Pope John Paul II unwinds with a beer, some pretzels, and an hour or two of television. What programs are His Holiness's favorites? "Mostly game shows," says a spokesman for the Vatican, "along with westerns like 'Bonanza.'"

If you can handle then you should be A-OK with Unexciting Stories!

(The above exclamation point is in no way meant to alarm you.)

Take a deep breath, and fill out the back of this card.

FREE from excitement

HOLLYWOOD REPORTER

In September 1930, former film salesman William "Billy" Wilkerson published the debut issue of *The Hollywood Reporter*, making it the entertainment industry's first daily trade paper. Joined three years later by *Daily Variety*, the two papers now share the duty of dishing out the latest in entertainment news regarding deals, performance results, hirings and firings.

This parody first appeared in Dec 2002 as a National Lampoon special edition. Distributed in limited quantity, it managed to fool many Hollywood insiders, even prompting one studio executive to exclaim, "Script choosing parrot?... No wonder my projects never get picked up at MGM."

"I, me me me me me. I, me. Me? Me, me and my agent. Me! Me! Me!!!! . . . Wait, what was the question again?"

– Vin Diesel, actor, 2005. The question was, "What do you think of the Hollywood Reporter?"

THE Hollywood RETORTER

December 1-31, 2002   a NATLAMP parody ■ **$4.95** *(U.S.)* **$8.95** *(Canada)* ¥**9.25** *(Uzbekistan)*

Eisner, Diller, Katzenberg form JewTV

By Dan Rubin

Jew

After years of Jewish executives and producers concealing their Jewishness, Jewish entertainment moguls announced yesterday that they will form a new network, JewTV.

"It's just too much effort to hide it any longer. We spend so many countless hours trying to make characters that are so obviously Jewish seem gentile. It's just not cost effective anymore," said Jeffrey Katzenberg.

"Look, it's all Jewish anyway. Take 'Seinfeld.' Even George Costanza, who's based on Larry David, is a Jew. Why not just call a spade a spade and make it all JewTV," continued Katzenberg.

Barry Diller echoed Katzenberg, also believing that television is essentially a Jewish medium. "Archie Bunker is really Norman Lear's uncle, a Jew. And Meathead is a NYC left wing radical. Everyone knows they're all Jewish; it's a Jewish show. Strangely, the only character that isn't Jewish is the token Jew they would parade around now and then wearing a yarmulke and quoting Talmud — obviously way too Jewish to actually be Jewish."

See **JEWS** *on page 12*

CNN shoots 'The Kennedys'

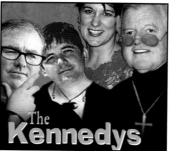

By Ann Barnard

HYANNISPORT — Hoping to match the success of "The Osbournes," CNN announced it will throw its hat into the reality ring with a new hour-long series featuring hard-drinking Senator Edward Kennedy and any family members of his who are both alive and unincarcerated at the time of shooting.

According to CNN's Ted Turner, " 'The Kennedys' will have the kitsch of 'The Osbournes,' but with the uncertainty element of 'Survivor.' And it's got the sex appeal of 'Temptation Island.'

If the Kennedys hold true to form, viewers can expect to see intoxicated women in skimpy beachwear, getting

See **RAPED** *on page 60*

Penn pens 'Oscar' effort

By Sean Scott

Oscar?

After failing to win an Oscar for "I Am Sam," a movie about a retarded man struggling to keep custody of his beloved daughter, Sean Penn (ICM) is upping the ante. Penn is receiving a reported $9.3 million for scribe/starring duties on "Oscar," the story of a crippled, black homeless veteran with AIDS, cystic fibrosis and Parkinson's of the eyes who lives in a NYC garbage can.

Oscar befriends and mentors a group of under-privileged neighborhood children, who in turn teach the grouchy trash dweller to read.

The film is described as a cross between "Awakenings," "Finding Forrester," "The Deer Hunter," "Roots," "My Left Foot," and every Lifetime Networks film ever.

"Oscar" Oscar buzz has already reached a fevered pitch, and the script, which is still 82 pages away from completion, is being lauded by no less than 15 separate charities and organizations as "finally voicing the concerns of society's dark secret."

A creative-infringement lawsuit with the Children's Television Workshop is pending. ■

Ovitz to launch 'Artist's Valet & Parking Group'

By J.K. Cummin

Mike Ovitz today announced the formation of Artist's Valet and Parking Group, which the one-time Hollywood super agent promised would reinvent how parking was conducted in this town.

"The first step to closing any deal is finding a place to park," explained Ovitz. "Disney may want a certain actor, but without a parking space that actor isn't even going to make the meeting. By controlling the cars of the top stars, I can control everything," Ovitz added with a menacing laugh.

Under the current system, an actor, writer or producer drives their car up to a talent

See **OVITZ** *on page 7*

Tom Hanks can't lose

By Joe Brown

When box-office darling Tom Hanks decided to produce "My Big Fat Greek Wedding," he knew the quirky film stood a strong chance of losing money. "I liked the project, but honestly I thought it was going to be my big fat Greek flop," confessed Hanks.

Over $100 million later, Hanks realized he was mistaken. "When we crested into nine figures, I had this disturbing sensation that everything I do is blessed. That I can do no wrong."

This feeling of destiny was so powerful that Hanks decided to test his impression by writing "Alabama Porch Monkey," a comedy about a lovable animated lawn jockey.

When the script was pur-

See **BIG FAT WINNER** *on page 7*

Congratulations to us... Winners of ShoWest's "Formula of the Millennium"

"Find a formula, and stick with it." That advice is as true today as when Uncle Michael first said it in 1987. From that adorable Arab boy and his magical genie, to that endearing Asian girl and her magical dragon, to the recent pairing of that pudgy Pan-Asian and her magical alien, the Dinseey formula of pairing ethnic protagonists with magical, lovable creatures, is proven BOX OFFICE GOLD! Let "Forty Acres and his Magical Mule" into this formulaic equation and into your hearts in June 2003!

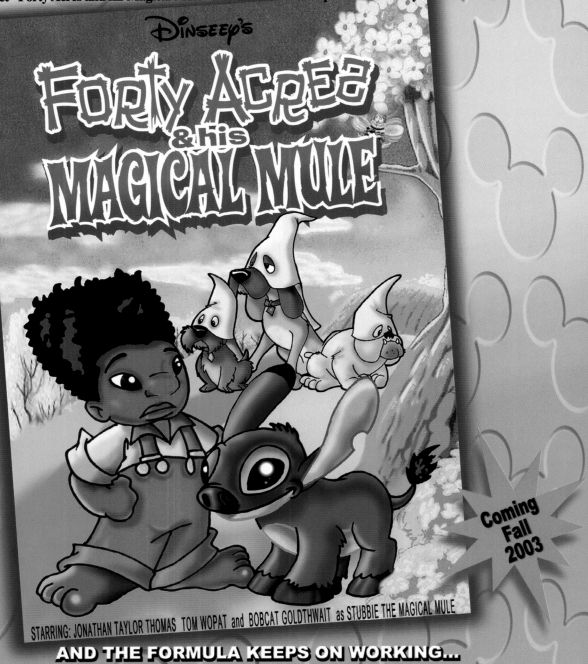

DINSEEY'S
FORTY ACRES & his MAGICAL MULE

Coming Fall 2003

STARRING: JONATHAN TAYLOR THOMAS TOM WOPAT and BOBCAT GOLDTHWAIT as STUBBIE THE MAGICAL MULE

AND THE FORMULA KEEPS ON WORKING...

A CHINK IN THE ARMOR

The enchanting story of an orphaned Chinese boy, Pu, and his wise cracking crane, Fu

Abandoned on the doorstep of the evil warlord, Tzing Tsong, Pu with the help of Fu not only saves the day, but saves face when he accepts Marx's early writings that man does not advance society through creative discovery, but instead argues that society advances according to mechanistic laws through a natural progression, from ancient society, to feudalism, to capitalism, to socialism, to communism.
Spring 2004.

VOODOO-ALITY

The bewitching tale of a shaman boy, and his wise cracking, undead zombie chicken brother

Meet Rasta, a Caribbean shaman boy who would like nothing better than to go about his business as an intermediary between the natural and supernatural worlds. Unfortunately for Rasta (portrayed deliciously by comic genius Arsenio Hall), his deceased twin brother Mojo, (also Hall) has inhabited the body of a farmyard animal and has become the wacky, undead zombie-chicken sidekick.
Christmas 2004

clips

Roberts 'Boards' SKG

SKG is adding another partner to their ruling board and another letter to their logo. "SKGR came about from a trip we paid to the international film buyer's market at AFM in February," explained David Geffen. "We saw Eric was starring in or was attached as a producer to no less than 26 films playing during the first day alone. We knew he was our way into AFM. Finally, we can distribute our films overseas."

Hacks

A Comedy Writers Against Ageism summit was disbanded after it was found out that most writers over 50 were not being discriminated against, merely completely unfunny. "The head writer of 'She's the Sheriff' kept telling me how all comics today work blue," said one twenty-something TV exec. "Then he told me some long-winded yarn about his prostate."

History Repeats

A New York City teenager is in hot water after trying to extinguish the entire Jewish race from the face of the earth on Tuesday. The 16-year-old boy had apparently seen a similar stunt nearly pulled off by the Germans on the History Channel and was trying to imitate it.

Kattan: Code Red

Homeland Security Director Tom Ridge put the nation on "high alert," warning that, despite 'Corky Romano,' Chris Kattan may yet strike again with another film based on one of his paper-thin 'SNL' characters such as Mongo, Mr. Peepers or Professor Sandwich-hands.

Case of the Scooby scribe solved

By Scott Mason

Warner Bros. long search to find a scribe capable of handling the third installment of the Scooby Doo franchise has ended with the hiring of Dan Foreman and Paul Foley.

The announcement comes as a welcome relief to Warner Bros., which was forced to seek a new writer after James Gunn (author of "Scooby Doo's 1 and 2") reportedly turned in a script consisting entirely of the question "What have I become?" typed over and over for 335 pages.

With Gunn effectively out of the picture, Warner Bros. immediately approached a number of top talent, but to no avail.

"Steven King gave us an elaborate treatment, and we were totally with him, until it turned out that his monster was actually real," stated WB distribution president Jake Soto. "I'm not sure that a ghost torture master who feeds on human pain was going to play to our key demographic of 5 to 12 year olds."

But finally Warner execs saw what they were looking for.

According to Soto, "Foreman and Foley came in and really wowed us! They understood exactly what we were after, like they were reading our minds! From the moment the Mystery Machine broke down in front of a spooky resort hotel to the discovery of strange gooey black stuff seeping out of the ground to the arrival of the swamp creature who had been scaring away guests, we were hooked!"

"The plot is perfect!" continued Soto. "It's really touch-and-go for a while there. And talk about a twist! Real 'Sixth Sense' stuff! We're making the press sign releases not to discuss the ending in their reviews because we don't want anybody spoiling it."

"But I will tell you to keep your eye on Old Man Hawkins," continued Soto, winking broadly. "There's a reason that crotchety Old Man wants to keep the kids away."

An ecstatic Warner Bros. believes that Foley and Foreman's efforts could be the beginning of a beautiful friendship.

"They've got this idea for the fourth movie in which Scooby and the gang team up with the Harlem Globetrotters!" gushed Soto. "I mean, these guys are on fire!" ∎

MGM's script-choosing parrot dead at 14

By James Foster

Feathers, the Executive VP of Development at MGM, died in his cage this Monday of parrot-related causes, surrounded by close friends, small, blunt-edged mirrors and durable tingly bells. He was 14.

The parrot had worked at MGM since 1991, greenlighting various projects throughout his tenure by nodding his head at one of a fan of scripts laid out in front of him. Many credit him with singlehandedly jumpstarting the once-ailing studio.

"Feathers had a gift," stated MGM/UA President Michael Nathanson. "For a bird whose brain was roughly the size of a plump raisin, he had a keen eye for scripts that perfectly mirrored what America wanted to see at a given time."

"I'd ask him, 'Feathers, how do you do it?'" marveled Nathanson. "And he'd always come back with 'Pretty Bird! Pretty Bird!' God, I'll miss him."

Detractors, however, main-

**Feathers
1988 - 2002**

tained that Feathers picked scripts based only on the color of the string used in the binding, and that unscrupulous producers knew to take advantage of the bird's instinctual weaknesses. Indeed, Bruce Willis reportedly went so far as to smear peanut butter on the cover page of "Hart's War."

Even so, no one can deny that the avian executive, who lived in a two-by-four-foot cage blanketed with its own defecation, knew what "clicked" with audiences, compiling a track record with a total gross of over $5 billion.

MGM, while saddened by the loss, is still well-positioned for future success, upping Barky the talking seal ("Windtalkers," "Jeepers Creepers") to the top script slot. ∎

Chabon grocery list optioned

By Evie Crespo

Wunderkind scribe Michael Chabon ("Wonder Boys") has

sold the rights to his latest work, a grocery list, to Scott Rudin for an undisclosed amount somewhere around the mid six figure area.

"His writing has a gentle, orderly way of bringing you into the story," stated Rudin. "By the time I got to 'milk,' I was about ready to burst from all the emotions roiling around my insides." ∎

Diesel shifts into high gear

By Gunther Brykman

Vin Diesel keeps the pedal to the metal as he signs on to the Original Films remake of Orson Wells' classic, "Citizen Kane," for $20 million.

According to Neal Moritz, the new version will feature Kane rediscovering his childhood by riding his snowboard, "Rosebud," through a series of high-speed chases and harrowing explosions. ∎

Lifetime sickened by cure

News of advances in the field of cancer research has caused shares of the Lifetime Network to plummet as analysts fear the network may run out of projects within the next 10 years. "If cancer is cured," stated financial analyst Fred Light, "then the network will be forced to rely exclusively on pregnancy mishap shows, and I just don't think there's enough lingering, relationship-intensive tragedy to fill the gap."

CFO, VP, EP, EVP, SUV-VW crash

An SUV filled with MGM VP's collided with a UA VW microbus causing a bizarre acronym mix-up. "I was CFO of MGM. Now I'm the FVS of AOL! What the hell's an FVS? Somebody please tell me, 'cause I got a job to do!"

CBS Prez too busy for 'Becker'

CBS Entertainment President Nancy Tellum acknowledged last week that she had never seen the network's flagship sitcom, 'Becker.' "I've been meaning to get around to it," stated Tellum, "but something always comes up. I'm pretty busy. I'm sure it's good, though." Continued Tellum, "That Sam Malone's a very funny guy. When's it on, anyhow?"

WB first in sequels

By Ulf Weismuller

As of Friday, Warner Bros. became the first of the major studios to adopt an all-sequel based strategy for film production. "Treading new ground just isn't cost effective," said WB TV Pres. Peter Roth of the move. "We own the rights to over 600 films. It would be a misuse of those rights if audiences weren't ever allowed to revisit the worlds of films like 'The Life of Emile Zola,' 'Deliverance,' or 'The Ten Commandments.'"

The maiden voyage of this daring policy, however, will be helmed by what the studio is calling a "super-sequel," a remake of the classic remake of the Rat Pack classic, "Ocean's 11."

Director Steven Soderbergh and the entire cast have signed on to reprise their duties for "Ocean's 11 II," a shot for shot remake of the remake, but to keep the film from appearing stale, the cast will be shuffling their roles: George Clooney, formerly Daniel Ocean, is now playing Matt Damon's part of Linus (originally Dean Martin). Andy Garcia, formerly Terry Benedict, is replacing Brad Pitt as Rusty Ryan, who will be stretching his acting chops by taking over the role of Tess Ocean, last played by Julia Roberts (first played by Angie Dickinson), who is also stretching her talents to play Terry Benedict, now a beleaguered mother and not a greedy casino owner. The role of Turk Malloy, last played by Scotty Caan, will be played twice, simultaneously, by former Reuben Tishkoff, Elliott Gould as well as by former extra from the original movie, Holly Darnell. ∎

Astronomers discover fifth Baldwin

By Lindsay Bing

Hubble scientists working at Palomar Observatory yesterday stunned the scientific community when they announced the existence of a fifth Baldwin brother.

"We were aware of Alec, Stephen, Billy and even Danny," stated Dr. Brian Janikowski. "But no one had ever even speculated about the possibility of

MX 53-7

another one. Sure enough, there he was, just outside of the lab door. Apparently he's hungry."

The new brother has been named Janikowski Baldwin (MX 53-7), after the astronomer who first spotted the rogue sibling. ∎

1,2,3 'Redlight'!

By Raegan Holdsworth

Dreamworks gave the thumbs-up to "Redlight," a project designed to put the kibosh on scripts that must never, ever be made into movies. Said Steven Spielberg, "Beyond forcing the writer to toss the thing in the fire, this is the surest thing we can do to keep another 'Sorority Boys' from ever happening again. We've estimated 'Project Redlight' will save the studio hundreds of millions, perhaps billions, annually."

Projects already slated for "Project Redlight" include "Asthma Man," "Cop Rock in 3-D" and "National Lampoon's Yom Kippur Vacation." ∎

Sony's dreams come true

By Rumpus Frelinghuysen

TOKYO — Having established itself as the dominant player in the TV, film, cable, internet and video game markets, Sony has announced an exciting new initiative to provide exclusive direct content for the human subconscious.

"We did market research and were very disturbed to discover that the average person spends almost one-third of their lives asleep. That's six to eight hours a day completely outside the reach of commercial media!" said Sony spokesman Micky Otaki, "That is way too much time to be left to your own imagination. Most people are simply not qualified to provide exciting, fast-paced dreamtime entertainment on their own."

Sony America CEO Howard Stringer added his own perspective: "I know I don't enjoy my dreams. I find them predictable and repetitive. How many times can people find themselves back in high school taking an exam for which they did not study? When I dream that, I am not anxious. I'm saying, 'Seen it!'" ∎

Bye, Bi-Mafia

By Mary Vinton

Ridiculed by the Harvard Mafia and reviled by the Gays, the Bi-curious Mafia has finally decided to pack it in.

"We were tired of getting it from both ends," said spokesman Andy Dick. "Our members are real sore about this."

The female branch of the organization, however, is expected to continue as long as men want women to "experiment" in college. ∎

Dennis Woodruff finally admits 'too small' for porn

By Stan Kesmodel

How could the man who spends his life degrading himself in the hopes of landing a small acting role have not tried porn?

"I'm too small," admitted a tearful Woodruff, while gluing little plastic Emmy awards onto a '79 Dodge panel van. "And my car won't make it to the valley."

It is one of the great ironies of Hollywood that the man with star dreams was born with just a bit part. "And it curves to the left," he added. ∎

Bruckheimer sets Morocco 'Ablaze'

By Gary Fullmer

Industry mogul Jerry Bruckheimer took production value to the next level by setting the entire country of Morocco on fire for one shot in his newest film, "Ablaze," a fast-paced orangutan/cop buddy film.

Unfortunately, the shot, which cost more than $100 billion, had to be cut from the final print.

"It just didn't make sense from a character standpoint," said screenwriter Greg Francis. "Orangutans hate fire."

"Besides," continued Francis, "I'd forgotten that Morocco was mostly sand. Sure, pour some oil all over it and it'll go. But is it in the end believable? I think not."

Bruckheimer remains undeterred. "We're setting explosives across every square inch of this land. It's going to be huge! Kaboom!!!" ∎

the vine

Heard around town

Jolie not jolly

Angelina Jolie expressed a fatuous opinion on an irrelevant non-issue on Tuesday, when she said "I think it's really important that the moon remain land-mine free. It would be terrible if one small step for a man resulted in the loss of a limb."

NBC to fatten Roker

Network execs at NBC have demanded that Al Roker re-gain any weight he may have lost in the past few months, citing his

Funny

Unfunny

gaunt, non-jolly appearance as a probable cause for their slipping ratings. "We hired a fat guy, and we're going to get a fat guy," stated news head David Schlicter. The extra weight, it is believed, will take 10 years off Roker's life, "but the years he does live will be highly rated."

Howser strikes gold

After searching for California's gold for over a decade, Huell Howser has finally found it: "Turns out there's a large ore-bearing lode directly underneath my backyard," beamed Howser. "Ironic, isn't it?"

'Bram Stoker's Count Chocula'

The box office success of this summer's cartoon-driven fare, "Spiderman" and "Scooby Doo," can not be argued, but Jonathan Demme's reimagining of everyone's favorite vampire achieves artistically what they did not. "Bram Stoker's Count Chocula" is a tense and toothsome treat that leaves the audience wired and wanting more.

This bloody and erotic retelling of the oft-filmed story is, to date, the most faithful to the initial literary source, although some purists to the original may get

BY MIKE OESTERLE

the bottom line

This deliciously evil film will sate even the most ravenous of appetites.

upset that Renfield (Sonny the Cocoa Puffs Bird) has given up eating insects in favor of Post's Honey Bunches of Oats.

Demme's coldly majestic style and Chocula's raw animal sexuality blend as nicely as bananas and corn flakes. The story is familiar to most: The vampire king plots his conquest of Britain, which involves transporting coffins filled with his native soil and plenty of chocolatey marshmallow goodness, all the while infecting the populace via incarnations as bat, wolf and a milky mist. Suffice it to say

that Count Chocula chews up the scenery in his first appearance on the big screen.

Chocula the thespian was born a Chocovanian nobleman in the 13th century and became a classically trained dramatic actor, before joining the ranks of the undead. It was at the London Academy of Music and Dramatic Arts in the late 60s

BRAM STOKER'S COUNT CHOCULA
General Mills Productions

Credits: Director-screenwriter Jonathan Demme. **Cast:** Count Chocula; Sir Grapefellow; Twinkles; Colonel Corn Burst; Snap; Crackle; Pop; Apple Jack; The Wizard Of Oatz, Toucan Sam; Dig-em the Frog; Boo Berry; Teddy Graham Bear; Super Sugar Crisp Bear; Cap'n Crunch; Smedley the Elephant; Quake; Quisp; The Cookie Crisp Trolls; Cookie Jarvis; King Vitaman; Trix Rabbit; Lucky the Leprechaun; Cheerios Kid.
Rated R, running time 250 minutes

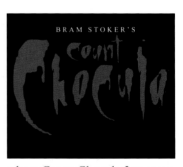
BRAM STOKER'S Count Chocula

where Count Chocula first met a young jazz dance student named Francis Nicholas Berryman (later changed to Frankenberry). The two teamed up to become arguably the greatest cereal-selling duo in the history of the genre.

Their well publicized break in 1985 is a typical Hollywood story. Egos, drugs and Dyan Cannon

See **US RDA** *on page 72*

Attention Networks

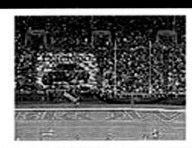

INCREASE YOUR
AD REVENUE POTENTIAL

If you're watching a ballgame on ESPN, chances are you don't know whether the logos on the field really exist or whether they're just digitally-created illusions. But why stop at sports?

At VirtAdvert, Inc., we won't let you waste any valuable airtime with revenue-free content! From breaking news to classic footage, you'll never miss a placement opportunity again!

VirtAdvert: The only thing that's real is the profit!

Actual stills from our Clio award-winning virtual insertion, "The Zapruder Spot," as seen on the History Channel.

VirtAdvert 10850 Wilshire Blvd. Suite 1000 Los Angeles, Ca.90024.... contact Vantro Ruiz at VirtVant@VirtAdvert.com

cries and whispers

"When you fight for me you're fighting for all surgically-altered, chimpanzee-loving, elephant-man-skeleton-owning, gay-porn-producer-hiring, hyperbaric-chamber-sleeping, allegedly viteligo-suffering, quote unquote black men dead and alive."
— Michael Jackson during press conference re: his suit against Sony

"How did you get in here?"
— Heather Locklear on how 'Cries and Whispers' editor Ben Levitz got into her bathroom vent

"You think I could at least get some free cookies?"
— Billy Bob Thornton while trying to donate the vial of Angelina Jolie's blood he wore around his neck to the Red Cross

Ovitz

Continued from page 1—

agency, obtains the services of a "parking valet" to park the car and then must walk inside and rely on a separate "packaging agent" to put together a TV or film deal.

By providing parking, however, Artist's Valet and Parking Group, or AVPG, can take care of everything right there in the lot. "It streamlines what had become an antiquated system," explained Ovitz, whose "packaging valets" structured the sequel to "The Whole Nine Yards" while backing Bruce Willis' Lexus into a tight spot. Added the consummate deal maker, "And we saved him anywhere from $1.50 plus tip to $4.50 plus tip."

With headquarters on the corner of Victory and Brand, AVPG has promised to stop at nothing in an effort to recapture Ovitz's former clients. Already, Tom Cruise felt the pressure as the megastar was unable to park his BMW Z3 in Ovitz's parking lot after freezing the "uber valet"

out of a deal. "I wanted him to valet my car," said Cruise. "Simple. But thanks to Mike's new policy of package-parking, I can't find a spot until I pay for the parking of two of his newer clients. Ridiculous."

Cruise spent nearly 45 minutes circling around Burbank for a parking spot.

Whether AVPG will help resurrect the fallen Ovitz's career, however, remains to be seen. After the demise of AMG in June, the man once described as "The Most Powerful Man in Hollywood" found himself downgraded to "Second Most Powerful Man in his Own House" over the July 4th weekend. "I planned a trip to Sea World for the whole family, but my son Brett, who just turned 17, wanted to hang out with his friends. After a brief discussion, Brett grabbed my throat, and it was then we decided the most amicable solution was to let Brett spend time with his pals."

But lest anyone count Mike Ovitz out just yet, Brett Ovitz was forced to park five blocks away after returning from his friend's house. ■

NATIONAL LAMPOON ®

Vol. I, No. 1
Copyright © 2002 by National Lampoon, Inc. All rights reserved.
No part of this publication may be reproduced, stored in any retrieval system or transmitted in any form or by any means – electronic, mechanical, photocopying, recording or otherwise – without the prior written permission of the publisher.

Editorial, Corporate Headquarters
10850 Wilshire Blvd. Suite 1000
Westwood, CA 90024
Phone: (310) 474-5252
Fax: (310) 474-1219

Scott Rubin (Editor-in-Chief)

Editorial
Mason Brown (Managing Editor), Steven Brykman (Managing Editor), Sean Crespo (Sr. Editor)
Joe Oesterle (Sr. Editor), Pete Cummin (Sr. Editor)

Reporters
Pete Cummin, James Pinkerton, Mark McCarthy, Dan Bialek, Shannon Hall, Arthur Bullock, Shalom Auslander, Gary Greenberg,
Alex Burger and Matt Ornstein, Steve B. Young

Art
MoDMaN (Sr. Art Director),
Joe Oesterle (Art Director), James Silvani (illustration),
Steven Brykman (Layout)

Photos
Donna Korones, Steven Brykman,
Joe Oesterle, Peter Martin

National Lampoon's The Hollywood Retorter is a newspaper of parody - satirical parody, humorous parody, and sometimes stupid parody published by The National Lampoon as parody. It is not endorsed or affiliated with The Hollywood Reporter or VNU Business Publications in any way. The National Lampoon uses invented names in all its stories, except in cases when public figures or companies are being satirized, which in this case is often. Nothing in this publication states or implies actual facts or events about, or conduct of, any person or company. Any other use of real names is accidental and coincidental. None of the stories herein are intended to be taken as expressions of truth, and are published as parody for humorous and satiric purposes only. Now lighten up.

98° scrapped for parts

By Balthazar Silvani

The moderately-successful boy band 98° was sold piecemeal at a sparsely-attended Orlando auction.

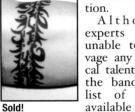

Sold!

Although experts were unable to salvage any musical talent from the band, the list of items available for sale was impressive, including two barbed-wire tribal arm tattoos, an extensive collection of pouts, scowls and poses, and a cocksure attitude that was unable to meet its reserve price.

Motown execs plan to put all unsold parts into a smelter and recycle them into a new guy group tentatively entitled BoyKrush. ■

Cruise

Continued from page 1—
protests too much. ■

2002 fantasy Jew rotisserie leagues start new fall season

By Jay Lemieux

At agencies throughout L.A., assistants and CEOs alike are poring through their Hollywood Creative Directories, getting ready for this season's Fantasy Jew Rotisserie league drafts.

With points scored for achievements in such categories as marrying a trophy shiksa, making a "Survivor" rip-off and furthering the career of Adam Sandler. Hebrew rotisserie is rapidly rivaling Fantasy Baseball in popularity.

"You have to do your

Waiver Fodder?

research," noted long-time rotisserie enthusiast Jay Green. "Picking the right Jews can be tricky. Last year, I went with Eisner #1, and he tanked. Worse, I had to leave in the middle of the live draft and let the computer take over. The stupid cyber 'Juru' picked Strauss Zelnick. I mean, sure he was the head of BMG, but for crying out loud, now he's

promoting bike races and National Lampoon. The only thing that saved me was that I picked up Sumner Redstone as a free agent. I guess people didn't know he's Jewish."

Surprisingly, the game is proving exceptionally popular among industry gentiles.

"My Fantasy Jew team is as close as I'm going to get to being on the Inside," explained Ron Howard ("A Beautiful Mind," "Apollo 13"). "When I follow my team, it's like I'm a real Hollywood player!" ■

Big fat winner

Continued from page 1—

chased on spec by MGM for $10 million against 25 gross points, Hanks next tried to self-destruct by enjoying a full-release massage from a leprous Bombay hooker, then telling his wife about it afterwards.

"Rita was ecstatic that I trusted our marriage strongly enough to tell her about my actions," stated Hanks. "Not only that, I

also contracted a slight case of leprosy myself — but I suffered only enough nerve damage to minimize the sensations in my penis. Now I can last for hours and hours, enabling me to bring any woman to a multitude of continuous climaxes. I was shocked."

Determined to harm his career, Hanks pushed his theory to the limits the next day, hurling human feces at the elderly in a Hollywood nursing home.

"They loved it," confided Hanks. "They kept saying how

happy they were that somebody was finally paying attention to them, especially a big movie star like Tom Hanks. I'm telling you, no matter what I do, people will always like me. It's scary!"

The two-time golden man winner now plans to release a non-consensual nun-fisting movie on Pay-Per-View in December. "And if that gets me another Oscar, I'm going to recite my winning speech from 'Philadelphia' word-for-word. That ought to make somebody hate me." ■

$217,0

THE ADVENTURES OF
PLUTO NASH
THE MAN ON THE MOON

"... ASTONISHING WEEKEND!"
- Broadcaster's journal

"UNBELIEVABLE ... I AM DUMBFOUNDED"
- Wall Street Journal Investor's Daily

"... WE'RE GOING TO BE TALKING ABOUT THIS ONE FOR A LONG, LONG TIME."
- LA Times Business Forecast

00,000*

* inflation adjusted to the year 2087

A grand Endeavor

By JRodney Holtz

Assistants at Endeavor can breathe a one-sided sigh of relief this week. Inside sources report that scripts will no longer have to be copied two-sided. This frustrating process is largely cited for the cycle of emotional abuse in Hollywood.

The inevitable breakdown of Xerox machines during the delicate two-sided copying process forces assistants to store their pupal anger for years at a time, before maturing and metamorphosing into full agents, managers or producers, at which point the anger reaches the adult stage of full-grown rage and is loosed almost haphazardly on assistants and small-fry clients over such minor incidents as lost calls or the discovery of the small selection of fonts for P-Touch label makers.

"I had to fix that damn copy machine everyday," said former assistant to Endeavor's Phil Raskind, Bart Shinseki, last week. "It was always when I was on the last few pages, too. Suddenly the last hour of my life was gone and I'd have to make like another 70 copies of pages 34-97. You know, because that's what I wanted to be when I grew up, the Xerox Guy."

Bart got the bump to full agent yesterday. Lester Klum (mailroom) was tapped for Shinseki's new assistant today based on Endeavor's pre-hire psychological profile, which described him as "a malleable, weak-willed, powder keg."

"I think Lester and I will get along just fine," smirked Shinseki. "As long as those 40 copies of the 'War and Peace' 16-installment teleplay get out before lunch, right Les?" ∎

Producer has sex with own wife

By Spencer Troy

Paramount producer Steven Borzoi broke a two year streak of bedding down personal assistants, day-player actresses and madam-hired courtesans by engaging in the physical act of lovemaking with his wife of over 15 years, Melinda.

"I don't know what came over us. It was crazy, like we had just met all over again. All I had to do was come home on time, kiss the kids goodnight and wait for 'Law & Order' to end," said Borzoi. "It was so easy. And free!"

The newly re-enamored Borzoi later expressed regret over Melinda's long bouts of fidelity-induced sexlessness.

"To think, all these years I was away, she was just keeping herself for me, waiting to unleash all that sexual energy in one night of crazy, torrid sex! And now, just as we've recaptured that sense of

Borzoi

romance in our lives, I have to leave the next day for three months on a business trip with my new Swedish secretary ... and her sister."

Standing in the doorway, bags already loaded into an LAX bound limo, a teary-eyed Borzoi's request, "You'll wait for me again, won't you?", was interrupted by a spit-take from the on-break pool boy, Juan, enjoying some cherry-flavored Kool-Aid.

His devotion to Melinda reinvigorated, Borzoi was able to make it almost past his own mailbox before a female leg thrashed orgasmically out of the limo's open window.

The owner of the leg could not be confirmed. ∎

Big bucks for bin Laden's bangs

By Curt Asuncion

Al Jazeera has signed Osama bin Laden to a first-look deal for his next three threatening videotapes, each promising more blood-curdling threats against the infidels than the last.

"These things are practically free to produce," beamed Al Jazeera Prexy Mohammed Jassem al Ali, "and the kids love him, especially in the most desirable demographic of disaffected 18 to 35 year olds willing to die for Allah." ∎

NBC's vice president of diversity fires self

By Holmes Ludlow

LOS ANGELES , CA – John Maxwell, Vice President of Diversity for NBC, fired himself today making room for a minority candidate to fill the slot. "What gives me the right to be here?" asked Maxwell, "Because I'm white? Because I have Ph.D. in Sociology from Harvard? That's just not good enough anymore. I must go."

According to Industry insiders, Maxwell was in a meeting with "Friends" producers trying to persuade them to make the Rachel character African-American for the show's final season, when suddenly he caught a glimpse of himself in the smoked-glass mirrors just behind executive producer Todd Stevens' bar. He suddenly burst out, "Oh my God! I'm a white guy! I'm really a white guy! We're all white, look at us. Somebody has to go." After getting no response from the others in the room, Maxwell shouted, "Well I guess it's going to be me! ... I'm fired!" Maxwell, hysterical, picked up his laptop and stormed out.

NBC programming boss, Jeff Zucker, was upset at Maxwell's dismissal and believes the intense pressure of the position, combined with the former executive's deep commitment to fair treatment for all minorities finally got to him. "We had ice cream last week together and John managed to eat all 31 flavors. He is so sensitive that way. It doesn't surprise me," said Zucker.

Although Maxwell had a very difficult challenge convincing Hollywood producers to use a more diverse palette when casting their shows, he does leave with some successes: convincing NBC anchorman Tom Brokaw to speak with a lisp, making him appear more closely aligned with the gay community; demanding that "SNL " keep Tim Meadows despite his being 28 years older than the nearest cast member; pressuring "Saved by the Bell" producers to focus more on Screech in an effort to reach out to the mentally handicapped; and applying red highlights to the hair of "Weakest Link" host, Louise Wallace, in an attempt to give viewers the impression that she might be Irish.

Maxwell's job prospects look bleak. White is simply the most inappropriate skin tone for a former diversity executive. Nearly all of the Fortune 500 companies' diversity executives are either African-American, Asian, Latino or Slavic. When Maxwell was made aware of this racial profile he was stunned, "My God. I'm a minority in my own career ... Wait, this is great, I can get my old job back!" ∎

on screen

Young Howard Taft thwarts Philippino insurgents by blocking the doorway with his massive bulk in "The Adventures of Young Howard Taft, opening Friday via Dreamworks.

The Adventures of Young Howard Taft — The future 27th President of the United States finds himself in an international imbroglio in the Philippines. Trapped by madman/progressive William Jennings Bryan, Taft must eat his way out of danger or be crucified on a cross of gold. The Dreamworks picture opens in wide release Friday.

Can You Hear Me Now? — Based on the popular Verizon ad campaign, Mike Meyers stars as a mysterious telecommunications technician who wanders America, encountering many strangers and having minimal effect on their lives. Meyers also plays a secondary character with a Scottish accent. Artisan opens the comedy Friday.

Kotto makes Zsigmond see black

By Reno Jones

Oscar-award-winning cinematographer Vilmos Zsigmond has decided to put the lens cap on his career after repeatedly failing to capture Yaphet Kotto on film during principal photography of Miramax's new comedy, "Idi Amin's Night in the Coal Mine."

"He was so black!" exclaimed Zsigmond. "I hit him with every light I had. The man just absorbs light! I spent a month doing AfterEffects on one frame, and all I got were his eyes and his teeth! I quit! I have failed! I am nothing!"

Zsigmond's retirement is just one in a series of mishaps on what has been by all accounts a very difficult shoot, marred by a swirling vortex of free-flying metal objects and erratic discharges of deadly gamma radiation.

"For years, scientists have speculated on the possibility of mini-black holes, tiny gravity wells which suck in space, light and time itself," stated Cal Tech Astrophysicist Matt Kingsley. "We just had no idea that one of them was the star of such films as 'Live and Let Die' and 'Brubaker.' That's a very black man."

"We lost a make-up artist who was trying to apply a foundation to Mr. Kotto," said one source close to the set. "Zsigmond believes that the poor woman simply passed Mr. Kotto's 'Event Horizon' and was sucked in."

The affable Kotto was available for comment, but his quotes won't reach human ears until 2025. ∎

Indie fest gets 'Cagey'

By Karen Weiss

Sundance is cutting its last three days for "Nicolas Cage: A Retrospective," defending itself by citing that the various major studios Cage has worked with are "independ-

ent" of one another, thereby complying with the festival's definition. The 42 theater, three day event will push the remaining 115 films into a narrow two-hour window, which will be projected simultaneously onto one wall in a recently renovated mine shaft. From 4-am to 6-am. Next year's "Travolta: the man, the leg-

See WHORES on page 41

AOL Time Warner: synergeriffic!

By Jane Holiday

After a rocky start, the much-touted synergies behind the merger of AOL and Time Warner are finally beginning to pay off.

"We used to be very disparate entities, without a lot of communication," stated CEO Richard Parsons. "But now we're really starting to feed off of each other, and use each other's strengths."

"Why just the other day, 'Time' magazine was running short of ideas, and then, bingo, it hit us, how about an article on how AOL's blundering mismanagement has ruined the pension plan of most of the executives here at Time-Warner."

AOL'er Steve Case is equally excited about the new, open atmosphere.

"After seeing TBS' 'Atomic Twister,' a lot of our programmers realized that they could help out our compatriots in the so-called 'creative side,'" stated Case. "So they used our Instant Messaging system to bombard Warner Brothers execs with innovative, high-concept movie pitches such as 'I'm an Arrogant Fuck from Time Magazine' and 'All My Thinking is Done by Focus Groups.'"

"We're very impressed by the AOL team's ideas," beamed Parsons. "I'm pretty sure we're going to develop some of them

into features with only a few minor changes, maybe to the title. We were thinking, 'I'm An AOL Homo Who's Never Dated A Real Woman And Masturbates Constantly.' Plot's pretty much the same. We've just added a love interest. If you can call your own hand a love interest." ∎

Diesel

Continued from page 20—

following the "Citizen Kane" box office wipeout.

"E! True Hollywood Stories" defended their decision to release the show portraying Diesel as a washed-up drug-addict as "something that's obviously going to happen." ∎

Diller sues Viacom for rights to former self

By Ruby Love

Phyllis Diller, who was recently refused a series of residual checks from Viacom due to improper identification, joins Richard Chamberlain, Carol Burnett and Michael Jackson in a multi-million dollar lawsuit against the entertainment giant.

"Why should this strange woman receive royalties from any of Phyllis Diller's work? I don't care how much I.D. she shows me. The two look nothing alike," said Randi Price, Viacom's controller. "This other woman looks great but she's not the hideous creature that paraded around in a 'fright wig' in the 60s and 70s."

Diller, who has tried numerous times to collect the residual, has even showed up at Price's office in person but Viacom still couldn't make the match.

"This woman thinks that she can put on an old ratty wig and tell a few old jokes but I can do that too," said Price. "I'm sorry. She's just not the same woman as in that 1969 'Love American

Diller   "Diller"

Style' episode. Should I give you Rip Taylor's residuals just because you found a bad toupee and tossed a few limp-wristed handfuls of confetti?" continued Price. "I don't think so. I could get fired for that."

Carol Burnett had to recently undergo a retina scan to prove that she was in fact Carol Burnett and entitled to receive her residuals from the old Carol Burnett Show. But nothing compares to what Richard Chamberlain had to endure to receive his back residuals for "Dr. Kildare." "I had tiny silicone implants inserted under my eyes to recreate the bags I had at 43. They had to undo my face lift, pluck out half my hair plugs,

and remove my penile implant. It was the most painful thing I've ever felt."

Diller's attorney, Michael Lawstein, disagrees with Viacom but acknowledged he has an uphill battle in proving Diller is Diller. Official efforts to identify Diller as Diller ended last week following unsuccessful photo, dental, fingerprint and urine content match-ups.

"We're still early in the game," said Lawstein. "We still have blood tests, DNA, internal organ core samplings and 3D Computer Generated Imaging. Trust me, she assures me she's her."

Price contends that Viacom's policy toward Diller is fair and justified. "We can't be expected to pay out monies to people who are simply not themselves. There wouldn't be money for anybody else who are actually who they say they are, let alone for people who pretend to be who they think they are but who aren't who they are because it's quite obvious who they are now is not who they are anymore. Now that wouldn't be fair." ∎

Paramount releases junket rules

Paramount studios has released its newest junket guidelines to the press. Excerpts of this year's changes are reprinted below:

...You may be tempted to ask the actors about other projects. This is fine so long as the questions are limited to the following:

1.) I understand you have a new film in which you play a _____ on the edge.
  a) Cop
  b) Scientist
  c) Navy seal
  d) Ex-cop

2.) Congratulations on your engagement to that famous _____.
  a) Model
  b) Actress
  c) Singer
  d) Model/Actress
  e) Singer/Actress
  f) Actress/Singer/Model

3.) I understand you have an interesting anecdote in which you:
  a) Refer with self-effacement to the talents of your more

famous co-star of whom you were in awe.
  b) Tell an amusing story about some quirky method of getting into your role.
  c) Relay an anecdote that shows how you chose to pay-your-dues despite the connections of your celebrity relatives.
  d) Discuss how jail was good for you.

...One A-list actor is very proud at having "recently completed a screenplay on Abraham Lincoln." Should he insist on showing it to you, please do not mention that it is in fact a place mat from a pancake restaurant.

...You will notice that today's actors have a variety of tattoos. You are encouraged to mention them as it adds to their so-called "street cred." However, we ask that you ignore any that say "Expiration Date__/__" This is for internal studio use only and is meant to be kept confidential, particularly from the actors themselves.

...There are certain "negative" words that may come up in interviews. We strongly recommend the following proactive

NEGATIVE	POSITIVE
"Violent"	"Energetic"
"Sadistic"	"Visceral"
"Illiterate"	"Post-Literate" or "Visceral"
"Forced Community Service"	"Giving Back"
"LA County Dept. of Corrections"	"Stella Adler Studio"
"Visceral"	"Sexy"

alternatives:

...Occasionally an actor may have trouble distinguishing the difference between a one-on-one press junket interview, and a session with a psychotherapist. If an actor should become physically excited or utter the words "I hurt! I hurt so much!" the interview is over. Should you attempt to continue the discussion, you will be charged with practicing psychiatry without a license.

...The main thing is to have FUN, be objective and remember three fundamental things: We all work for the same media conglomerate, we know where your kids go to school and drifters owe us favors.

See you at the premiere! ∎

Jews!

Continued from page 1—

Jewish producers are thrilled by the announcement and are lining up to turn many of their hits into JewTV shows.

"What a relief," said James L. Brooks (Jew), producer of "The Simpsons." "Now we can finally stop this nonsense of making Bart and his family appear white trash and just make them Jews already."

Renamed "The Simpsteins" for JewTV, Homer Simpstein will own a small check-cashing business and be a little more successful then his Simpson counterpart, while Marge, a compulsive, high strung career woman, will be racked with guilt for not properly mothering her children to death. Bart will be a hypochondriac obsessed with anti-Semitism, who will constantly nudge his dad to describe the deaths of many his dead relatives who died in the Holocaust.

And Ed Weinberger (Jew), creator of "The Cosby Show," looks forward to making the show Jewish. "There's really not much to do except add an occasional line that they just returned from Florida. It's already there. He's a doctor, she's a lawyer. Come on, don't tell me anybody really thought they were a black family."

The all Jewish web acknowledged that sports programming could be a problem but feels confident with their recent acquisitions. "We've just signed-up 75-year-old Marv Levy, the former Buffalo Bills coach and Shawn Green of the Dodgers, I mean how great is that?!" said Michael Eisner, who plans to pair the two Jewish sports stars in a remake of "Home Run Derby." "Marv will pitch to Shawn as contestants wager on how many times Shawn can hit it out of the park. It's testing through the roof."

Also slated is a reality series that will follow the lives of Jewish owners of NFL franchises. "A Day in the Life of Art Model," followed by "A Day in the Life of Al Davis" will show Jewish Sports Owners trying to bring their club's roster under the salary cap while strategizing which city they should move their team to next. ∎

Real Estate

Shattered Dreams Realty

ROBERT DOWNEY JR. ADJACENT!
17 BRs means you'll never know where he'll turn up. Judging by the sound of bongos, Matthew McConaughey may be in the basement. MUST SELL!!!

WOW!
Rare property, magnificent grounds, former home of famous SNL comedian and his meshugina wife. Bedroom has been repainted, all bullets removed from walls and floor, and crime scene has been cleared by LAPD. CHEAP!

REDUCED
Must see, former home of famous athlete, recently refurbished after girlfriend set it on fire. Kitchen has marble counters, wine cellar and built-in steroid refrigerator. Crime scene has been cleared.

Seattle Spectacular! Once owned by famous grunge musician. Everything perfect, master bedroom has jacuzzi and steam room. Most pieces of brain and skull retrieved by Forensics. Please call Courtney at 323-555-2387.

BARETTA FANS!
Beautiful Los Angeles estate for sale. 6 BRs, 3 baths, in-ground pool, tennis courts and a separate guest house for the bitch to live in while you find someone to kill her. MUST SELL. Willing to trade for cigarettes and a shiv.

Stunning estate property situated in the Hollywood Hills. Former home of Ray Combs, beloved host of Family Feud. Note: Ray only *attempted* suicide in the master bath with cedar trim and Mexican tile; the actual death occurred at the hospital, which is, along with schools and synagogues, within walking distance.

ELEGANCE!
Sprawling estate originally purchased by Britney and Justin, and Justin's now with Janet, but Britney doesn't need Justin, she just wants to move on with her life and new album which goes on sale Jan 2. MAKE OFFER.

Because famous people suck

For Sales Contact 310-474-5252

Real Estate

PRODUCTION OFFICES

Need quiet space for production? Unique opportunity in my mother's basement. 600 sf at affordable prices.

CALL JIM BEFORE 9PM. (323) 555-1414

Out of State

Manhattan Pre-War

Seller won't specify war. One bed/one bath. Great Location near Port Authority! Only $6.75 million

Lyle Kirkwood - Prudential Estates

The Greatest American Car Lot

You don't need magic jammies to know a good deal when you see one. Fly on down to North Hollywood Used Auto. If I can't find you a car you can afford, I'll let you wear my tights and cape home. And that's a promise.

LANKERSHIM & MAGNOLIA

LOOK FOR THE 🏠 IN THE WINDOW

Help Wanted

ACCOUNTANT

Mini-major seeks Arthur Andersen grad who's ready to really cook! Great pay + options, options, options!!!

ted@launder.com

Secretary

needed for high powered music exec Dirk Kilbus. Temp. position. Contact Janice Queijo b4 Thurs. Claustrophobics need not apply.

(818) 555-1111

RECEPTIONIST

For prestigious production company in Tarzana. Must be able to type 36 to 24 to 34 wpm. Great oral skills required. Must take dictation. No fatties.

Fax resume to 555-474-1519

ACTORS!!!

Hone your craft for pay! Motivated sellers needed to read scripts over the phone! No memorization! Make the elderly happy as you inform them of lottery "winnings"!!!

$250/wk + commission.
PO Box 245, Beverly Hills

Real Estate

MAKE MONEY ACTING!!!

The Winona Ryder Acting Academy is now enrolling students.

Don't just "play" act. "Be" act! One of our light-fingered method actors has earned as much as $5,560.40 preparing for a part as a mere shoplifter.

Call girls, drug barons and contract killers can make even more!!!

Contact Winona@sanquentin.ca.gov
There's a method to our madness!!!

Entourage Needed

"B" level star looking to expand. Need 10-12 large men to wear shiny jewelry, sing my praises.

Contact bowwow@netzero.com

Post Engineer

Anne Heche/Tom Cruise vehicle needs chemistry added.

It's in post, now fix it!

Call 310-555-5252

THIRSTY AGENT NEEDS A DRINK

Get me a cola, Intern!

Knowledge of vending machines, currency necessary. Credit only. Let's get something straight right now. You're an imbecile.

Send Resume to:
shark118@caa.com

Workshops

THE WELTON WAY

Donald Welton, featured in such shows as "The White Shadow," "Scarecrow and Mrs. King," and "What's Happening Now," shares the secrets to great acting. Past students include: Dustin Diamond, Mark Price, and That Guy in the Soda Commercial.

Don@Weltonway.com
Complimentary audiocassettes available with six-month class purchase.

Equipment Rentals

LARGE FURNACE NEEDED

Nights only. Privacy a must! No questions ever, especially about hammy smell. Will pay cash.

Mind your own business!
e-mail JoelSilver@aol.com

Auditions

ACTRESSES

Needed for new high-budget production.
Get on the road to success!
La Brea Motor Lodge #121
This Friday @ 3 pm
**Please knock three times.
Then wait. Then knock twice.**

Investments

INVESTORS WANTED
Return to Cutthroat Island!

Modine on board!
Inquiries to box 12J

Yard Sale Sat.

Reclining chair, lava lamp, Rosebud.
Vin Diesel
Downtown LA - Igloo #2
(just beneath 110 freeway)

Scripts

HIGH CONCEPT!!!

**Guy + Girl + Sparks = $$$
Just add Adam Sandler.
Can't Miss!!!**

Call Greg. (323) JKL-2033

Professional Services

NATIONAL LAMPOON'S

YOUR NAME HERE!

Align your movie with the #1 brand in humor! Slots open for '03 and '04. Scripts not required, cash + points only.

THE GREAT LIFE

Your name in my classified! Cost: speaking part + meal tab Last night, my dinner companion was: Barbara Lazaroff!

E-mail: Georgechristie@aol.com

Caption the Flag, Inc.

 #3 in quality captioning since 1990

Our customers ask us to improve, but we don't.
Why?

"Because - Frank my dean, we don't give a man."

Accredited Member, National Captioning Association 1992, 1997, 1998

Hope

MISS KANSAS RUNNER-UP '01

Finally bringing my dreams to the
City of Angels!!
Talented, bright, beautiful, loves life! Full of positive energy. Suck me dry.

(818) 555-6826

events

Today

"Look at us, we're black!" Networking Conference. Roscoe's on Pico.

Walk-a-thon to Beat Death. Purchase a black ribbon and join us in the quest to live forever! 1K stroll starts at Restoration Hardware at Century City Mall and ends at Houston's Steakhouse. Sat. 1 to 1:15 pm. Bring water!

FREDXPO!!! Come and meet me, I'm Fred. I'm lonely. Fred's house, Sunday 8 am - 6 pm.

Silent Auction for the Deaf. Fundraiser. Location TBA. Look for signs. Sat. Noon - 4 pm.

West Covina Short Internet Film Festival. Hosted by radio personality Malibu Dan. Watch over 3,200 60-second films at 800 x 600 resolution. No downloads!

2002 Awards Show Awards Honor the best of the best at the Sportsman's Lodge, Sherman Oaks. 7-9pm

A Perfect Cast: A Celebration of Body Doubles in Plaster! With special appearance by Shannon Hall, finger double in "Coyote Ugly." Armand Hammer Museum Courtyard. Sat.

B-CONCERNED >>

events that have people talking to their lawyers

Thursday night's gala charity dinner to supplement B stars' straight-to-video incomes went off with a B-ang! The members of B-LIST, an invitation only club for B stars, turned out by the B-unch: **Eric Roberts, C. Thomas Howell, Dolph Lundgren, Dan Cortes, Lee Van Cleef, Marc Singer, Brigitte Nielsen, Rae Dawn Chong, Lisa Bonet, Justine Bateman, Ernie Hudson, Josh Brolin, Andrew McCarthy, Kevin Sorbo, Martha Quinn, Bruce Boxleitner, Jeff Conaway,** and **Billy Drago** all attended. "I happened to be free tonight. Lucky thing," confided each attendee at one point during the party.

The evening was interrupted by the arrival of **Jaleel White,** who caused a veritable stampede of Bs attempting to curry favor by asking for an autograph or a handshake from the "Family Matters" star.

A highlights reel, featuring scenes from some of the actors' 204,032 collective "films," like the classics DEATH RING, DEAD FIRE and THE HITCHER II: I'VE BEEN WAITING, was interrupted by a very un-B-coming argument started by **Billy Drago,** upset that people might confuse him with table-mate **Dolph Lundgren,** who played the character Drago in Rocky IV.

Garrett Morris stated he was just happy to be there.

FIGHT NIGHT >>

Following **Michael Buffer's** signature opening, fight fans were treated to a fast and furious charity bout in which 51-year-old **Robert Hegyes** (Kotter's Juan Epstein) soundly trounced **Vin Diesel.**

"This was the saddest spectacle I've ever witnessed," stated pugilophile/Nazi Hunter **Simon Wiesenthal,** who came as the guest of **Jaleel White.**

Exiting crowds were also treated to an unscheduled display of the sweet science, as **Matt Damon** and **Ben Affleck** got into an embarrassing, hair-pulling slapfight.

GIEL-GOOD GRIEF ∨ ∨

The premier of **"Weekend At Bernie's 3"** starring the corpse of **Sir John Gielgud** as Bernie was marred by a tug-of-war over the deceased knight's body between **Catherine Zeta-Jones** and **Lara Flynn Boyle**. Fighting ended when the arrival of **Jaleel White** caused a veritable stampede of A-List film actors, infuriated to the point of violence at the 1990s TV star's appearance.

Brian Grazer's hair also attended.

BIG OPENER >>

Mariah Carey at the gala opening of her legs to Island/Def Jam president **Lyor Cohen**, with whom she has recently penned a $20 million deal, including her own record label.

Also in attendance were celeb couples **Will Smith** with wife **Jada Pinkett**, and **Jennifer Aniston** with husband **Brad Pitt** who later announced they would be swapping spouses next week.

"It's been approved by our PR people," defended Pitt, who spent the evening humming the title track to **Spike Lee**'s **"Jungle Fever."**

obituaries

Reviled by many, hated by all, **Ted Nussbaum** (William Morris) finally died, almost amazingly of natural causes. He was 78. Services will be held at Forest Lawn on Tuesday. Few, if any, are expected to attend. Perhaps not even the Rabbi.

Sidney Gold, 75, manager for more than 40 years, whose clients over the years included pre-"Arthur" Dudley Moore, pre-"Different Strokes" Gary Coleman, and post-"Pluto Nash" Eddie Murphy, was found dead of a self-inflicted gunshot wound to the head in his half of a North Hollywood efficiency.

Ailing Universal Music Exec., **Dirk Kilbus**, 72, has begun preparations for his journey into the afterlife with the sealing up of personal secretary **Janice Queijo** into his family's pyramidal shrine. Dehydration is expected to take her on Thursday at which point her organs will be replaced with spices from the Orient and her brains extricated nasally. Queijo would have been 32 on Friday. Kilbus, maker of such multi-genre classics as "The Scurvy Rodger," "D.O.D. (Dead On Delivery)," and "Caboose!" will be holding services for himself tomorrow. The Kilbus family requests that all donations go to their charity of choice, the Kilbus Family Shrine Refurbishment Fund. Graverobbers are forewarned that a curse has been placed at the shrine entrance, and that an elaborate series of booby traps and undead guards exist in the inner sanctum.

When **Danny Aiello's** chartered plane hit unexpected turbulence last Tuesday, one **Other** passenger died of a heart attack. Other is survived by his wife and two others. Aiello was fortunately uninjured.

Tony Danza's career died peacefully when he took the stage at San Bernadino's Candlewick Dinner Theater to perform his one-man show, "Tony Danza's Atlantic City."

Hollywood's favorite lead in any number of failed TV pilots, Danza's demise was relatively painless, as the former "Taxi" heartthrob sang, danced and joked his way through a monopoly of Baltic, Atlantic and Pacific Avenue references, delighting a near half-full Friday night crowd, undoubtedly drawn by Candlewick's famous all-you-can-eat Bufferama.

Danza's career was 35 years old. It is survived by the careers of Christopher Lloyd, Danny DeVito and Alyssa Milano.

CORRECTION: Earvin "Magic" **Johnson** is not yet dead.

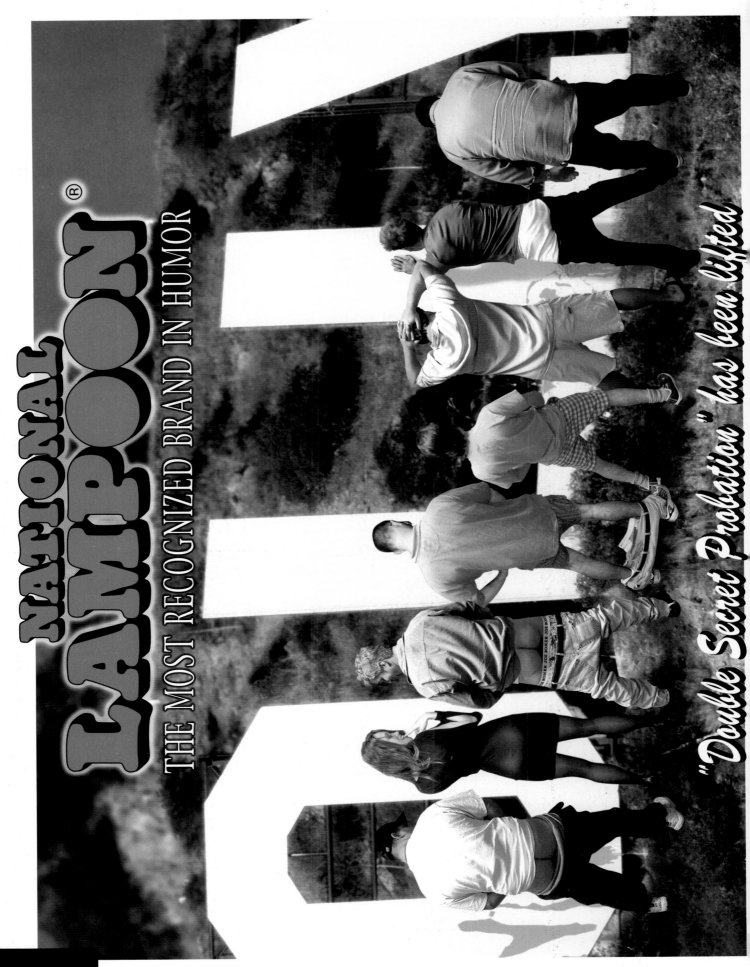

NATIONAL LAMPOON®

THE MOST RECOGNIZED BRAND IN HUMOR

"Double Secret Probation" has been lifted

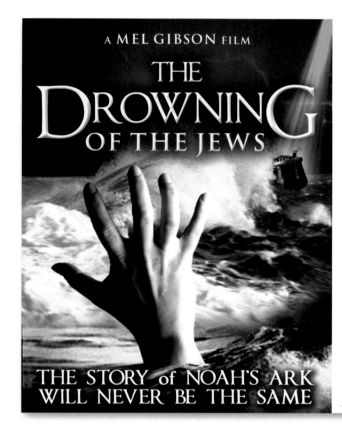

"Give me a magazine targeting kids, and give me two healthy fourth-graders and a spear, and I'll show you a great party game."

– William Randolph Hearst

CHILDRE

MAD MAGAZINE

Founded in 1952 by publisher William Gaines, *MAD* was initially circulated as a comic book under the name *Tales Calculated To Drive You Mad*. The magazine was famous for its goofy spoofs, ad-free pages and, beginning in 1964, a "fold-in" that appeared on the inside back cover of each issue. But undoubtedly *MAD*'s most enduring image is that of its gap-toothed cover boy, Alfred E. Neuman, asking "What? Me worry?"

Since both *MAD* and *National Lampoon* targeted similar subjects, even using many of the same freelance artists, they were often thought to be 'sister publications,' a fact which angered both because it sounded a lot like being called a 'Nancy magazine' or a 'Wussy rag.'

This parody first appeared in the November 1971 issue of National Lampoon.

"I want to say to all you terrorists and all you nations that harbor terrorists: I do NOT look like Alfred E. Neuman. So stop it! It's insultiating."

– President George W. Bush, 2003.

A NATIONAL LAMPOON PARODY OF

MAD

No.
147
Nov.
'71
3310

IND

®

OUR PRICE

40¢

YOU GET
WHAT YOU
PAY FOR

JOHN ROMITA

WHAT, ME FUNNY?

SCENES WE'D LIKE TO SEE

NUMBER 147   NOVEMBER 1971

MAD

"I grow old, I grow old . . ."—J. Alfred Newman

JOHN BONI, SEAN KELLY, HENRY BEARD *writers*
MICHAEL GROSS *art director* ELLEN TAURINS *production*

RALPH REESE, JOHN ROMITA,
JOHN LEWIS, ERNIE COLON, AL WEISS,
BABI JERY, STUART SCHWARTZBERG,
JOE ORLANDO *artists*

DEPARTMENTS

CITIZEN GAINES

THE MAD MAGAZINE PRIMER

YOU KNOW YOU'VE REALLY OUTGROWN MAD WHEN . . .

THE LIGHTER SIDE OF DAVE BERG

HORRIFYING CLICHÉS

ONE DAY IN THE PARK

THE SOUND AND THE FÜHRER

At last someone had the spunk to portray Hitler for what he was—a rotten, cold-blooded murderer. For too long, people have been led to believe that he was a misunderstood kid who took a wrong turn at Bavaria. Now MAD has told it like it is!

Jerry Kosinski
Painted Bird, Wyo.

Heil MAD! You really did in old Adolph! It's bound to cost you some German readers, but I guess that's the price of being gutsy! Keep those right-on spoofs coming!

Art Decco
Bangor, Maine

Stalin, Mussolini, and now Hitler. How about taking a poke at Marshal Pétain next? He's really due for a bringdown.

Rosemarie LaBinaca
Los Angeles, Calif.

A MAD LOOK AT MOTHBALLS

"Mothballs" was the funniest article I ever read in MAD. I especially liked the part about how they smell so funny and break into lots of little pieces when you drop them on the floor.

Noreen Klevish
Naismith, Ore.

I smiled at your "MAD Look at Sash Weights." I chuckled at your "MAD Look at Linoleum Floors." I guffawed at your "MAD Look at Shoe Polish Tins." I howled at your "MAD Look at Mechanical Pencils." But I just went into fits over your "MAD Look at Mothballs!"

Lionel Trilling
New York, N.Y.

YOU KNOW YOU'RE REALLY HOT WHEN . . .

Great article, but you forgot "You know you're really hot when . . . you perspire!"

Patsy Tramming
Brooklyn, N.Y.

I thought your article was swell, but you missed one—"You know you're really hot when . . . your shirt sticks to your back!"

Vince DiMuerta
La Cacca, Calif.

Terrific! But you left out "You know you're really hot when . . . you drink a lot of water!"

Frank Craspi
Gentian, Pa.

BEHIND THE SCENES

"A MAD Peek Behind the Scenes at a Coat Closet" was your best yet. It was even better than your "Peek Behind the Scenes at a Glove Compartment." How do you do it?

Richard Gasvin
West Newt, Ariz.

I didn't realize just how true your "MAD Peek Behind the Scenes at an Invisible Reweaver" was until I went to get my cardigan last Tuesday. Sure enough, you could see the stitches!

Anne Fusco
Coriander, Fla.

Congratulations on your "Peek Behind the Scenes at a Christian Science Reading Room." You handled a potentially tricky subject with taste and tact.

Miriam Plesher
Caster, N.J.

MAD MOVIE SATIRES

Kudos on your nifty spoof, "Cleopasta." Although I am only fifteen, I certainly enjoyed your clever satire of what has to be one of the dopiest movies ever! Keep up the good work!

Terry Roberts
Wilmington, Del.

Many thanks for your jazzy takeoff, "The Pride and the Pasta." Your "usual gang of idiots" deserves cheers and applause, which is more than that dumb movie got. Keep up the good work.

Robert Terry
Wilmington, Del.

I read your delightful ribbing of Ingmar Bergman's idiotic film, "The Seventh Pasta," and I recommended it to my entire English class as a good example of how to write funny satire. Continue with the good work!

Bob Robertson
Wilmington, Del.

My hat's off to you for your hilarious "Moby Pasta" and last month's hysterical "Marjorie Pastastar." They're the funniest things I've read since your classic "Pastacus"! Up the work keep good!

Rob Terryson
Wilmington, Del.

I thought your worthless satire "2001: A Space Pasta" was really stupid. Good the work upkeep!

Terry Robertson
Wilmington, Del.

"The Owl and the Pastacat" was great! Work good keep the up!

Bert Roberty
Wilmington, Del.

Congratulations on that great series of letters, Sol! They read just fine, and I especially like the one about the kid who thought "2001: A Space Pasta" was stupid — it kind of gives the thing credibility.

Al Feldstein
New York, N.Y.

PHILOSOPHY LESSON

Do you call your magazine trash because you believe it to be trash; or do you believe it to be trash and call it trash to anticipate the arguments of those who, believing it to be trash, would logically call it trash; or do you believe it not to be trash, a priori, and call it trash in the hopes that those who believe it to be trash will reject the evidence of their senses rather than accept a nomenclature which they must regard as only another aspect of its trashiness? I, for one, think it's a piece of shit.

Jean-Paul Sartre
Paris, France

A FAITHFUL FAN

· I take your magazine with me wherever I go.

Tommy Tongyai
Atlanta, Ga.

MAD WINS AGAIN

When I wuz smart I uset to read Nashinul Lambpoon but now I read MAD.

Charly
Boston, Mass.

SATISFIED READERS

All of the unicellular flagellates in my petri dish read your magazine. We may be pretty low down on the Great Chain of Being, but we think it's great!

Bifistula Ciliati
Sandham Laboratories
Travis, Okla.

Bifistula and his friends reading the latest issue.

Hey, gang, have ya noticed how over the years a certain magazine has dropped its standards, its values, its commitment—but NOT its price? Didja ever wonder, "Wha hoppen?" Huh? Didja? Well, wonder no further, for here's the epic struggle of that mag's downhill metamorphosis as presided over by its publisher...

WRITER: JOHN BONI

ARTIST: ERNIE COLON

CITIZEN GAINES

...satire...

All right. That issue tells us about Gaines the **publisher**. What about Gaines the **man**? Namely, **how** was **he** different from **other** humormongers like Thurber, Benchley, Will Rogers —

They made you laugh.

No, you **idiot**. His **last words**. That's what distinguishes a man from **other** men. Gaines's **last words** were **satire**.

That's only **one** last word.

So what does it **mean**?

I dunno!

Beats me.

Intriguing, **right?** Here was a man who **assembled** and **controlled** the **Establishment** humor magazine, yet at the end, the **only** thing on his **mind**, his **last words**, were **satire**. Why?

That's **still** only **one** last word.

Maybe it's something **funny**.

Are you **kidding**? Don't you read MAD?

Bring me **"satire"** dead or **alive**. It's probably something very **simple**. Go ask everyone who made Gaines **laugh**.

That lets out MAD's **writers**.

Then ask everyone **he** made laugh.

And that lets out MAD's **readers**.

Ask anyway. Start with Gaines's editor, **Al Feldstein**.

Satire!? Is it a **word**, or **what?** Well, it doesn't have **anything** to do with MAD or **I'd know** about it.

Wait!!...Seems to me...something Gaines once said...

Al, as MAD's **new editor**, it's up to you to keep our readers laughing. It **won't** be **easy**.

Is that because **first-rate** humor is so hard to come by?

Nope! Because I won't let you print anything **funny!**

Only **kidding**, Al. But **seriously**, we're tightening our **funny belt** in order to reach a **wider** audience, namely, **dolts** and **idiots**.

So **go easy** on the **kind** of **humor** we've been printing up to now. You know, what **Kurtzman** used to call...

...to call...sorry, can't **remember**. It's been so long. I tell you what. Go to the **library** and read **Sol Furd's** memoirs. Maybe satire's in it. **Sol** was an agent who had a **lot** to do with Gaines's **youth**. He was a real **sweet** guy.

What's the book called?

"10% or Your Life!"

EDITOR'S WARNING: Flashbacks may be harmful to your health and this **furshlugginer** movie is filled with them.

Now, I meets the Gaines kid when he was eight. His folks rented a room to one of my acts, a deadbeat comic who skips town owing them money. Then the guy dies on me in Peoria—and everyplace else—and in his will he leaves the Gaines kid all of his . . .

Jokes??! He left my son jokes?! But we need **money.** not jokes!

Look, **sweetheart,** you want **money,** you shouldda rented to a **banker.** You rent to a **comic,** you get **jokes!**

Kid, **listen!** Schecky's jokes can make you in-**dependently funny.**

My **son,** the **joker**

I can't believe it! The dumb #f*% u@$c*k%! left us jokes!

I don't want your ratty ol' jokes.

But I does right by the brat anyway and invests his gags in tax sheltered comic books, plus I gives him a nice allowance of socko punch lines and setups, which he squanders on his pals . . .

Hey, didja hear the one about . . .

Take my wife . . . please!

There was this **traveling** salesman, see . . .

. . . so the Indian says, "Mat zos? I thought they were **suppositories!**"

I know you're **out** there, I can **hear** you **sleeping.**

. . . the kid was great. He couldda been another **Henny Youngman,** but he meets this **Harvey Kurtzman** and . . .

I wanna start a comic book that people will **laugh** at. I'm prepared to invest **all** my **jokes.**

Save your jokes, Bill. I have something better—**satire!**

. . . I told him the idea is MAD, cause who knows from **satire** anyway? It always closes on Saturday night.

Nah, boss, not a **clue.** I'm heading **back** to MAD to ask the usual bunch of idiots there about **satire.**

Half man, half goat. **Right?**

Wrong! It's a streetcar, like in a **Streetcar Named Satire.**

Uh, puddon me. I'se lookin' fo' mah wife, **Satire!**

Don't ask me. I only draw what they give me.

Satire? It's a Jewish holiday.

Maybe there's a primer on it.

Satire! Sounds familiar. Didn't we used to do that once?

I'm in circulation.

These **dolts** are no help. I'm gonna try the guys who **used** to write for MAD.

Siegel or De Bartolo would know, but they're not here.

Satire? I can't **conceive** of such a thing.

It's just like Gaines to say a dumb thing like that.

HI! I'M MAX BRANDEL

CHAPTER 1

See the reader.
He is very loyal.
He wouldn't miss an issue of his favorite magazine.
Even when its price went up,
He kept right on buying it every month.
Why is he such a loyal reader?
Because he likes a magazine that rejects silly old shibboleths
And takes a bold stand on important issues
And treats difficult topics in a mature way.
Of course, his mother buys him MAD
So he reads it, too.

ARTIST: AL WEISS

CHAPTER 2

See the editor.
He is very harried.
He is editing an article for the next issue of MAD.
He has a deadline to meet.
The article needs a lot of work.
To start with, it's too long.
The editor has to take out some words.
Most of the words he is taking out have only four letters,
But boy, they sure do add up!
The article also has problems in "pacing" and "timing."
There's a reference to an ethnic group that breaks the pacing.
And there's a joke about a major religion that spoils the timing.
Being an editor isn't easy.
To be a good editor there are three things you must have:
An eye for talent.
An ear for good writing.
A nose for new ideas.
To be a MAD editor, there is one thing you must not have.
Balls.

CHAPTER 3

See the writer.
He writes for MAD.
See him flog a dead horse.
Flog, flog, flog.
Take that, Hollywood bigwigs!
Try this one on for size, Madison Avenue phonies!
Later on, when he really gets warmed up,
He'll attack rigged TV quiz shows
And automobiles with big tail-fins
And segregated lunch-counters.
Well, maybe not segregated lunch-counters.
After all, fun's fun, but you have to draw the line somewhere.
Nobody minds a little ribbing now and then,
But there is such a thing as knowing when to stop.
Look at Lenny Bruce. If he knew when to stop,
He could be a great comedian.
He could even be a MAD writer.
He's what? When did that happen? No kidding!
Well, that just goes to show you!

You Know You've REALLY OUTGROWN MAD When...

You Know You've REALLY OUTGROWN MAD When . . .

. . . you start going to movies they don't do spoofs of.

You Know You've REALLY OUTGROWN MAD When . . .

. . . you discover that you have acquired a secret power that enables you to know the contents of every issue before you even open it.

You Know You've REALLY OUTGROWN MAD When . . .

. . . you adopt complicated ruses to avoid being seen reading it so your friends won't consider you "immature."

You Know You've REALLY OUTGROWN MAD When . . .

. . . you realize that the "Now" in their "Then and Now" articles is 1957.

You Know You've REALLY OUTGROWN MAD When . . .

. . . you find a richer source of humor in everyday things, like rocks.

You Know You've REALLY OUTGROWN MAD When . . .

. . . you find out what @@%$&$%@ means.

ARTIST: JOHN LEWIS

You Know You've REALLY OUTGROWN MAD When . . .

. . . you give the charity drive a hamster cage, your brother's chemistry set, a butterfly net you used to catch crappies, *The Golden Book of Squids, Meet Mr. Weather,* and all your back issues.

THE LIGHTER SIDE OF DAVE BERG

Thanks for coming over, Mr. Berg. I wish **more citizens** had your **community spirit**.

Just **doing my part**, Officer. I was a kid once, **too**, you know.

Sure you're **confused**, son, and maybe a little **bitter**, too, but, **heck**, who wouldn't be in this crazy, mixed-up world, what with **the A-bomb** and **the current wave of permissiveness**. Let's face it— things are in one **hell** of a mess, **if you'll pardon my French!**

But when **the going gets tough**, that's when **the tough get going!** I mean, you want to leave the world **a better place** for your having been here, **right?** You see, I have this **theory** that **deep down inside**, people are basically **good**, and . . .

STOP!! I'LL TALK!! ANYTHING!! JUST GET THIS CREEP OUT OF HERE!!

. . . so then me and Jimmy, that's Jimmy Trinelli of 364 Baycrest, are you getting all this? Like I say, me and Jimmy took the stuff to Rico's, you know, to fence it . . .

O.K., Mr. Berg, I think that does it. If we need you again, we'll call.

Package for **Mr. Dave Berg**. Say, you aren't **the same Dave Berg** who draws for **MAD magazine**, are you?

That's me, young man.

No kidding, **you're the guy** who does that **Lighter Side** thing?

That's right, youngster.

Hey, **you're putting me on!** You **really** write all that stuff about **baby-sitters** and **blind dates** and **drive-in movies?**

Yes, I do, son.

Boy, are you an asshole!

FASCIST PIG! DUPE OF THE MILITARY INDUSTRIAL COMPLEX! ALL POWER TO THE PEOPLE!

COMMIE QUEER! PAWN OF THE KREMLIN SLAVE-MASTERS! GET A HAIRCUT!

There are **two** sides to every question. And after all, **everyone's** entitled to his **own** opinion. Variety is the **spice of life**, so let's **live** and **let live**.

You see, I've found that all it takes to **bridge** the **generation gap** is a willingness to meet the other guy **halfway**, a little **give** and **take**. Now I'm **sure** there's **something** you two can agree on.

WISHY-WASHY LIBERAL FINK!

WISHY-WASHY LIBERAL FINK!

ARTIST: RALPH REESE   WRITER: SEAN KELLY

HORRIFYING CLICHÉS

Insulting A READER'S INTELLIGENCE

Avoiding A DELICATE SUBJECT

Following A FORMULA

Blowing A JOKE

Belaboring THE OBVIOUS

Raising A DEAD ISSUE

ONE DAY IN THE PARK

AY, JUST HOW
DID YOU MAKE
MAD INTO THE
HARD-HITTING
TIRE MAGAZINE
IT IS TODAY?

HERE WE GO WITH ANOTHER REVOLTING
MAD FOLD-IN

"The magazine developed through the years from a somewhat sophomoric, meat-cleaver type of humor into what I regard as the sharp satiric style it features today."* To see how this wonderful transformation was accomplished, fold page in as shown. *MAD writer Frank Jacobs, in the Travel section of the *New York Times*, Sunday, July 11, 1971

FOLD PAGE OVER LIKE THIS!

A▶   **FOLD THIS SECTION OVER LEFT**   **◀B FOLD BACK SO "A" MEETS "B"**

TIST: RALPH REESE

WELL, THERE THEY ALL ARE, OR WERE, WHEN YOU WERE ONLY A KID. WE
JUST PRINTED THEM FOR OLD TIMES' SAKE. JUST IN CASE YOU FORGOT
RIDICULOUS AS THAT SOUNDS. YOU MUST STILL HAVE MEMORIES OF ALL OF
THAT INCREDIBLE CAST OF CHARACTERS. SUPERDUPERMAN, THE MOLE. DUMB
KIND OF QUESTION TO ASK. NO ONE COULD FORGET ELDER'S OR WOOD'S STUFF.
IT WASN'T SATIRE, THOUGH, WAS IT? JUST SOPHOMORIC HUMOR. HUMOR'S EASY.

A▶   **◀B   END**

WEEKLY READER

Weekly Reader was founded in 1928 as a weekly newspaper designed to keep elementary school children abreast of current events. With hard-hitting journalism and a no-bullshit attitude, it's no wonder *Weekly Reader* is still the nation's top scholastic paper.

This parody first appeared in the September 1971 issue of National Lampoon.

"I always tell children, 'The only thing better than reading the *Weekly Reader*, is reading the *Weekly Reader* in bed on a Sunday morning with Mr. Fumbly Fingers.'"

– Michael Jackson, entertainer, 2005.

My Weekly Reader
®
THE CHILDREN'S TABLOID

News Story

Vol. 51 • Issue 28 • September 2, 1971

Luis' sisters play at scene of bizarre meal.

Boy, 9, Trapped in Refrigerator Eats His Own Foot to Stay Alive

Nine-year-old Luis Obispo of San Remo, California, spent two days and nights locked inside an old refrigerator. He was lucky that there was enough air to breathe. He was unlucky that there was no food in the refrigerator. He got very hungry.

When the policemen who found him opened the door to let him out, they saw that Luis was eating something. Then they noticed that one of his feet was missing. They put two and two together and realized that it was his own foot that Luis was eating!

"Luis may grow many more inches," quipped Officer Banfield at the time, "but he won't grow another foot!"

The refrigerator was in the basement of the apartment building where the Obispo family lives. Mr. Obispo fell into a cement mixer a year before Luis was born and was chopped up (if you have the March 5, 1961, Weekly Reader, you can read all about Mr. Obispo).

Mrs. Obispo and Luis' ten brothers and sisters live on food stamps. Food stamps are not like the ones you put on letters. Instead they are used to buy food. The government gives them to people like the Obispos so they won't have to eat their feet.

It's "ankles aweigh" as Luis bites into some "sole food."

News Here and There

Mini-Mugging

A boy in Newark, New York, has a funny way of asking for toys. He hits the other children over the head with a lead pipe. Then they let him take a turn.

He is the leader of the other children. They all have lead pipes, too. Some of them have sticks and knives.

One day this boy and his friends got some gasoline. They poured it on a school bus. Then they set the bus on fire. What fun they had!

A <u>Weekly Reader</u> Exclusive **Cribside Confession**

Girl, 6, Feeds Baby Brother to Hungry Hamsters

In the Rampagno household, it was the job of Linda Rampagno to feed the hamsters. "Have you fed the hamsters today?" Mother Rampagno would ask. "Oh yes, Mama," little Linda would say. But sly little Linda wasn't feeding the hamsters at all. On purpose she was turning them into ravening (RAHV-en-ing), savage, hunger-crazed creatures. Little Linda gave them a little salt and then took away their water so that they were hungry and thirsty, too. Then Linda put her baby brother in the hamster cage.

Linda says that her mother always called the baby "my precious little new arrival," and that this had caused her to take a violent dislike to the child. The crazed hamsters not only ate most of Baby but also an expensive squeeze toy and a box of Pampers.

Maid in the Shade

Summer's here, but cute, curvacious Carolynne Kefauver, last year's Miss Pompano Beach, believes in keeping it under her hat!

Science News

Doctor Warns of New Diseases

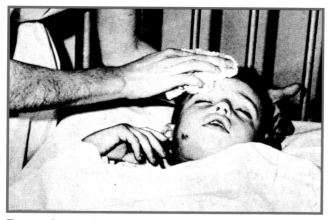

Tommy Prenz, 11, wishes he hadn't clapped so many erasers.

Stutterer Punished

Cute sub-debutante Joanie Krasner, age six, had an annoying habit. Sometimes she would get to a letter in a word and she would pronounce it about a dozen times before going on to the next letter. At first, classmates and teachers tried to "kid" or "josh" little Joanie out of her annoying habit. "C'mon, dumbo, spit it out," they would say with a grin. But soon people began to lose patience with Joanie. Finally, the class, tired of Joanie's selfish attitude, pushed her down a playground slide coated with a thin paste made from glue and broken bottles of Yoo-Hoo Chocolate Beverage, Yogi Berra's favorite drink. Joanie's teacher reports that Joanie had most trouble with the letter "V" and the word "indivisible." "I swear I could have taught the class their whole nines table in the time that child took to say 'indivisible.' It just wasn't right."

Do you know that there are loathsome (LOW-th-some) diseases that only little boys and little girls get? A scientist, Dr. Hans Amps spends all his valuable time thinking about these diseases. He comes up with several new diseases each year. This year Dr. Amps says we should look out for:

1. Playground Plague. A victim of playground plague blows up like a balloon and actually explodes. You pick up playground plague on slides, usually. "You see," says Dr. Amps, "some little boys and girls have trouble controlling themselves on the slide, so that little bits of number one and number two may accumulate, spreading the dread plague. I recommend that all slides be dismantled or sponged down with Lavoris."

2. White Lung. White lung happens when a little boy or a little girl is a little too eager to help teacher. Little boys and little girls who volunteer to help teacher in the hope of winning favors usually end up clapping blackboard erasers. If little boys and little girls clap blackboard erasers too often, they will get dread white lung due to chalk-dust inhalation, "which," says Dr. Amps, "is exactly what they deserve, if you ask me."

Aunt Em Tattles

Hi Again, Girls and Boys,

   Well, it's been quite a week for "Tales Told out of School," believe you me ... I've just heard that Michael Jackson of the Jackson Five is almost a thirteen-year-old! But he's still pretty sexy, and will be until his voice changes ... It's no secret that off the set young "Eddie" does more in the courtship line than his "father" ... he keeps a list of starlets on the inside of his toy box and checks his conquests off, one by one... His mummy Jackie is doing her best to keep those fabulous photographs of JohnJohn doing number one over the side of the *Christina* out of the scandal sheets ... Although they portray bitter enemies onscreen, in real life Puffenstuff and Witchypoo are *that way* ... mini-genius Charlie Van Doren, Jr., expected to blow the lid off the hushed-up "Sunrise Semester" rigging scandal with his memoirs in next month's *Humpty Dumpty*....

Love to all squealers,
Aunt Em

Coming Next Week

A Third Grader Asks,
"Do You Want to See My Little Breasts?"

Behind Closed Doors:
Principal's Office Torture Orgy

Cribside Confessions:
"I Threw Up in Math Class!"

A Weekly Reader Exclusive!
Baby Lenore Tells Her Own Story

Just for You Things to Do

1. See if you can find any, abandoned refrigerators where you live. If you do, leave a peanut-butter-and-jelly sandwich inside, so if someone gets trapped in it, they won't suffer the fate of unlucky Luis.
2. Get your teacher to have all your school's slides disinfected, and find a safe place to have the erasers clapped.

Uncle Funny Money   *By Dom Rodriguez*

INVASION OF THE BODY SNATCHERS

The Invasion of the Body Snatchers is a classic 1956 horror film, considered by many to be a powerful symbol of postwar America's fear of global communism. In the movie, an alien race takes over a town by transforming its citizens into emotionless nonhuman replicas of their former selves. Parodying the film as a comic book called Status Quo, National Lampoon told the story of an evil race of Jews infiltrating the good town of Whiteville. **Warning:** readers easily frightened by tales of pastrami on rye might want to skip this one.

This parody first appeared in the May 1981 issue of National Lampoon.

"You said 'snatch'. Hehe hehe hehe..."

– Beavis, cartoon actor of Beavis and Butthead, 1998.

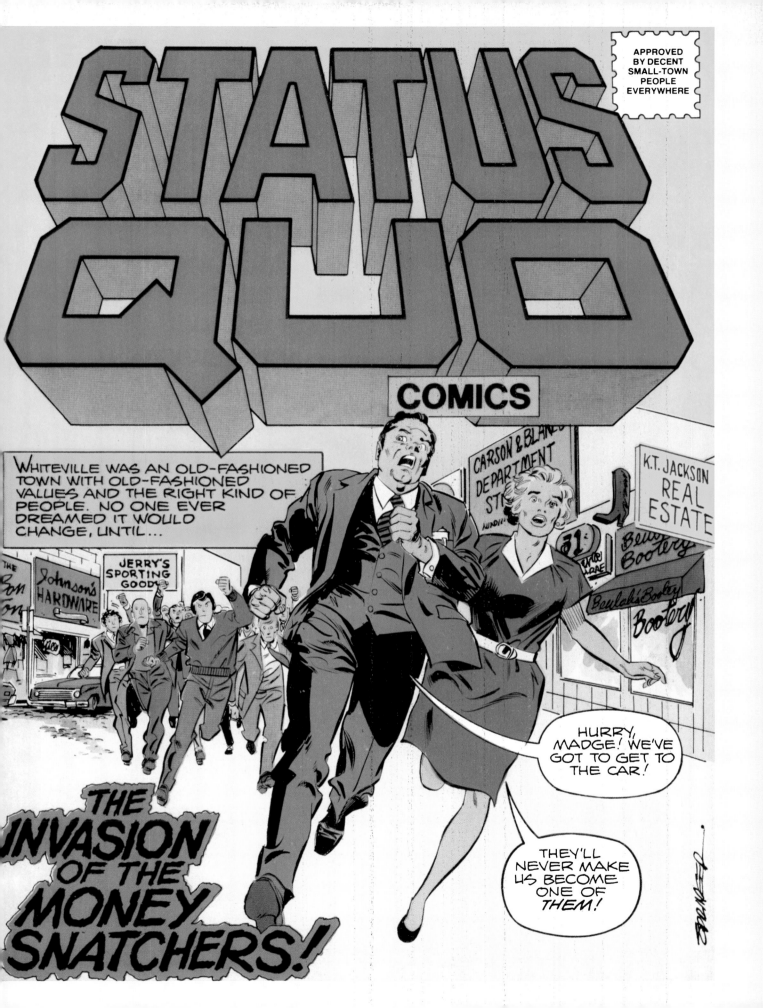

"The Riding Lesson"

Announcing a Limited Edition of Gen-Tiles, Hand-Painted Ceramic Tiles Depicting Classic Scenes of Non-Jewish Life

ONLY $69.95 EACH

Your brother drowns because he didn't wear his life jacket at sailing camp.

Here is a rare opportunity to collect a truly unique group of ceramic tiles surely destined to become priceless treasures in the years to come. Introducing Gen-Tiles, a collection of tile paintings created by the leading Gentile artists of America.

Each Gen-Tile is a beautiful hand-painted scene that is familiar and memorable to you and your family—scenes from childhood, school years, marriage, parenthood, and the golden years of retirement. These are memories that only you, as a pure Gentile, can appreciate and cherish.

Some Gen-Tiles will have special appeal to women, such as "Piano Teacher Exposing Himself to Young Female Student" or "Boyfriend Paralyzed from the Neck Down in Drunken-Driving Accident After Homecoming Party." Others will have a decidedly masculine flavor, such as "Your First Hangover" or "A Mild Coronary on the Country Club Tennis Courts." No matter what the subject, it is captured at its peak, its moment of truth, to become a timeless, classic, and soon to be highly valuable work of art.

The Gen-Tiles are rendered in rich yet subdued colors, creating a burnished look that will give your collection an image of old masters, rare works of art. And in the generations to come, your Gen-Tiles will attain an even richer, deeper patina of comfortable age and gentility—and, most important, a higher market value.

Available for a limited time only

You must order your set of Gen-Tiles before July 31, 1981. Only one set is available per person. Each set is numbered and carries the crest of the American Gentile Association. After the above date the Gen-Tile Collection will never be offered again. If you subscribe, you will receive one Gen-Tile a month for twelve months at the price of $69.95 per tile. Each Gen-Tile arrives meticulously wrapped in a genuine cotton chamois carrying case and is ready to hang on your wall or be displayed in your china closet.

Please act now if you wish to obtain this rare, limited collection.

Spilling red wine on your white ball gown at the Cotillion.

Limited Edition of Gen-Tiles. Limit: One set per person.

Must be postmarked by July 31, 1981.

The American Gentile Association, Philadelphia, Pennsylvania

Please enter my subscription for Gen-Tiles, the collection of hand-painted ceramic tiles depicting classic scenes of non-Jewish life. A Gen-Tile will be sent to me every month for twelve months, at the rate of $69.95 per tile. I will also receive a genuine cotton chamois carrying case for each. I need send no money at this time. I will be billed $69.95 for each monthly shipment.

Mr.
Mrs._____

Address_____

City_____ State_____ Zip_____

Drunk husband falls asleep on your wedding night in Bermuda.

IT ALL STARTED ON THE NIGHT OF APRIL 12, 1980. I WAS JUST ABOUT TO CLOSE MY DRUGSTORE WHEN *MADGE JOHNSON*, AN OLD FRIEND, CAME IN. MY NAME IS *BILL BRADFORD*, BUT EVERYONE CALLS ME DOC. MY FAMILY HAS BEEN LIVING IN *WHITEVILLE* FOR A LONG TIME. *WHITEVILLE* IS WHAT I CALL A *NICE* TOWN. WITH *OUR* KIND OF PEOPLE, IF YOU KNOW WHAT I MEAN.

YOU'VE *GOT* TO SEE MY BROTHER *EARL*, DOC. THERE'S SOMETHING *WRONG* WITH HIM. HE'S... *HE'S NOT MY BROTHER ANYMORE.*

NOW, MADGE...IF YOU'RE UPSET, I CAN PRESCRIBE A *DRUG.*

EARL *LOOKS* THE SAME, BUT HE'S NOT BEHAVING LIKE THE EARL I KNOW, I'M *SCARED!*

MADGE WAS *RIGHT.* EARL LOOKED THE SAME, BUT HE *HAD* CHANGED. AND SO DID HIS HARD-WARE STORE. IT USED TO BE A CLUTTERED, FRIENDLY PLACE. NOW IT LOOKED *WEIRD*, SORT OF *FOREIGN.*

LIKE...THE...WAY...I...FIXED...UP... THE...STORE, DOC?...EVERY...SECTION ...IS...A...HARDWARE...LIFE-STYLE... CONCEPT.

SEE WHAT I *MEAN*, DOC?

AS THE WEEKS WENT BY, I REALIZED THE *WHOLE TOWN* WAS CHANGING. LIKE ED WILSON, OUR LEADING BANKER. HE RAISED HIS INTEREST RATE TO *35 PERCENT* AND YET HE WAS LENDING *MILLIONS.*

WILSON SAVINGS & LOAN

ED'S MONEY FOUND ITS WAY TO OUR BUSINESSMEN, AND PRETTY SOON WE HAD A NEW SHOPPING PLAZA—WITH STRANGE NEW STORES.

INSANE IRVING
HI-FI

20TH CENTURY LOX
AND BAGELS

MARTY'S NO MIDDLE MAN FACTORY-TO-YOU DISCOUNT MEN'S & WOMEN'S APPAREL

BARRY FOO'S CHINESE RESTAURANT

OUR TOWN HOSPITAL WAS SUDDENLY RENOVATED.

BRAD & MARTHA CALDWELL CANCER CLINIC

RALPH & CORA SMITH MEDICAL & DENTAL SCHOOL

WHITEVILLE JUNIOR COMMUNITY COLLEGE WAS ENDOWED WITH NEW BUILDINGS AND PROM-INENT SCHOLARS.

BEFORE I KNEW IT, WE HAD OUR OWN CULTURAL CENTER.

WHITEVILLE Symphony ORCHESTRA CONDUCTED BY LEONARD BERNSTEIN GUEST SOLOIST ITZHAK PERLMAN

BUT IT WAS THE PEOPLE WHO REALLY FRIGHTENED ME. NICE PEOPLE I KNEW ALL MY LIFE WERE SUDDENLY GET-TING PUSHY AND LOUD AND USING STRANGE WORDS.

DOC. GIMME...SOMETHING... FOR...MY...HEARTBURN. IT'S ...DRIVING...ME... *MISHUGA.*

THE GIRLS I GREW UP WITH...THEY SEEMED SO *SPOILED* AND *BITCHY.*

HE...DOESN'T...HAVE...ESTEE ...LAUDER. HE...DOESN'T... HAVE...REVLON. HE...DOESN'T ...EVEN...HAVE...MAYBELLINE. CLARENCE, I'VE...GOT... TO...GET...MY...NAILS ...DONE.

STOP...NAGGING. HERE'S...ONE... THOUSAND...DOL-LARS. GO...TO... THE...BEAUTY... PAR-LOR.

EVEN THE KIDS CHANGED. WHITEVILLE HIGH USED TO HAVE PRETTY FAIR ATHLETIC TEAMS. BUT NOW EVERYONE WANTED TO BE A WRITER OR PLAY THE VIOLIN.

IT WAS MADGE JOHNSON, ONCE AGAIN, WHO FOUND THE ANSWER—ABOUT TWENTY MILES OUTSIDE OF TOWN.

DOC, WHAT YOU'RE GOING TO SEE ISN'T PRETTY.

THERE'S SOMETHING IN THOSE THINGS THAT'S MAKING WHITE-VILLE VERY *STRANGE.* IT'S AS IF WE'RE BECOMING...

DOC, WHAT ARE THEY EATING?

I DON'T KNOW. IT'S SCARY...! BUT IT SMELLS *FANTASTIC!*

BUT IT'S SO SPICY AND SO *FOREIGN.* AND IT LOOKS SO ICKY AND FATTY.

EVEN THE MUSTARD SMELLS GOOD.

MY OLD BUDDY WALLY CUMMINGS MIGHT KNOW WHAT THEY ARE. WALLY WENT TO MEDICAL SCHOOL IN NEW YORK. I HEARD THEY'VE GOT SOME PRETTY WEIRD FOOD THERE.

IT WAS SOME KIND OF REDDISH MEAT WITH LOTS OF FAT ON IT—ON RYE BREAD. IT NEARLY GOT TO ME, WALLY.

SOUNDS LIKE A *PASTRAMI SANDWICH* TO ME. IT'S A HIGHLY SPICED BEEF THAT *NEW YORK JEWS* LIKE TO EAT.

AMAZING. THOSE SANDWICHES EVEN HAD THE MOST TEMPTING *MUSTARD* I EVER SAW.

SURE. A...GOOD ...PASTRAMI... SANDWICH...HAS ...TO...HAVE...A ...SHMEAR.

A *WHAT?*

I...MEANT...A... *DAB.* A...DAB...OF ...MUSTARD.

DOC, LET'S GET OUT OF HERE!

THEY...KNOW...EVERY-THING. WE...MUST...*CON-VERT*...THEM. GET...THE ...SANDWICHES...READY.

I'VE GOT A *GUN* IN THE STORE. I THINK WE'LL NEED IT.

IT'S TOO LATE, DOC. IT'S TIME YOU AND MADGE BECAME ONE OF *US!*

I WAS ONE OF THE FIRST TO BE...CONVERTED. IT TAKES A LITTLE TIME TO LEARN TO SPEAK FAST, LIKE THE JE...

HOW COME YOU SPEAK NORMALLY, INSTEAD OF SLOW?

I KNOW WHO YOU ARE! YOU'RE *JEWS!* YOU'RE NOT WHITEVILLE PEOPLE ANYMORE. YOU'RE MONEY-GRUBBING, GREEDY, KIKEY *JEWS!* NOW YOU'RE TURNING OUR TOWN INTO *NEW YORK!*

SOON WE WILL BE MORE... SOCIALLY ACCEPTABLE. FIRST WE HAVE TO MAKE *MONEY* AND LIVE LIKE NOUVEAU RICHE. THEN WE ASSIMILATE AND BECOME JUST LIKE GENTILES—ONLY *SMARTER.*

SGT. NICK FURY

Marvel Comic's WWII hero, Sgt. Nick Fury, burst onto the scene in the 1960's. In true jingoistic fashion, this tough, cigar-chomping soldier led his 'Howling Commandos' in the endless fight against various Super Nazis. Later reinvented as Nick Fury, Agent of S.H.I.E.L.D, he continued the fight, this time against Super Commies. However, it wasn't until this National Lampoon parody that America finally got to see their hero fight some Super Nazis with truly super asses.

This parody first appeared in the February 1978 issue of National Lampoon.

"Ahnold luv dis comic. You will luv dis comic. But don't give lick to women in dis comic because ink will come off. And den you have ink tongue. Again!"

– California Governor Arnold Schwarzenegger, 2005.

SGT. PENIS AND THE BRASSBALL BATTALION GET
"HARD-ONS FOR HITLER!"

JUST ANOTHER DAY FOR NICK PENIS AND THE BRASSBALLS -- A GOOD, TOUGH WORKOUT, AND MAYBE A LAUGH OR TWO. BUT, LIKE HIS MEN, PENIS WAS ITCHY -- ITCHY TO GET BACK INTO ACTION, TO WIPE MORE NAZI SCUM OFF THE FACE OF THE EARTH. AND PENIS -- THE MAN THE GERMANS CALLED "DER GROSSEGRÜNESCHWANZ" -- ("THE BIG GREEN SCHWANZ") -- WAS THE MOST IMPATIENT OF THEM ALL...

HARDER! HARDER! LET'S GO, YOU GUYS! WHAT IS THIS, A TEA PARTY?

OY VAY, I'M GIVING YOU SUCH A HIT ON THE HEAD, OLAF...

YA, PY YIMMINY, IZZY, BUT SURE I TINK OLAF IS HAVING GOOD TIME, HE IS A BIG STRONG BOY, YA!

MAMA MIA! THE RIFLE, SHE TASTE GOOD! LIKE A LASAGNA!

DIS HERE SITTIN' 'ROUND GWINE DISS-TURBIFY MAH NATCH'L FIGHTIN' RHYTHM, SHO' NUFF!

HOOEE, SARGE WE GONNA GO BACK TO THE FRONT AND FIND US A LOTTA THEM THERE FRAÜLEIN LADIES AND HAVE US A LOTTA THEM THERE OR-GASMS?

I KNOW HOW YA FEEL, GUYS! BUT WE GOTTA WAIT FOR THE FAGGOTS AND DESK JOCKEYS AT GHQ TO GIVE US NEW ORDERS! MEANWHILE, WE KEEP SPINNIN' OUR WHEELS!

SGT. PENIS! MAJOR DAVIS WOULD LIKE TO SEE YOU IN HIS OFFICE. HE'S DE-BRIEFING A SOLDIER WHO JUST ESCAPED FROM STALAG 13. AND WOTTA STORY THIS GUY HAS TO TELL...

IT'S HER! -- HER! ILSE! IT WAS HORRIBLE! SHE MADE ALL THE P.O.W.S WEAR DRESSES LIKE A BUNCHA DAMES! THEN WE HAD TO SIT AND LISTEN TA HAYDN QUARTETS WHILE SHE AND HER LESBO STAFF SAT ON EACH OTHER'S FACES! AND WE HAD TA WATCH!

A GUY WATCHES STUFF LIKE THAT, HE STARTS GETTIN' IDEAS...

"Give me a magazine with a naked woman on the cover, show me to an empty lavatory, and I'll see you next Tuesday."

– William Randolph Hearst

MEN'S

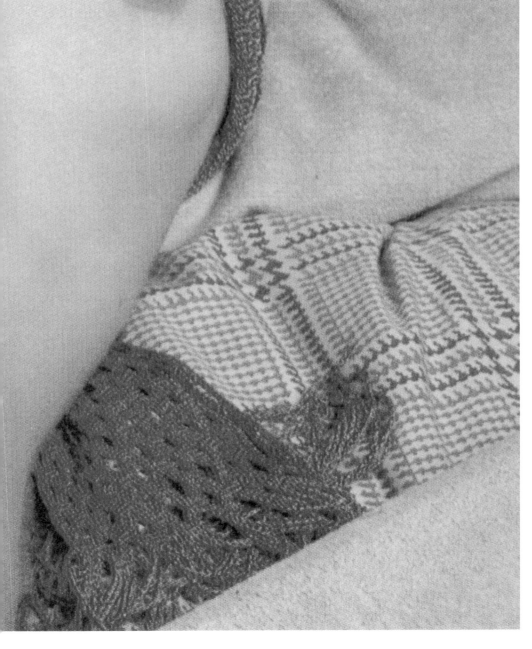

MEN'S HEALTH

Men's Health was founded in 1986 by legendary bodybuilder and nutritionist Joe Weider. It rode a wave of male fitness magazines – including *Men's Journal, Men's Fitness* and *Flex* – that began to hit newsstands in the 1980's and early '90's. With muscular cover models, tips on bigger biceps and sexier abs, and numerous ads for protein supplements, these homoerotic magazines seem determined to outdo the women's fashion industry when it comes to making you feel like crap about your appearance.

This parody first appeared in June 2002 on NationalLampoon.com.

"It took the hard-hitting journalism of *Men's Health* to finally open my eyes to all the carbs that are in Communion wafers. From now on, we're using wine and bacon."

– Pope John Paul II, 2005. The statement has since been retracted by the Vatican.

A man's lifestyle package, straight to you

Man'sHealth

CHESTS 'N TRIS DUKE IT OUT WITH BACKS 'N BIS

FREE LATS INSIDE!

PROSTATE of the UNION

5 WAYS TO AVOID DYING FROM CANCER

NUTTY ABOUT FITNESS:
tone your seminiferous tubules

SEX

Will it make your cancer jealous?

How One Man's Ripped Abs Saved His Town from Ruin
A HARROWING TALE OF WILLPOWER

SPECIAL REPORT

Are you still not talking to "it?"
peehole puppetry tricks to make it seem like he's really talking!

6-Pack Your Bags– You're Going to Abville

91 BE A LIFE SAVER WITH BROCCOLI

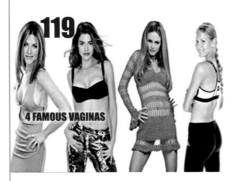

106 WRESTLERS WAX ROMANTIC ON PAST LOVES

119 4 FAMOUS VAGINAS

Tons Of Useful Stuff...

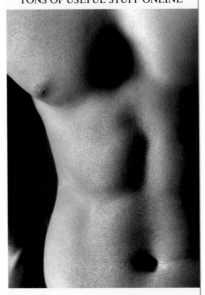
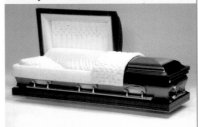

The Dutch created the many dikes that exist across the countryside for one reason: to ensure the continued existence of their red light districts. Nowhere is this more important than in Amsterdam, home of Holland's flagship Red Light District... and Gene Aurebacher.

FITNESS WITH A DUTCH TOUCH

A single child, born to a single father, neither Gene nor his father Joort knew his mother. Gene spent his youth growing up in the seedier sections of Amsterdam's open-minded and culturally diverse Red Light District, earning his keep working as a navel piercer in his father trendy tat bar, the Poonch ot Hule ent Tattork der Joort ot Sonnes. This is where Gene's love affair with fitness was born.

On any given day, Gene's regimen includes: shadow boxing tourists; Marine pushups on his head; racing trains (in his car); hang glide jousting and catching cannon balls in his teeth.

THE DUTCH (STARSKY AND) HUTCH

On the evening of Monday, April 15 at 2:05 am, fluctuating wave intensities and increasing Ph levels caused the unthinkable: Oosterscheldedam, about an hour and a half outside Amsterdam and the only barrier between the North Sea and the Red Light District, sprung a leak.

While the rest of this open-minded and culturally diverse Red Light District was resting in a sauna or oiling up for their next rendezvous, a certain someone was in the middle of his morning 100k sprints; when a four-foot diameter leak with the force of a thousand well-tossed bowling balls began pouring its contents into the basin that would eventually lead to Amsterdam's open-minded and culturally diverse Red Light District, only one person was available to deal with it: Gene Aurebacher.

With no one nearby to alert the authorities of the impending submersion of Amsterdam's open-minded and culturally diverse Red Light District, Aurebacher was forced to consider his options alone, a possibly lengthy process for a man with a resting heart rate of one beat per minute. After a few moments, it was obvious there was only one choice... bailing.

LUCKILY THERE WAS A WOODEN BUCKET THERE.

Gene began the seemingly impossible task of reclaiming the land from the ravenous North Sea, repeatedly filling the bucket then tossing the contents over the dam wall. Realizing the water was gaining, Gene saw he was in need of a singular motion, swift and easily repeatable, not the ungainly 'scoop and lob' thus far so ineffective. Gene asked himself one very important question: What was his greatest strength?

As he pondered, the skies themselves opened, letting forth a brilliant and dazzling shaft of sunlight. The heavenly ray, as if focused by God's magnifying glass, alighted upon the midsection of Gene's neon white jogging suit. The answer had been delivered.

Through his abs, the simplest and most perfect motion in the world–the sit-up–would save Amsterdam's open-minded and culturally diverse Red Light District. Gene began what would become a grueling 5 day, one muscle group workout session.

LAY BACK, FILL BUCKET, SIT-UP, TOSS, REPEAT.

Estimates later figured Gene performed anywhere from 900 million to 1.2 billion sit-ups before the Holland Autorutedam arrived. Only one life would be lost in this entire incident, and that not from the water at all. When the Chief of the Autorutedam approached Gene, still in the middle of his Herculean task, a small stone caused him to trip and land on Gene.

The Chief's easily combustible flesh was almost instantaneously converted into smoldering ash upon contact with Gene's furious abs. A group of well-intentioned rescue workers also suffered 3rd degree facial burns when they looked directly into Gene's navel to search for the Chief's remains.

In order to avoid more deaths, Gene's abs needed to be cooled. And still, the leak had yet to be contained. A few hours had passed since the Chief had been burnt to ashes, giving Gene's heart a chance to pump a few more times and giving Gene a chance to hammer out a plan.

As per Gene's instructions, a construction crane was rushed in from Amsterdam and hastily tried to grab Gene within its claws. It took four tries and three melted claws before the crane was able to lift Gene by his white jogging suit and surgically insert his abs into the dam's leak. The hole was sealed within seconds as Gene's thermally enhanced abs temporarily liquefied large portions of the dam's steel and concrete face. As a side benefit, millions of gallons of water inside the dam were instantly vaporized, which later precipitated in a drought-racked region of Holland's farming counties, saving up to 90% of Holland's agricultural exports for that year from a dry demise and averting an almost certain recession.

After being summarily cleared of all homicide and arson charges, Gene began using his new found celebrity to tour as a motivational fitness expert. And to this day, the city of Amsterdam uses the heat from Gene's abs to power a small geothermal plant located inside his one bedroom flat.

Asked if he felt he had proved himself to his father and his friends, Gene replied only, "Now I am the bull."

And that's ab-solutely the truth, Gene!

"I AM LIKE MANY CATS. I AM LIKE A PUMA OR A LION."

"I AM LIKE A TIGER BUT NOT LIKE A PANTHER. "I AM NOT LIKE A PANTHER BECAUSE THEY ARE BLACK."

"I AM SOMETIMES LIKE A CHEETAH OR A COUGAR. THE EYE OF THE COUGAR TOO."

MH: Gene, where did you find the will power to achieve your goals? I didn't find it. I engaged it.

MH: Some people in America have complained that some of the motivational advice on your latest calendar loses something in the translation. Of this there are many consequences. If you came to my country and did not use verbs so much, we would have no problem to make a better one. Most people there speak two or three.

MH: Americans are notorious for being picky though. Do you think future products will have to go through a more stringent translation process? (standing up) Time in again, I am to find mine self confrontational avec les oeufs, uh, how to say, with those who did not get much learn. The new calendar and everything on it have been more translated better. If this is not to work, what will? You know, I have many skills. Many that I have made for after when Oosterscheldedam went to the holed. Is this not the way with all of the great?

MH: Well, certainly, in America, yes. What are these feats of which you've found yourself capable since that fateful day you saved Amsterdam? Watch. I will toaster to make exist.

A fully-functioning toaster appeared on the small table between Gene and MH interviewer.

MH: That's amazing! Is there bread in there? How did you do that? Not "how," but "For." The need to impede, my friend. Stronger than love, not so strong as excellence.

MH: Can anyone will a toaster into existence? Toaster is easy. Memorabilia much harder.

MH: Like old lunch boxes or political campaign buttons? No. Memorabilia, uh, how to say...what has happened in passing and you know.

MH: Memory? Yes.

MH: Wait, you're saying you can alter people's memories and make them believe anything you want? Tough but yes, this I have can.

MH: What's to stop you from taking over the world one person at a time then? Nothing. This does to scare you?

MH: No. I am grateful for to have the chance to excel to you. This is goal number one. You will do of the well, my friend.

MH: I thank for you. End.

HEALTHBERT

THERE ARE ONLY 2 KNOWN WAYS TO GET A BODY IN SHAPE!

ONE: YOU CAN WAKE UP EARLY EVERY MORNINIG. JOG 12 MILES, LIFT ENORMOUS AMOUNTS OF WEIGHT, GIVE UP RICH SAUCES, DESSERTS, AND BEER, AND OF COURSE REPEAT THE PROCEDURE BEFORE YOU GO TO SLEEP EVERY NIGHT...

OR TWO: DEVOTE ALL YOUR FREE TIME TRYING TO FIND SOME SORT OF ARABIAN MAGIC WISH-GRANTING GENIE.

WHERE ARE YOU GOING?

PRICELINE.COM... I NEED TO GET A FARE TO BAGHDAD.

PENTHOUSE

Penthouse was founded by Bob Guccione in 1965. As a racier competitor to Playboy, it became the first mainstream publication to show pubic hair. When Playboy eventually followed suit, Penthouse took us even closer to the action. God bless them. The magazine is also known for its Penthouse Forum, a section of "real" stories submitted by readers that often begin with the phrase: "I never thought the letters in your magazine were true until I had a similar experience..."

Recently, sales of the magazine have been in sharp decline due in large part to the Free Smut Emporium, also known as the World Wide Web.

This parody first appeared in the January 1974 issue of National Lampoon.

"If you bedded a Playboy Playmate, you'd brag to everyone. But if you bedded a Penthouse Pet, you'd leave $100 on her dresser, drive home to your efficiency apartment in the Valley and viciously scrub yourself with soap."

– Hugh Hefner, publisher Playboy Magazine, 1984.

PETHOUSE

THE INTERNATIONAL MAGAZINE FOR MALES

JANUARY 1974 ONE DOLLAR

THE NAKED NAKED APE

VIVISECTION
TWO LEGS ARE
BETTER THAN NONE

SPAYED CATS

SADOMASCOTISM
THE LAST TABOO

Belgie 60 frs./ Danmark 10.25 Kr inkl. moms/Deutschland 5.60 DM/France 9 NF/Israel 5.35 Israeli Pounds/ Italy 800 Lire/ Japan 450/Yen.
Nederland 5.25 FL/New Zealand $1.00/Norge 10.50 N.kr/Oesterreich 35 Sch/Philippines 12 Pesos/Schweiz 5.30 frs/Sverige 7.50 kr. inkl. moms.

PETHOUSE
FARMYARD

in which dogs have their day, cats are let out of the bag, sheepish readers get monkeys off their backs, old dogs learn new tricks, bitches get squirrely, and everyone gets our goat. **Letters for publication should carry pawprint and pedigree** though these will be withheld by the Editor on request. All submissions may be reacquired at a later date upon payment of an appropriate sum. Send to Pethouse International, c/o Umberto's Clam House, Mulberry St., New York. The views expressed in this column are not those of the editor and are usually stupid.

Dago plaint
Wassermatteryou, Bob? You no like a guinea fowl? Howsabout a nice a fat guinea fowl soon, eh? Sit on you face. Mmmmm. Nice, nice.—*C. Cacciatore, Salerno, Pa.*

Autophilia up
I can eat myself. I don't mean eat myself the way you'll think of it—I mean *eat* myself. I'm eating myself right now. God, I'm delicious. What's more, I don't make a bump in me. I make me a little thicker but I don't make a bump in me. Yummy nums. I'm half way up me already and still eating.—*Willie "The Snake" the Snake, Ariz.*

Peg o' his heart
I'm a pretty normal well-balanced tuna who digs a salty piece of *Thunnis alalunga* as much as the next guy but recently I've found my blood practically freezing at the very thought of an amputee mate. Is there some service available that might put me in touch with such a dreamboat or am I just one sick, sick fish?—*Charley T., Hairless, Mex.*

Yes, you are sick—looks like that mercury might finally have gotten to your minute nerve center. And even though there probably is some sweet-lipped pathetic denizen of the deep limping around the seabed on her dorsal, her poor darling finless stump of a tail dragging around behind her like a lost memory, defenseless against all kinds of unspeakable sexual assaults from stronger, faster fish who might kiss or lick or suck or even gnaw on her poor, helpless, delicious, salty stump, you should see a doctor immediately.—Editor

Second helping
I tell you I can't believe I never tried this before. I'm the best thing I ever tasted. The further up me I go, the yummier I get. What's more, the parts of me I've already eaten are even fatter and juicier than the parts I haven't, because there's more of me in them. Right now I'm coming up to the part of me with my tail in it. It's so fat and thick and juicy I can't believe it. And do you realize that I'm just going to go on getting fatter and thicker and juicier the more of me there is in me? Up yours, Puccione, eat your heart out. Can anything this good be wrong?—*Willie "The 'the snake' Snake" Snake, Ariz.*

Spray plaint
Is it OK to spray? Even though I've mounted a million chix I still spray all the time. Wherever I am, I spray indoors or out, day or night. I must spray sixteen or seventeen times a week. It is OK?—*Mitten, Kans.*

Our medical advisers lead us to believe that advertent or inadvertent spraying, even though it is perfectly normal, can eventually lead to galloping myopia and/or serious cataractual detriment with possible loss of vision. There are also less substantiated reports that constant spraying may result in capillary growth on the hard underside or pad of the paw. If you must spray, although in view of this information it seems unwise, our advice would be to just do it 'till you need gloves and glasses.—Editor

The problem down there
I have had this really strange experience. I don't know if it's normal or not but I'd like your advice. I am a perfectly ordinary haddock and I've been seeing a really cute little mackerel named Jill. Anyway, one thing has led to another and the other night I went down on her for the first time. The thing is, her cooze was real cute and everything but it *stank!* As a matter of fact it smelt just like a human—you know, those things that bloat up and float around. Is this normal or should I give my girl a little present?—*P.J., Reykjavik, Iceland*

It is unfortunately entirely normal for the average female's privates to exude a definite odor and many have considered it not unlike the odor of humans. However any well-educated mackerel should know how to practice hygiene in this area, although your girl may be too inexperienced to be aware of it. Drop her a hint next time by something simple like throwing up or playing dead.—Editor

He can't believe he ate . . .
Boy am I full! I just ate the part of me that had the part of me that had my tail in it. That means I've eaten my tail three times already. I look like a huge green doughnut. I tell you I'm beginning to wonder if my eyes weren't bigger than my stomach.—*Willie "The 'the "the snake" snake' Snake" The Snake, Ariz.*

Coming, coming, gone
I have a real problem. I take too long to come. Most of my bitches are through in two or three seconds but I often take four or five to pop my wad. Trouble is, the next guy in line can't usually wait that long so I'm always getting it up the Old Dirt Road. What to do?—*(Name and address withheld)*

Turn gay. Ahahahahahaha.— Editor

Chicken of the sea
I just wanted to write to you because I am so happy, so happy to be alive, so happy to be in love. How many people can there be who could have such a wonderful husband, one who is so understanding, so loving, so gentle and faithful, above all who cares for you so much. You may wonder why I am writing this and why you are printing it. Well, it is quite simple. You see, I have a terrible handicap. I am an amputee tuna. Every morning when I wake up it is not like other fish. I must limp pathetically along the seabed with my defenseless pink stump trailing behind me, looking for breakfast, which of course it is terribly difficult for me to catch. Many fish would spurn me or even try take advantage of me by licking or sucking or biting on my pretty stump but not my husband. He just kisses my stump gently in the center where it's tenderest and lays me down between some comfortable rocks so that my stump can be soothed by the current washing it slowly back and forth like an exotic dish, and finds me some breakfast before he leaves for work. Often when he is gone I am frightened that I will be attacked by some larger fish and I will be unable to get away because of my poor, useless, pathetic, helpless stump and whoever it might be will dash at my stump and rip and tear at it till it bleeds and the water all around is a seething mess of red whirls and torn flesh, but I know that he is never far away. And then I thank God that despite my stump I have still a beautiful family of three hundred and forty thousand like any other healthy tuna lady and though I sometimes worry that this will be the day when my disgusting ugly slimy sickening stump will finally mean that he never comes home—he always does and kisses and fondles my stump as if it were the most precious part of me and puts it in his dear mouth and soothes its throbbing pain, and then I know the wonderfulness of a true love. And I know that when we go to sleep that night my man will take my hacked-off limb and hold it between his fins and rub himself gently up and down up and down up and down until . . . until we both fall into the deepest slumber.—*(Name and address withheld!)*

I wrote this one How'd you like it?—Editor

Another stupid letter
I gotta repeat a paisan whatsa wrong with you? Howcome no a guinea pig? Hows about a real nice a guinea pig soon, eh?, Sit on you face real a good. Dump one a right in you mout. Mmmm. Nice, nice.—*Involtini di Vitello, Palermo, Mo.*

Objection to age-old tradition
Must I return to my vomit? Who made me that way? I don't like wallowing in great piles of blown lunch—why should I? It's disgusting—*Pickles, England*

We sympathize as a matter of course with anyone who writes us with his problem, but this time we have to say just who the hell do you think you are? What do you think you're descended from, fella—an ape? You're descended from a goddamn turnip, that's where you are on the chain of being. You've got a brain the size of a peanut. You don't have any feelings. You're not capable of them. You don't have to know why you're made that way. You are. That's it. So just cut the crap, and get back to that vomit Jesus, these kind of letters make me mad—Editor

Après moi, le déluge
BLLLLLLLLLEEEEEEAAAAAUGGHHHHHH! !!!—*Willie the Snake, Ariz.*

Cave canem...

NANA

Nana is now. Nana is yours. Nana is soft, hard, cold, warm, stunningly, sleekly clean. Dirty. As you wish. Nana relaxes. Nana seduces. Nana checks with her answering service. Nana. An enigmatic bundle of furry, feathery fantasy, a million strands of unconditioned reflex, from which the hidden secret suddenly peeps, like a peach in a bucket of meat. Who knows Nana? If she's aware of the ontological dichotomy in late nineteenth century Hegelianism, she isn't telling. And why should she? In the end those deliciously stubby little legs say it all, a four-square invitation to live with her, in her, on her, through her, for her. Nana has a word for it. Arf. And I have a word for it. Crap. Why do I write this? No one ever reads it. All they're interested in is glomming this month's mess of pussy or doggy or sheepy or goaty and locking the bathroom door

You think Puccione gives a shit? Nah. All that tacky wop cares about is getting his ashes hauled with whatever he's pointing his Pentax at and keeping out of the cement overcoat the boys in the back room have ready for him if he drops below 110 percent annual growth. You realise that seventeen times in the last seventeen months right here on these very pages I have *quit? And no one has ever noticed?* It's fucking incredible. Well, this is it, boy. No more cameras smeared with so much vaseline they look like dildoes at a Mattachine Ball, no more creaking premises for Pooch's crotchshots. This time I'm walking. Period.

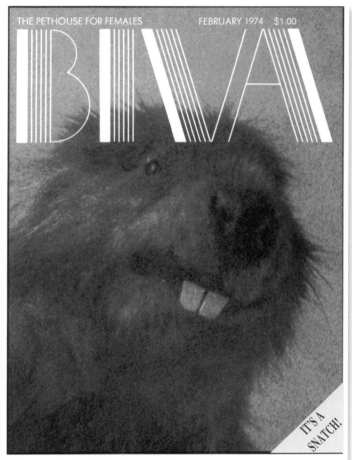

THE PETHOUSE FOR FEMALES   FEBRUARY 1974 $1.00

BIVA

IT'S A SNATCH!

FOR BITCHES SOWS COWS EWES DOES HENS MARES VIXENS NANNY GOATS AND CLAMS!

The same kind of magazine
for the same kind of audience . . .

If you're one of those sexual dodos who gets off on the seamy pockmarked fur we flash in *Pethouse*, then *Biva* is for you. *Biva*—the same old junk thinly disguised as a magazine for females, and created in response to a demand we whipped up by sending ourselves thousands of phony letters.

PLAYBOY

Founded by Hugh Hefner in 1953, *Playboy*'s first issue featured a two-page spread of a very naked Marilyn Monroe. It immediately sold out, helping to launch an empire that would include clubs, jazz festivals, cable stations and those infamous Mansion parties.

While competitors such as *Hustler* and *Penthouse* began cropping up in the 1960's, their racier photos were no match for *Playboy*'s brand recognition, which included its bunny logo and the ubiquitous claim that "I buy it for the articles."

This parody fist appeared in the January 1973 issue of National Lampoon.

"The other day, I'm reading a *Playboy* to my eight-year-old son, and he looks up at me and says, 'Daddy, where's the pink?'"

– Bob Guccione, publisher Penthouse Magazine, 1984.

INTERMENT FOR MEN

JANUARY 1973 ONE DOLLAR

PLAYDEAD

PLAYDEAD PICKS THE PIGSKIN PLANE-CRASHES OF '73

13 PAGES ON THE GIRLS OF FOREST LAWN

SHROUDS OF SPRING: FASHION FORECAST

SUBURBAN GRAVE-SWAPPING

THE NUDIST SHARON TATE EXHUMED

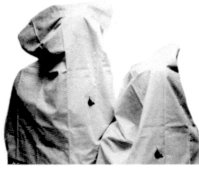

THE PLAYDEAD ADVISOR

I have a delicate problem. My girl friend is a lifelike dead person who is "passing," and she is very intolerant of my family because they aren't "up on" the latest grooming techniques and don't look as lifelike as she does. She is especially hard on two uncles of mine who have decomposed. I am embarrassed that my uncles don't take more pride in their appearance, but I can't help loving them and I can't help being hurt when my girl friend refers to them as "those old stiffs." What can I do to change my girl friend's attitude?—Y. M., New Hope, Pennsylvania.

Uncork the bottle one half hour before you plan to serve it, and you will enhance its bouquet and avoid the "vinegary" taste you mention.

I'm writing you because I'm just too embarrassed to ask anyone else. I had always thought that in subtraction the number on top was the minuend and the number on the bottom was the subtrahend, but in a bus the other day I happened to overhear a remark which indicated that it was just the reverse. Can you set me straight?—C. P. A., Wilmarth, North Dakota

Glad to help. The sweater you saw was a cardigan. One reason you were confused is that in France all sweaters are called "pullovers," even if (as is the case with your cardigan) the sweater buttons down the front and is not "pulled over" the head.

The flesh is beginning to fall away from my right arm in chunks. I have consulted my mortician, and he assures me that the situation is completely normal for my time of death (I passed away six months ago), and he tells me not to worry. Still, it is alarming to see my very own flesh come off by the handful. Is there anything I can do, or must I resort to long-sleeved shirts?—C. S., Essex Fells, N. J.

No, you lose your bet. Frankfort isn't the only town with a "wide open" section where prostitutes can ply their trade legally and under the supervision of trained medical authorities. Brussels and Milan have similar arrangements, and Copenhagen has a "kennel district" where animal contacts are supervised by the state.

Now, with my nose drops is it three drops every two hours or two drops every three hours?—M. L., Norfolk, Virginia

Not in this day and age. Five years ago it might have been necessary to tell your hostess in advance that you planned to bring a dead date to her dinner party. Dead people are now so much in evidence at nearly every "live" event that your question would be embarrassing as well as superfluous.

The other day I went to a restaurant in a part of town I rarely frequent. I ordered a steak and a salad. I was halfway through my meal before I noticed that there was salt but no pepper on the table. When I complained to the waiter, he came back with a funny-looking wooden thing the size of a bedside table. He turned this thing once or twice and something that looked very much like pepper came out. What gives?—L. M., Quincy, Massachusetts

It could be an allergy. Even lifelike dead people develop new likes and dislikes after death. The fact that you were accustomed to eating strawberries without experiencing aftereffects during your life does not directly bear on your après-death situation.

My stereo goes whurra-whurra whenever I turn it on. Then it makes noises like dentures going down the garbage disposal. Then it backfires. Then the turntable speeds up to about two hundred rpm's. Then it goes blurp-a, blurp-a and stops completely. Frankly, it's been a long time since I've really enjoyed listening to music on my machine.—G. H., Greenwich, Connecticut

Be thankful you have a wife who will speak to you frankly about her sexual needs. Encourage these discussions. Sometimes the sex life of a married couple can be enhanced by a "change of place." Suggest to your wife that you make love in the cellar, the laundry room, or under the dining-room table.

PLAYDEAD INTERVIEW: DAN BLOCKER

a candid conversation with ole hoss cartwright of the ponderosa, tv's latest pulmonary embolus

---

It's no secret to any casual observer that the new mortality is here to stay. It has only taken a few short years for it to make its way from the closed tomb to the drawing room. Sanctified by the public's demand, this once grave subject is now the topic of major motion pictures, best sellers, nightclub acts, reviews, and the like. Even the predictable standard fare generally offered to television viewers has taken steps in this new direction to give its public what they've been craving for many years.

One early pioneer in this area is the fifteen - year - old - and - still - going - strong "Bonanza." Though still subject to a great deal of criticism by true aficionados who claim, "Yes, they've killed a lot of people on the show, but they do nothing with the bodies afterward. What's that? That's garbage to us," "Bonanza" has *been* responsible for over 1,247 TV deaths. One hardly can think of "Bonanza," though, and not think of the lovable, gullible second son, Ole Hoss, played admirably by Dan Blocker.

Born Daniel Blocker in Bowie, Texas, of monied parents, he was bent on an acting career from the start. His parents encouraged his vocation by sending him to Yale, where he studied drama and became president of Bubble and Sweek, the college's acting society. After a stint in the Korean War, he earned his master's and half a Ph.D. and was hired to appear on "Gunsmoke." In his first TV role he lassoed and dragged Chester fifteen miles out of Dodge. Marshall Dillon caught him but had to release him when Doc said that Chester would live. Still furious, Dillon took him out behind the jail and beat him into unconsciousness. That was in Dodge. He then headed as far West as you could go and not be in California: Nevada . . . and was given two brothers and a father whose penchant for riding into town, riding around their ranch, and asking each other questions was boundless. It was on this stretch of land, the Ponderosa, that Ole Hoss made the show a success and himself a wealthy man.

PLAYDEAD *sent our own handgun editor, Kevin Dowd, to interview Dan Blocker and had this to say about him:* "The first thing you're struck by is the man's size. Figuratively, not literally. He's enormous. I talked with some of the extras he'd work with, and they'd always like to say, 'Why he's so big he has to go out of the bunkhouse just to change his mind.' Lorne Greene, who plays his father, asked me to change that 'bunkhouse' to 'main house' because he didn't like Hoss going into the bunkhouse when he had a perfectly good room right upstairs. Greene expressed some confusion when I suggested that Hoss is really Dan Blocker and not his real son. "There were two separate interviews. The shooting schedule of the show demanded most of his time, but I was able to ride with him for the two-hour drive to and from the set. The producers of the show explained to me that they plan to alter his character somewhat this season and have him play the part of a comatose shut-in. The nature of the program led me to my first logical question."

PLAYDEAD: After fifteen years of high riding, ranch tending, and shout-outs in and around Virginia City, Nevada, you've become an institution and a very wealthy man. How much of the show's success would you say is attributable to your gun vis à vis your brother's and father's guns?
BLOCKER:

PLAYDEAD: In your present situation, how often do you get laid and blowed and see other dead people naked?
BLOCKER:

PLAYDEAD: We don't want to put any words in your mouth but . . .

"   " "   " "   "

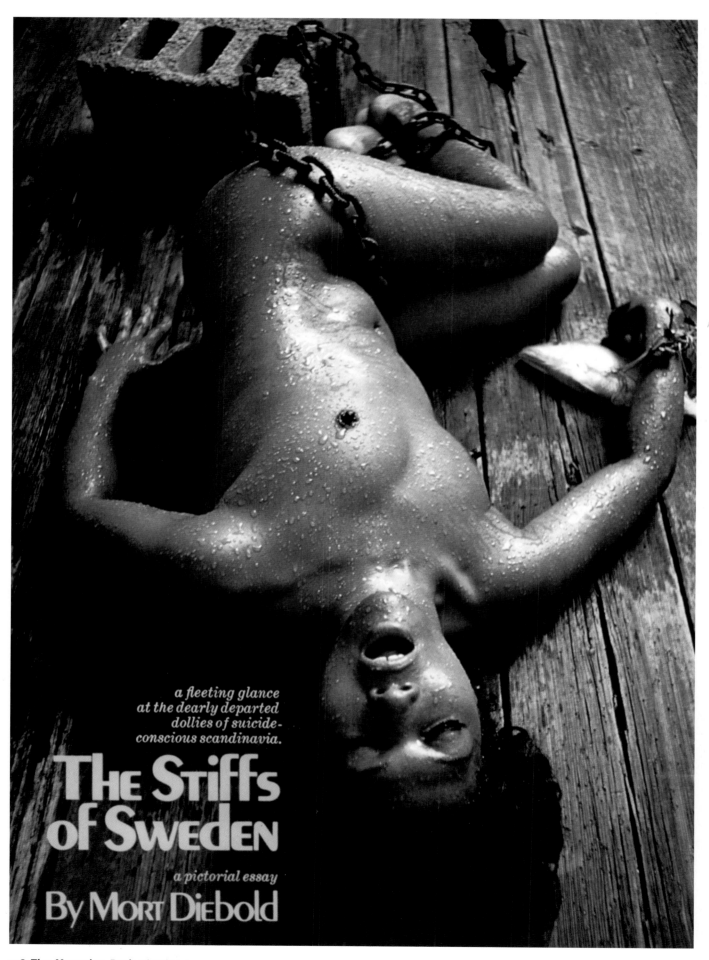

a fleeting glance
at the dearly departed
dollies of suicide-
conscious scandinavia.

The Stiffs
of Sweden

a pictorial essay

By Mort Diebold

While Paris may sizzle and Rome may burn, no place can satisfy the multi-faceted desires of today's sophisticated necropolitan male quite like Sweden. The signs are all about in this land of the moonlight sun—from the grammar-school chants, "You can rig a soccer match,/You can rig a tortoise,/You can rig a sailboat,/But you can't rig a mortis," to the nation's top songs, which freely extole the virtues of virulence. In 1967 Sweden played host-country to the first International Death Fair. Though other nations have attempted to repeat this fatal phenomena, their brands of dead reckoning left much to be desired. The Japanese, who rank second to the Swedes in per capita suicides, were able to capture some of the cryptic celebration but fell short inventively when they tried to recreate the individual body-embalming exhibits, the grave-digging displays, and the corpse-stripping and hefting-and-running events.

(continued on page 125)

With over twenty-seven arrests and eighteen convictions attributed to her clan-destine undercover-work, gangland gossip Penny Soljivon (left) seems a little morti-fied as she's dragged from her visit to the deep six while Songe Korjoe (right), the daughter of a minister, finds it all in keeping to spend her day off hanging around the attic.

Debbie Peterson (below), a true organic gourmet, winds up cooking her head off and reminds us to pick up some buns on the way home tonight; and certainly worth stairing at is pert Miss Mia Fojrd (left), a former airline stewardess who knows how to take steps in the right direction.

MISS JANUARY 17, 1947–JANUARY 5, 1973

PLAYDEAD'S PLAYMORT OF THE MONTH

PLAYDEAD'S PARTING JOKES

Our Disinterred Dictionary defines a *posthumous erection* as vigor mortis.

The homosexual necro went down to the morgue for his weekly dalliance.

"Slim pickings today," said the friendly mortician, "all we've got today is a beautiful, sexy, young housewife who slashed her wrists."

"Oh, well," sighed the disappointed sodomite. "Buggers can't be choosers."

Then there was the newly widowed husband who thought his wife's body would look good in something long and flowing, so he threw it in the Mississippi.

The Texas cowboy had been pursuing a beautiful dance-hall girl named Eugenie. When he finally got her into bed she begged him to do it with his Colt instead of the usual weapon. He got so excited that at the crucial moment he accidentally pulled the trigger and creamed his Gene.

It's an ill whore that blows nobody any good.

The three conventioneers out on the town for a little old-fashioned necro, found Madame Fifi LaJambe's stiffs the best looking they'd ever seen. Each retired to a separate room to sample the delights of the house and after a decent interval emerged to compare notes.

"The best ever," said the first. "Stiffer than a Marine sergeant on V-J day."

"Just the greatest," said the second. "Tighter than a thirty-foot putt on the eighteenth."

The third was silent.

"How was yours?" asked the other two.

"She moved," was the glum response.

Our Disinterred Dictionary defines a *homosexual necrophiliac* as someone who's always running into a dead end.

Then there was the frustrated cancer patient who had himself cremated in a whorehouse in the hopes of one day having his ashes balled.

And Ernest Hemingway—always shooting his mouth off.

There was a jazz player called Coors,
Whose riffs drew fantastic applause.
When asked why this was,
He said, "It's because
I'm constantly shooting up 'whores'."

The travelling salesman was quite lost in the wilds of the Middle West. Despairing of finding a place for the night, he stopped at a nearby farm and was taken in by the hospitable master of the house. After a hearty dinner the salesman began to feel some rather basic urges and inquired of his host where he might satisfy them.

"Well," said the farmer, "I do have a daughter, but she's dead."

The salesman, too horny to object, followed instructions and found a beautiful girl with no legs hanging in the barn, three months dead. After a wonderful night, he was overcome with remorse and buried the corpse.

"The rice in her cunt was delicious," he explained to his host the next morning, "but I had to pay her my final respects."

"That's O.K.," was the matter-of-fact reply. "Most guys just left her hanging there. And by the way, that wasn't rice, it was maggots."

These days those sex-and-death orgies in California are being referred to as gang bang-bangs.

MODERN DYING
The Playdead Pad/A Tomb With a View

Presented on this page are plans for the ultimate in funeral digs, an *après-vie* retreat, which, in the opinion of the deaditors, provides a fine and private place for the discriminating playbody with a penchant for post putrefaction.

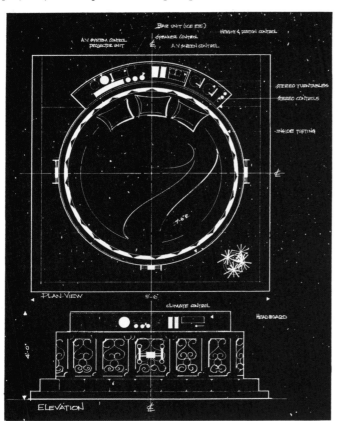

From the heavy-duty iron doors through whose keyhole our ghostly host issues forth to greet us, to the sunken necreation area where most of the moldering goes on, this mausoleum is a monument to easy afterliving. As we enter, we note that solid prestressed-concrete construction throughout protects our postmortem companion both from a yegg in his bier and from crypt-crashing maggots who might want to nosh in his kniche (see Thomas Mario's *Food For Worms*, PLAYDEAD, November 1969).

Passing into the vault, we reflect on the good taste of this forever chamber's ossuarial occupant in selecting a last-straw bury-preserve that embodies so many of the amenities of the good death, and frankly we're too polite to mention that his *chateau* with an *accent grave* seems to have mausitosis. But the catafalque hasn't got our tongue when it comes to commenting on the charnucopia of posthumous possessables that litter his litter, a testament to the grin-and-take-it-with-you attitude which PLAYDEAD has long espoused (see *The Playdead Necrology*, part 1, January, 1958; part 2, March, 1958; part 3, June, 1958; part 4, August, 1958; part 5, December, 1958; part 6, February, 1959; part 7, May 1959; part 8, July, 1959; part 9,

(continued on page 336)

From the moment when he kicks the bucket (burnished copper with brass handles: $24.95, from Necrotics) until the last trump sounds, the man with *savoir mourir* will be on shroud nine in the Playdead Circular Coffin. Amply proportioned, richly appurtenanced, and lavishly accoutered, this Mama Cassket has room for the carefree carcass and his sepulchritudinous corpa delicta to peter out on their pall and stay merry as they decay *à deux* in Seventh-Sealy-Posturepedic comfort. While magic fingers massage the abra-cadavers, a cross-the-bar offers a wide selection of exotic embalmables and an automatic eternal sound system plays music to rot by, allowing our dead man-in-the know and the nookie in his nook to turn into mulch in tasteful entombment.

"Don't pay any attention to her. She doesn't know whether she's coming or going."

"I said, 'ashes to ashes,' Mr. Abernathy."

"I'm not paying. You said she was a virgin."

END

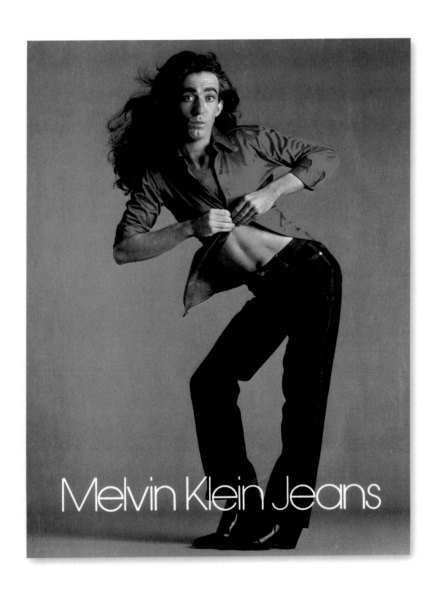

Melvin Klein Jeans

"GOING POSTAL"

On August 20th, 1986, an employee from the Edmond, Oklahoma Post Office gunned down 14 of his co-workers before taking his own life. Although senseless, this tragedy was not without merit as it inspired both the comically descriptive phrase 'Going Postal' and the National Lampoon piece, *Berserk!* Written as a newsletter for the disgruntled man, *Berserk!* takes aim at violence-based publications like *Guns and Ammo* and *Soldier of Fortune* — and at a society that refuses to recognize its problem with gun violence. Now, nearly two decades later, everything from school shooters to suicide bombers suggests that the world has gone *Completely Berserk!*

This parody first appeared in the April 1987 issue of National Lampoon.

"If you can spare ten minutes, I'd like to ring for my nurse, so she can help me out of this chair, walk me over to that desk, pull out my revolver, and hold my arm steady while I shoot you."

- Charlton Heston, former president of the NRA, 2002.

BERSERK!

The Controlled-Circulation Newsletter for the Frustrated Man

Stray Slugs

Dead Letter Office

The Dustbowl Blasters, a berserker club from Enid, Oklahoma, is petitioning the United States Postal Service for a commemorative stamp honoring Pat Sherrill, the "Post Office Killer" who sent his co-workers a volley of lead thank-you cards this past summer after being laid off from his mail carrier job. "This guy's a real American hero," says Blaster president, Smitty Wesson. "I mean it, he's the Oliver North of mail delivery. Everybody's always bitching about too much bureaucracy and lousy postal service. But whoever really went into a post office and cleared out the deadwood until Pat went on his spree?"

Move Over, Yuppies

The FBI's National Crime Advisory Board is predicting a lively summer for 1987. According to the experts, we'll be seeing a sharp increase in berserk high jinks over the coming months, as long-term low gas prices lead to a real recession, with all those layoffs and pay cuts that really get under our skins. Increasing waves of immigrants should meanwhile continue to make blue-collar Americans feel overwhelmed and worthless, while recent Reagan decisions are expected to increase international tensions and add to that I-may-as-well-go-out-on-my-own-terms sense of fatalism. And anyway, it's a non-election year, so we can look forward to a slow news summer…and that means plenty of publicity for our kind of action. It looks like impotent

Let 'Er Rip

In this world of overrated pleasures and underrated treasures, sometimes it's hard for a man to know just what he needs to be happy and content with himself. Everything in today's media screams "Success! Money! Power, power, power!" One gets the impression that one has to be lean and tanned, dressed in YSL sportswear and a Rolex watch, gunning a new Porsche at full speed down a freeway while a $2,000 car stereo blows a high-powered Nikki Sixx solo right through the juicy middle of the moist-mouthed huge-titted blond harlot snuggling next to you *and offering you sex and power and cocaine to zing through your mind screaming faster bigger better more*

But how is a regular guy, a decent guy, not a genius but not a real dumb guy, a guy who just wants a little respect and his fair share of the good things in life, just a job and a house of his own where he can take care of his family and his semiautomatic weapon collection…yeah, just a guy like you…how is a guy like that supposed to make his way through this sleazy world? How is he supposed to keep them from tearing him apart? What's he supposed to do when his wife starts screaming "Gimme this, gimme that," and the kids are whining for the Masters of the Universe toys you can't afford and you lay it out for the boss why you need more money and he provokes you into arguing with him so he can fire you for being belligerent and then they call you unemployable *and they all turn against you and all you wanted was a little human dignity but they can't even give you that and they beat on you and beat on you and beat on you until you have to fight back*

Well, it just makes you wonder what to do, doesn't it? Surely we'd all like a simple solution, just one quick stroke that could cut through all the confusion. But does the media give you that solution? Hell, no. The media just says buy, buy, buy. The media just wants to exploit your dreams. The media just wants to suck your blood. So let's give them what they want. Let's give the sons of bitches what they want. You want blood? Is that what you want? Blood? You want blood to put on the news, want blood to juice up your film at eleven, *blood to spatter in the faces of the little people while you pretend to be horrified by it pretend to be disgusted while you're hungry for it flowing dripping spattering you hypocritical bastards if that's what you want*

Psychologists tell us that letting stresses build up is unhealthy, that a quick, sudden release is often the best therapy for life in our complicated times. Maybe that's why more and more people every year are turning to berserk rage as a solution to life's little trials. And why many others, not yet prepared to make that dramatic, and often fatal, step, seek to gain a little pleasure and serenity from planning their own Big Burst and from enjoying vicariously the accomplishments of other berserkers.

But enough philosophizing. We've got an exciting issue for you this month, beginning with more of those hot news items from the crazy world of mass homicide. So let's charge in and have a blast…and remember the song of the berserkers:

When they've got you on the run,
Don't cave in or go limp,
Just come out with your favorite gun
And show 'em you're no wimp.

Gerard Jones
Editor

Stray Slugs

rage may be the fad of the future! Better get out there and get shooting before the herds of human sheep start trading their BMWs and coffee grinders in for semiautomatic arsenals!

High-Powered Therapy

Did we say "fad"? Take a look at what criminal psychologist A. K. Kalashnikov told the American Psychiatric Association recently: "We must not confuse the single-outburst rampage killer with the pathologically sado-erotic 'serial murderer.' With the constant Approach/Approach and Avoid/Avoid dichotomies of our society, the rampage can be a traumatic self-therapy for cognitive dissonance. The violent reach outward is, in effect, a violent journey inward in search of the individual's human essence." Sounds like we're part of the health craze now, like fiber and vitamin C. Maybe next time you go on a spree you can tell your victims that you're just searching for your human essence—while you're splattering theirs all over the walls!

Slow and Steady

Healthy or not, those darned serial killers have topped us again in the annual body count. Nationwide figures for 1986 show habitual killers with a tally of 102, with berserkers dragging in at only 88. But there's one bright note: counts for both groups are sharply up from 1985. We're still way behind jealous spouses and drug-gang hit men for the lead, but we're gaining!

BERSERK. *The Newsletter for the Frustrated Man,* is published in occasional outbursts by One Shot Publishing, 14 Tower Street, Austin, TX. BERSERK is the only journal representing the American mass murderer and the man who just wants to feel like one. The publishers do not endorse any activities described herein. We are doing this solely to protect your First Amendment rights. Believe it. Subscriptions are available if you think you'll be around long enough to care.

MASS MEETING

Yeah, we've all heard the one about America being tilted toward the west (so all the loose nuts roll into California). Well, the Golden State has its defenders and its detractors, but surely no other clime has been home to so many berserk heroes, from Theodore "Silver Hammer" Straleski to the "I Hate Mondays" gal to the famous cop-turned-berserk-politician who is honored every year with our highest award (below)…not to mention more serial killers and cult murderers than you can shake a buck knife at. And after all (sorry, New York!), California has become the undisputed capital of the broadcast media that give us our number-one reason-to-be. So what better setting for the biggest, most explosive annual American Berserkers Convention yet than beautiful Los Angeles?

And what more beautiful representative of the city than this gorgeous "California Girl," presenting the 1987 Dan White Award for Exceptional Violent Outburst to the urn containing Carl Ingle, the "Cable TV" killer of Menomonee Falls, Wisconsin. Ingle edged out the heavily favored Pat "Post Office Killer" Sherrill thanks to a slimmer pretext: where "POK" flew off the handle for being fired, Ingle's only excuse for shooting up a cable TV ofice was being turned down in a job interview!

These'll keep you up longer! Every berserker's favorite moment of the convention was the Protective Clothing Fashion Show. The maniac of tomorrow won't just wade into a crowd and start firing in his street clothes, only to get cut down by police bullets five minutes later. … Why waste a moment that comes only once in a lifetime? With a little advance armoring, you can stay on your feet for those few extra, precious shots.

And they can cook, too! Our beautiful hostesses served a real berserk snack assortment all through the convention: hamburgers chock-full of MSG (James Huberty's favorite!), plenty of strong black coffee and amphetamines, and, as ever, the famous White's Delight—the *de rigueur* Hostess Twinkle. When dinnertime came around, none of us could eat a bite. Boy, that's what we call diminished capacity.

Why don't women go berserk? That was the question being posed by this concerned panel of feminist researchers, led by criminal psychologist Myrna Koch-Heckler. Exploring the low incidence of random killings among women (and conveniently ignoring such *femmes fatales* as *60 Minutes* star Sylvia Segris), Myrna tried to convince the conventioneers that men should avert violence and become better human beings by "feminizing." After an hour of good-natured razzing and taunting from the crowd, Myrna grew so frustrated that she blew her cool and sprayed the hall with machine-gun fire.

YOUR BEST SHOT

Had a funny or exciting experience with violence lately? How about a fantasy your fellow connoisseurs of mayhem would like to share? We welcome all contributions from our loyal readers, whether you're letting fly wildly or dead on target. So come on, gang—shoot!

I Could Just Bust!
(What does it take to light your short fuse?)

Always such a quiet man. Never caused any trouble. Just a good neighbor, didn't know him very well, kept pretty much to himself.

Yeah, that's what they said. All up and down the street. And you knew what they were thinking. "Someday he's going to explode and kill us all."

You could see it in the way they'd pull their kids back, whispering, "Careful, Jimmy. That's the quiet man who minds his own business." At work I'd hear them whisper, "God, I hope they don't fire him. You know how those meek loner types are." Finally it was the cops, knocking on my door in the middle of the night, saying, "We hear you're a polite, retiring guy who doesn't make friends easily and never causes any trouble." "That's right," I said. "Okay," they said. "So how about showing us your stash of automatic rifles?"

The trouble was, I really was just a quiet, pleasant neighbor who kept to himself. I didn't have any automatic rifles. I didn't nurse any paranoid grudges, didn't have any unresolved hostilities toward my father. I didn't even go to Charles Bronson movies. But every time some assassin or psycho made the news, every time they started the interviews with shocked neighbors of the killer, I could see the eyes peeking out from between curtains when I walked down the street, see the glint of binoculars when I stood at the window.

So I changed. I turned myself into a loudmouthed, belligerent asshole. And wouldn't you know it, everything started looking up. I'd ram my neighbor's fender and jump out of my car screaming obscenities, and pretty soon the guys on my block were inviting me into their duplexes to argue about the Bears and the Raiders. I'd tell the boss where he could shove his unbalanced ledger and right away I was getting promotions. Oh, sure, everybody'd shake his head and say, "What an asshole" whenever I left the room, but at least I got respect.

Then it started turning sour. Guys picked fights with me in bars. I found myself going out with women who shrilly urged me to punch out other assholes in the stands at hockey games. The boss put me in charge of intimidating delinquent accounts. I found myself part of the climate of violence that's suffocating America, and it made me hate myself and everybody around me.

So I decided to mellow out. I made myself into a warm, loving, giving human being. I did favors for everybody in the neighborhood, putting in more hours and getting paid less than anybody at work. And they laughed at me. "Wimp." "Sap." "Sucker." Those are the nicest names they call me.

They all take advantage of me. I've quit my job, but nobody else will hire me. Too nice, they say. I go out of my way to do things for the neighborhood kids. They just ask for more and laugh at me behind my back. I give love, love, love. They spit on me.

Makes me want to kill somebody.
Walther Ruger
Winchester, PA

Is My Face Red!
(What was your most embarrassing violent outburst?)

Hoo-boy! What a goof-up I pulled last Friday! Luckily, I was able to make it all right in the end.

You see, it was the Negroes. I've always had trouble with Negroes. I don't cause them any trouble. Hell, I let them go their way just as long as they let me go mine. But they won't let me alone. Always showing me up at work, going faster than I can, carrying more than I can. Beating me out for raises and promotions. They win the football pools and I lose. You wonder why? Look what color those football players are. Those people stick together, you know. They won't just let a white man live his life.

Then there were these layoffs at the factory and I was out on my butt. I told the foreman he should fire the Negroes first, but he said he couldn't do that. They've got him scared. They stick together. I punched him. He said I would never work there again. The Negroes.

On the subway home a Negro boy wanted my money. I told him he had my money, he had my job. He laughed at me. I was hearing him laugh all the way home, even into my own home, even into that vodka bottle I was emptying. Well, my wife came home and I wanted to feel better, so I tried to make her make me feel good, if you get my meaning. And she slapped me and cursed me and started to leave. So I said, "I know where you're going, bitch! I know what you're going to! You're going to a Negro with a giant penis!" She laughed. And then I heard voices in my head, it was like the voices of all the white men who'd starved to death and been humiliated by the Negroes. Saying, "Put an end to Negro laughter, put an end to it forever."

So I fumbled around, and maybe I wasn't too clear in the head, and I fumbled some more until I found my Uzi. I'd bought it as a collector's item, but now I had a good cause I could use it for. I drove down to that place called the Arkansas Razorback Red Hot Bar-B-Q, where the Negroes hang out.

When I went in with my Uzi they started screaming, their white teeth shining like dice. I yelled, "The laughter of Negroes will be silent forever," and I opened fire. And what do you think came out? Nothing but water!

You see, I'd grabbed my son's water-gun Uzi, that fancy one he ordered from that Sharper Image place, instead of my real one. My son listens to Negro music. He has a poster of a Negro woman on his wall, looking at him with sexual proclivities. That's how they enslave you, with their sexual proclivities. My own son. The Negroes.

They laughed. Police came, Negro police, and asked me what I was doing, and they saw I was drunk and they told me to go home and sleep it off. On the way home I saw that I'd made a fool of myself, that I hadn't done the right thing after all. But I said, Well, Tommy, at least you didn't get yourself shot. It's not too late to set things right. At least you're still alive to fix up the mess you made. So I filled up the water gun with acid and I shot it in my son's face.

Yeah, I guess you could say my face was red. But not like his!
Tommy Thompson
Gary, IND

This'll Kill Ya!
(Heard a funny one about homicide lately? Shoot it to us!)

There's this manic-depressive chronic loser, see? And he's just lost his job, and these kids hassle him on the bus, and when he finally gets home he finds his wife in bed with another guy. So he goes for the Ruger Blackhawk .357 magnum he's got in his drawer, right? And he's about to go on this shooting spree, but suddenly everything seems so hopeless that even that doesn't seem worthwhile. So he puts the gun to his own temple and gets ready to pull the trigger, and he says to his wife, "You drove me to this!" And his wife starts laughing. She just laughs and laughs and laughs at this poor bastard, and he's standing there with the gun at his head. So finally he can't take it anymore and he yells, "Don't laugh, bitch! You're next!"

Get it?
Buddy Beretta
Remington, GA

SNIPINGS

Dear Editor,

Thank God for you berserkers. I'd never seen your magazine until I flipped through a copy in the waiting room at the trauma center of my local hospital, and, by golly, it did my old heart good to see somebody keeping alive the American spirit of guns, guts, and glory. Used to be, back in the good old days, you could bring a whole community together around some irrational violence. If we had a nigger gone bad we'd just get the town together and rehabilitate him quick, with the aid of a good strong hickory limb. Back in '17 the Jewish munitions magnates were trying to trick us into getting into that dirty world war in Europe, and we fought it hard. But once we finally got sucked into it for real, it was Look Out, Mr. Kraut! Now we screw around, tying our hands with due process and diplomacy. Just like in the days of the Wild West, it's come down to a few strong-minded individuals to show us what's got to be done. With any kind of luck, before I die I'll see a day when a man can't be fired without his wormy co-workers diving for cover, when a mother can't emasculate her son without every woman in America looking over her shoulder, and when every nigger on the subway is fair game.

Buck Shooter
Smallbore, TN

Dear Editor,

Ah, you Americans! Yes, yes, we call you Great Satan and Imperialist Empire and all this much of very too nasty names! But, yes, deep in our Moslem hearts we are envy you too much! What we must dress up in religious discipline and, how you say, fundamentalist fanaticism, you enjoy with such spontaneous and pleasure! If we wish to leap into the crowd and begin to blast with the guns, we have to make up the political causes and scream the crazy slogans. In the otherwise, nobody gives us the guns or puts us on the television cameras! But you too lucky Americans! Like the Diet Coke, you shed the blood just for the taste of it! Someday, someday, we will make Beirut and Jerusalem just like your post offices and your subways! *Salaam!*

Abdul ibn Budda-Budda
South Lebanon

Dear Editor,

Please be advised that your commercial exploitation of my client, Mr. Richard Speck, is in violation of trademark and is not protected by fair usage doctrine. The slogan "Born to Raise Hell" and the procedure of raping and strangling student nurses are trademarks of Richard Speck Enter-

prises, Inc., and any generic use of this slogan and this procedure constitutes a dilution of properties. In view of Richard Speck Enterprises, Inc.'s forthcoming book, film, music video, and other commercial enterprises, such dilution constitutes unfair and actionable competition. Please clear all future uses of the Richard Speck name and trademarks through this office.

Manny Slaughter
Slaughter, Slaughter &
Slaughter Assoc.
Chicago, IL

All right. Maybe it's about time that berserkers got a few rewards for laying it on the line. But as for the likes of you, Manny . . . well, we just wish we could dress you up in a little starched white dress and a funny cap some night and toss you into Dick's cell.

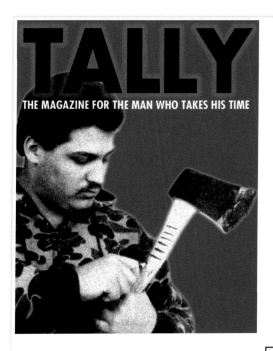

TALLY

THE MAGAZINE FOR THE MAN WHO TAKES HIS TIME

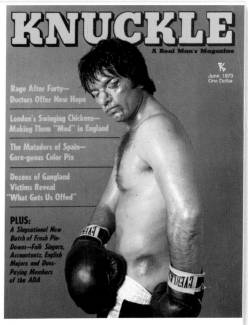

KNUCKLE
A Real Man's Magazine

June, 1973
One Dollar

Rage After Forty—
Doctors Offer New Hope

London's Swinging Chickens—
Making Them "Mod" in England

The Matadors of Spain—
Gore-geous Color Pix

Dozens of Gangland Victims Reveal
"What Gets Us Offed"

PLUS:
A Slugsational New Batch of Fresh Pin-Downs--Folk Singers, Accountants, English Majors and Dues-Paying Members of the ADA

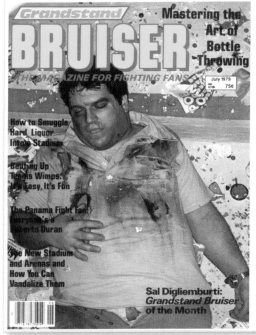

Grandstand
BRUISER
THE MAGAZINE FOR FIGHTING FANS

Mastering the Art of Bottle Throwing

July 1979
75¢

How to Smuggle
Hard Liquor
Into Stadiums

Beating Up
Tennis Wimps:
It's Easy, It's Fun

The Panama Fight Fan:
Everyone's a
Roberto Duran

The New Stadium
and Arenas and
How You Can
Vandalize Them

Sal Digliemburti:
Grandstand Bruiser of the Month

If you like BERSERK!, you'll go nuts for these titles...

NAME: _____

_____

ADDRESS: _____

_____

CELL BLOCK: _____

PAROLE OFFICER: _____

_____

CITY: _____

STATE: _____

M.O.: _____

Real He-Man No Pussies Publications
New York, NY

"Give me a magazine aimed at women, and I'll give you a bunch of dumb broads holding it upside down."

– William Randolph Hearst.

WOMEN

"TROPHY WIVES"

Working Woman, Working Mother, Ladies Home Journal, Oprah – the publication landscape is littered with magazines aimed at women, yet nothing speaks to the young, attractive gal who's willing to marry an older man in exchange for a pampered life of luxury. Well, in 2004, National Lampoon said, "Enough!" and published the first edition of Trophy Wife Magazine.

This parody first appeared in April 2004 on NationalLampoon.com.

"Opinions are like wives. I change mine every 13 months."

– Larry King, talk show host, regarding his seventh marriage, 2001.

"Opinions are like husbands. Both are easier to swallow if you're on a private jet."

– Melania Trump, wife number three of Donald Trump, 2005.

TROPHY WIFE
magazine

**TWM's
GUIDE TO
PREGNANCY**

STEPCHILDREN
The 'step'
between you
and your dreams

**ENDURING
B.J.'S**
What all aspiring
trophy wives
should know

PLUS
one trophy wife's private hell:
"I was on a starvation diet for 17 years"

The TWM guide to PREGNANCY

Staying thin, tight, and sexy is Job One when you marry the silver fox of your dreams. But how do you maintain your figure in a lifestyle where the richest and most fattening food, desserts, and liquor are always within reach?

As you know, the answer lies in what medical professionals call bulimia. TWM calls it "selective digestion."

We've gone into detail before about this controversial form of weight management, so we won't bore you gals by repeating its myriad benefits. Today, we want to discuss another important issue facing Trophy Wives: pregnancy. Eventually your wealthy spouse is going to want to turn your happy twosome into a happy family. After all, a rich man needs heirs like a woman needs jewelry.

If years of selective digestion haven't shriveled your womb like a sun-dried tomato...

If years of selective digestion haven't shriveled your womb like a sun-dried tomato, and if your C.E.O. hubby happens to nail a bulls-eye some drunken, grope-fest of an evening, you may be "lucky" enough to find yourself in a family way. That, TWM gals, is where trouble can start.

Having a baby will ravage your body like a gang of suburban mommies razing a discount table at Baby Gap. With pregnancy comes weight gain, followed by sagging and bloating–which can turn 'Mr. Right' into 'Mr. On-The-Prowl-For-Thinner-Better-Looking-Pussy' so fast it'll knock you off your Manolo Blahniks and onto your big fat ass.

The only way to stem this intractable descent into flabby, blubbery ugliness is to ensure you don't gain one ounce more than necessary while that future rival for Mr. Big's affections (a.k.a. the "bundle of joy") gestates in your ever-expanding belly.

What follows are a few DO's and DON'T's for maintaining a selectively digestive lifestyle during pregnancy:

DON'T stop purging. You're going to be ravenous to the point of mania. This is nature's way of making sure baby gets all the food it needs. Pregnancy can potentially add hundreds of pounds of excess weight to your body that has little or nothing to do with your baby. Purge or suffer the consequences.	**DO leave some food inside for the baby.** Once the little tyke is born you can deny it all the affection, attention, and love you want; but before that, you cannot deny nourishment. Where you once purged three to six times a day, cut down to two.
DON'T stay with your old doctor. Your sawbones will likely have some inkling that you're bulimic and may try to engage you in a "little talk, for the good of the baby." Trust us, find yourself a physician who's ignorant of your weight management choices -- or end up fat, poor, and single.	**DO listen to your body,** not the nagging, insistent voice of bulimia. Make purging a conscious choice, not a compulsion. The last thing you want is to vomit yourself into a miscarriage.
DON'T fall into the "diet trap" and start thinking that a well-balanced diet is better for you than your current system of weight management. Lord knows you have enough to think about without having to count calories and shop for good produce.	**DO exercise** ...kidding! Just making sure you're paying attention. Experts will tell you that physical activity in small doses is good for both mother and baby. But those are the same "experts" that tell you diet and exercise is the best way to stay thin.
DON'T forget to coat your throat with a liquid antacid before purging. The number one way bulimics are diagnosed and forced into treatment is by the inevitable wear and tear on the throat caused by acidic stomach fluids.	**DO practice good dental care.** Stomach acid can rot your teeth in the long run. Even if you remain thin, a set of grey, acid-mottled teeth will turn off hubby faster than cottage cheese thighs. So make sure to brush, floss, and visit the dentist.
DON'T worry about your dentist blowing the whistle on your bulimia. After all, he's not a real doctor.	**DO purchase flattering maternity wear.** Like it or not, you're going to have a larger than normal tummy. Well-styled clothing can hide the bulge that your bulimia-addled eyes will perceive as a disgusting hillbilly beer belly. Seeing that tub of guts reflected in shop windows may lead to excessive guilt-induced purging which can hurt your baby. Remember, it's not a gut, it's a bundle of "happiness".

Once the tot is born, your figure will not immediately snap back to its former sinewy glory. It may take a couple of weeks of dedicated gorging and purging for your body's 'natural' shape to kick in. This is a time to enjoy the process of selective digestion -- and the joys of motherhood ...And don't worry about the wear-and-tear of breastfeeding you've heard about. Your bulimia-shriveled mams will never produce milk. (Lucky girl!)

Enduring *B.J.'s*

what every aspiring trophy wife should know.

Let's face it, unless you're giving P-Diddy or Peter North a hummer, blow jobs are no fun.

They're work. And this work -- pardon the pun -- pretty much sucks. Here's a few tips on how to get through the many, many hours of cocksucking you'll endure in your pursuit of Mr. Right.

• Remember and repeat the Trophy Wife mantra: Jewelry, Jewelry, Jewelry When you're in the trenches, doing enough furious head-bobbing to buy your chiropractor a yacht, keep your mind on the prize. Granted that "prize" is the salacious old fart fondling your tits, but landing him gets you closer to Trophy Wife Nirvana: an account at Tiffany's. Keep bobbing, and keep repeating the mantra. Time will fly.

• Protect those knees. The CEO of Time Warner doesn't give a shit if his pool-house floor hurts your knees if you're servicing him while his wife entertains guests in the house. Kneepads went out with roller-skating, so be creative. Learn how to hunker in six inch heels for minutes at a time. Failing that, place your padded bra under your knees. For those with foresight, Proctor and Gamble produces a thin adhesive moleskin which, when applied to the kneecap under your stockings prior to going out, provides ample padding to get through an eight-minute hummer with no ill effects.

• Use the time to strategize. You already know how to give a heart attack-inducing blowjob on pure instinct. With your body thus occupied, use your mind to plot the next move. When you're finished, are you going to hit him up for jewelry, a Mercedes of your own, or keys to his summer house? You won't have time to think when he's zipping up and searching for a tissue to wipe his pants, so be ready.

• Treat it like a game. Remember, we're just fodder for these men until we trap, trick, or finagle our way into a Trophy Marriage. After a few hundred blow jobs, it's easy to get discouraged, so make a game out of sucking cock. Time how long it takes a prospective mate to blow his blubber, then try to beat that record with the next potential Mr. You. A group of Miami-based women, all of whom are now Trophy Wives, created an amusing gambling pool based on this concept.

Like the kids in the famous Armour Hot Dog jingle, you'll meet a lot of different 'hot dogs' on your journey from gal-on-the-make to trophy-wife-on-the-take: fats ones, skinny ones, even ones that climb on rocks.

Okay, maybe they won't climb rocks, but hopefully the owner of one such wiener might present you with a rock of the multi-carat variety if he's had an eye-rolling, mind-numbing, forget-my-wife-I'm-leaving-her-for-this-chick orgasm. Oh, and one last thing:

• Use a condom. Condoms protect you from diseases and, more importantly, from the awful taste of seventy-three-year-old-Oil-Baron man-goo which, trust us, tastes like expired mayonnaise.

STEPCHILDREN:
The step between you and your dreams

Statistics have shown that the average trophy wife is married to a man over forty-five, who has been married at least once before and has late teen or young-adult children.

In most cases, the grown children of your silver fox are less-than-happy about someone their own age taking Mom's place in Daddy's heart, home, and bed.

Hidden tensions and unspoken resentments can sometime bubble to the surface, putting you and your future goals in jeopardy. Here are seven strategies for maintaining peace on the home front:

1. Share make-up and clothing tips with his daughter. Show her that you're just another gal.

2. Listen to the stepkids' boring problems and offer pat, syrupy advice. Consult Chicken Soup for the Soul for appropriate anecdotes. This will build trust.

3. Encourage male children to pursue sports. Mr. Big Jr. is less likely to edge you out of Daddy's will if he's scuba-diving the GBR, parasailing in the South of France, or six feet under due to a heli-skiing accident.

4. Encourage female stepchildren to pursue modeling. Even if the girl in question is a hideous sea-donkey, the self-esteem she gains from wearing expensive clothes and lots of make-up will score you major points.

5. Put the family on a diet. If the diet is amphetamine-based, the kids will be way too busy to bother you. If it's a stupid fad diet, the kids will be too run-down to do anything.

6. Worst case scenario: If a stepson is causing you real problems, throw him a hummer. He'll be too horny to refuse and too ashamed to tell Daddy.

7. Worst case scenario, part two: If a stepdaughter is causing problems, 'arrange' for her plugged-in boom-box to find its way into the hot tub some late night when she's had too many Darvon and champagnes.

Remember, the loss of a child can be traumatic for your trophy husband. In the event one of his children is taken too soon (see #3 and #7) use it as an opportunity to practice being supportive. He'll remember your selflessness next time he's revising the will.

Letters To, Yana

Yana Raslovina's marriages to Sultan Ali-Al Jamal of Saudi Arabia, Earl "Big Earl" Carleton of West Texas Oil & Feed, and Bernard Zuckerfield of MGM Studios each left her with settlements that put her in the #1 spot in TWM's Fortune 300 list for six years running.

Yana has graciously offered to answer questions from Trophy Wives because, in her words, "I wanted to give something back that didn't involve money."

Dear Yana,

My trophy husband has stopped sleeping with me. I suspect he's cheating. What should I do?

Svetlana, Los Angeles CA

Dear Svetlana,

If he was so enamored of you that he forgot to put a prenuptial agreement in place, then hire a detective, catch him in the act, and smile—because honey, you just hit the mother-freakin-lode! Basically the sky is the limit—unless you're in California, in which case 50% (with some restrictions) is the limit. Enjoy.

However, if you do have a prenuptial agreement, and he decides he wants to trade you in for something new, there's nothing you can do at this point but pray that your lawyer got you a decent deal. If not, sorry sister, but you're going to have to start being a LOT more creative in bed.

Consider getting some friends involved in a threesome, foursome, or whateversome it takes to get Mr. Moneybags to pay attention. If you have to smuggle in some Korean ladyboys and a couple of midgets to make him smile, then start smugglin'.

Once he's face-deep in midget pussy with a ladyboy fist up his ass, mention that you wouldn't mind renegotiating the Pre-nup. It's a long shot, but if he 'nupped you at the start, it's the only shot you got, baby.

Good Luck,
Yana.:)

END

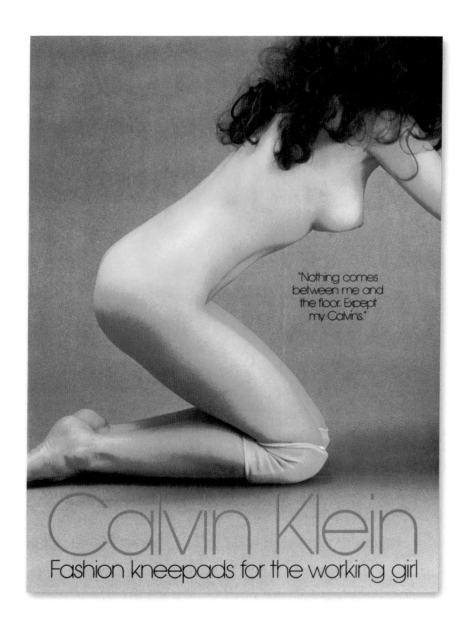

"Nothing comes between me and the floor. Except my Calvins."

Calvin Klein
Fashion kneepads for the working girl

WORKING MOTHER

While the feminist movement was proud of its achievements in getting women out of the house, by the late 1970's, many were concerned as to the effect this might have on their children. To help address these issues, *Working Mother* magazine was founded in 1979 by the same company that, in 1976, had founded *Working Woman* magazine. Demonstrating its ability to spot societal trends early, National Lampoon beat them all to presses, when it published *Negligent Mother Magazine* in 1975. Of course, this could also mean that *Working Woman* and *Working Mother* were actually parodies of our parody – in which case, we applaud them both for their dry sense of humor and their incredible, 25-year commitment to the joke.

This parody first appeared in the January 1975 issue of National Lampoon.

"I told my latest woman, 'If you get a subscription to *Working Mother Magazine*, I'm getting one to *Bitch Slapping Illustrated*. And making my comeback!'"

– Ike Turner, entertainer, 2002.

Negligent Mother

$1.00

January 1975

The Hows and Wheres
of Motorcycle Racing

Instant Vacations
Via Liquor and Loud,
Loud Music

Shoplifting
for the Hell of It

Baby Lenore's First
Real Whipping

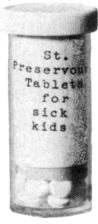
Negligent Mother

Well, hello again. Jesus Iced Christ, it's January already. The last thing I seem to remember was swinging into Thanksgiving and trying to pull myself together and cook a goddamn turkey to get what's-his-face off my back when Mona shows up with a Puerto Rican street gang she found so uniquely *entracté* she simply couldn't pass them up, and under her arm, and I'm thinking to myself when I see it, well, bless her darling soul, is a turkey. She struts past giving one of her butterfly waves and flings it in the oven. Meanwhile, the P.R. Rainbow Division is wandering all over the place *mira-mira*-ing everything and splitting their pants pockets with the crystal ashtrays which dictates my next martini to be no parts vermouth and two parts bourbon and I had it half down when Bozo the clown surfaces from the wonderful world of twenty-four-hour football and corners me with frantic whispers wanting to know what the hell is up. I tell him that it's Christian Charity Ungirdled Week and say hi to all our dinner guests which moves him to run upstairs and lock himself in the kids' room. Then out comes Mona drinking Manhattans out of a flower vase, shouting orders for everyone to turn on their little radios for Commonwealth Bandstand. No two of them could find the same station and between that and the table we broke and the smashed lamp, reenter Mr. Blue. This time with both kids clinging to Dwaddy's arms and tells me that he thinks it's a disgrace. I tell him that I know it's a disgrace but what's Thanksgiving without some wild Indians. That sets a couple of us woo-wooing and hop-stepping out the front door and that's when I passed out on the lawn. I got in about four hours before the Roberto Clemente fan club was dumping water on me and dragging me to the table for the Mona special. There sat Captain Mitty with the two kids all in pajamas looking like the Frank family. I poured myself a drink and decided I'd chew the ice cubes for dinner which was just as well because Mona doesn't know you have to thaw meat before you cook it. When she went in with a knife, I thought she hit an artery. The blood came out like spray paint. Well, I had about had it, so I gave my usual going-to-the-corner-for-a-pack-of-cigarettes chant which Mona thought was a swell idea. She grabbed all the bottles left and we headed out with Jack Armstrong yelling after me that it's three in the morning and it's a disgrace. I yelled back that it wasn't a disgrace anymore because it wasn't Thanksgiving anymore. We all got into their cars and started toward the park. Juan number one kept making me cognac and ginger ale while Juan number two kept making Mona wet. When we got near the zoo, Mona yelled stop and we all piled out. She wanted us to break into the administration building and screw around with the animals' records. And that's when it starts to turn to mush. I remember being pushed in a window, leaving my breakfast in somebody's out box, more blanks, a train ride to Trenton, New Jersey, waking up in a construction site with my underpants on backwards, and a fist fight in a Laundromat with a ten-year-old. If more of it comes to me, I'll let you know. Hope you like the issue.

Pamela Blair Stoner
Editor

PERSONALITY OF THE MONTH:
TIPPI DURERY

LOVING IN THE MOONLIGHT, LAUGHING IN THE DAYLIGHT, HAVING A WONDERFUL TIME

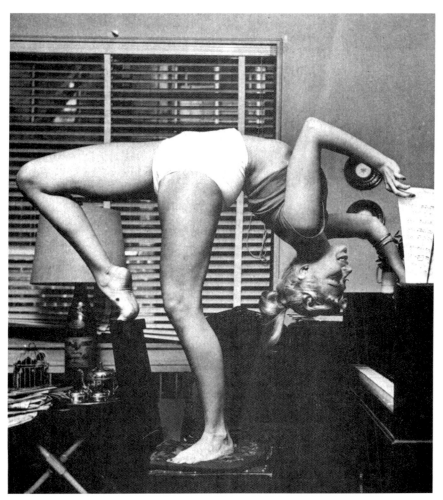

M is for the merriment she's made of. Tippi Durery with her figure back (above) makes a final check of the notes before she does her version of "Heart and Soul" for some off-camera friends. But (below) in a "before" picture, she is shown in a more serious mood, expressing an understandable degree of contempt for her second or third child for robbing her of her figure, which she jokingly refers to as "grand larceny."

There are no flies on Tippi; rarely are there even clothes covering her shapely thighs. Tippi is one of those few people who give meaning to the word *rompish*. From crashing a convention of tree surgeons to holing up with a gang of embezzlers, she's never at a loss for wringing those few extra drops from the towel of life.

Mother of two or three children, Tippi has never been the sedentary type. She told us, "That isn't me. That's somebody else. Oh, but I can be somebody else if I want to be, though. Like the time I dressed up as a ragpicker and pretended to sell my first kid to a childless car dealer for a new Impala. When I thought the joke had gone on long enough, I went back to return the car but the guy had moved. But that wasn't me. That was me as somebody else because I don't believe you can put a cheap value, such as a car, on a human kid."

But life hasn't always been skittles and beer for Tippi. The ravages of childbirth left her with a bad case of personal inflation. It took weeks of painful sit-ups and dieting until Tippi was back to her svelte self again. Misinterpreting the question, "If you had it to do all over again?" she snapped back, "I'd do it all over the mountains and the valleys. I'd do it in coal shutes and in grain elevators. And I do."

It's exactly this sort of energy that Tippi brings to all of her capricious

continued on page 40

MOMMA DON'T ALLOW...
Hints for home or wherever you hang your hat.

I came up with a neat rap I'd like to share with anybody who finds herself in a similar situation. It won't work for everybody, but it's worth a try. The next time you come home at four in the morning with your blouse half open, grass stains on your dress, and your lipstick smeared, and he wants to know "where the hell you been," try telling him you were just raped by men from outer space. If he's as dumb as most of the men I know, not only will he believe it, but he'll probably wind up giving you a grand for a special Martian abortion. But as I said, it might not work for everybody. Good luck.

Sylvia Schmid

LUCK BE A LADY
A lot of NMs find themselves at their wit's end when they first start making book. I know I did, what with all those little pieces of paper you have to keep track of and losing half of them. Well, I found out the best thing to do is go buy yourself a couple of twenty-five-cent composition notebooks and keep them right by the telephone. Clearly label each one with the different sport and that way you'll be sure to pay off the heavy bets as soon as they come in. And then you won't have to spend so much time worrying about having your spine broken because of some stupid lost paper.

Nancy Kagle

DOG DAZE
After I came home from the hospital with the kid, I couldn't help noticing that my two wirehaired terriers began acting very sickly. I brought them to the vet, but when they were there, they seemed fine and he couldn't find the problem. It took me about a month and a half to figure out what was wrong with them. It was the odor from the baby that was making them sick. If any of you have found this to be a problem, I've come up with a good solution. Buy some kitty litter from the supermarket and mix in a tiny bit of Clorox and pour it into the baby's crib. It worked perfectly for me and now my darling terriers, Mufkie and Pufkie, are as frisky as ever.

Kathryn Binder

SEW WHAT'S NEW
If you've published one hint about cleaning stubborn vomited wine stains out of dresses, you've published a thousand. And I've come up a cropper on every last one of them. I've even tried beating them against rocks and it's been no use. I don't doubt for a minute that it might be the acids in my own stomach that are setting the stain, but nothing seems to work. So I've had to come up with my own solution, and this can be added to the list, making it one thousand and one. I just go to the hem of the dress and cut off a patch and sew it over the mess. I admit it's not the neatest solution, but it's the only one that works for me.

Jean Dowling

SQUARING OFF
If you leave your kids in the playpen until they're four or five, and then take them out, they can only walk two yards in any one direction before they take a 90-degree left turn. This may not actually qualify as a hint, but I think it's good to know.

Elizabeth Hooper

WE WILL FIGHT THEM ON THE BEACHES
I've been in therapy for a couple of years, and though I can't say that the time has been wasted, I feel I spent much too much of it understanding my problem and not enough solving my problem. Which is, that I'm overwhelmed with impersonal liberal guilt: Vietnam, Hiroshima, Flanders, all of it. I wasn't getting anywhere. And then one day I was sitting in the living room feeling pretty despondent when I noticed my child. Do you remember when people used to say that all babies look like Winston Churchill? Well, mine did. I don't know what came over me, but I jumped up, grabbed the kid, and began demanding to know why he ordered the fire bombing of Dresden. I spent about a half-hour screaming at him, berating him, tossing him around, pleading with him, and then the whole feeling passed from me. I was completely at peace. It was terrific. I can't recommend it enough. If your child looks like Churchill and you have a bone to pick, don't hold back. It's the best thing in the world.

Dolores Knapp

We set up this little demonstration to show you our Bambee clothes for kids are not that flammable. This child, modeling from our Tundra Tog line, has walked quite a distance along the beach in the blazing hot sun and is still safe, snug, and free from any flames.

Bambee Clothes for Kids

END

Special Offer to readers of
Negligent Mother

ONE MONTH supply! FREE (4-pack)

SPARTIES
the 5-day live-in diaper suit

If you're like most mothers who just can't find the time or the stomach to change baby but refuse to put up with the constant crying, you'll want new Sparties, the five-day live-in diaper suit.

Sparties take the mess and bother and free you up to do the things you like.

And when the Spartie is filled up, simply untie the drawstring, lift baby out by the neck, and toss the old Spartie in the trash.

After baby's hosed down, it'll be ready for a news Spartie, and you'll be ready for another week of carefree living.

Sparties...it's in the bag

This coupon for a one-month supply of
SPARTIES (4-pack) redeemable at all
Quiquor Liquor Stores

LADIES' HOME JOURNAL

Ladies' Home Journal has been offering women tips on sex, hairstyles, health and fashion since 1883. And while most of this advice has been updated since the 19th century, some trademark features – like the 50-year-old column, 'Can This Marriage be Saved?' – simply refuse to die. Why is that?

This parody first appeared in the September 1974 issue of National Lampoon.

"I have been flipping through *Ladies' Home Journal* since 1981 and I can honestly say that this is the one women's magazine I have never been able to masturbate to. And I'm incarcerated."

- John Hinckley Jr., would-be assassin of Ronald Reagan, 2005.

OLD LADIES' HOME
Journal

SEPTEMBER 1974/60¢

GIVE YOUR BODY MORE HAIR,
BY THE AUTHOR OF
GIVE YOUR HAIR MORE BODY

THOSE NEW PRECHEWED FOODS:
Fancy Face-Saver or Foolish Fad?

GUIDE TO LOVE AND
HAPPINESS, PART I:
How to tell who the men are

"PERILS OF A WAXED HALLWAY"
12-part serial complete in this issue

How to Have Back-and-Forth
Conversations with the
People You Meet

New 23-Hour-A-Day Beauty Sleep Plan

How to Chart Your Own
Monthly Spite Cycle

How to Tell if You Had a
Better-than-Average Sex Life

How to Comb Your Wrinkles
into Today's Chic Styles

Why Men Prefer Women who
Remember Their First Names

The Clues That Tell You When
You Did Have a Visitor

WHY I'M NOT DEAD:
AN EXCLUSIVE INTERVIEW
WITH MAMIE EISENHOWER

LETTERS TO THE EDITOR

If known, name and address must be included with every letter. We will withhold both whether requested to or not.

Sirs:

Did I read the last issue of your magazine? What magazine? What am I doing? Am I writing a letter? Are you here to repair the telephone? Would you like to see a picture of my grandchildren?

R. M.

Sirs:

I wish to take exception to the article that appeared last month in your publication, entitled . . . I think it began with "The". . . I think it was about fire engines, pianos . . . have you met my son? . . . letter, letter. Sincerely yours, Dear Sirs, Would you like to see a picture of my grandchildren?

R. T.

Sirs:

One of my staples chairs told me this story I thought I would pass it on your tape, put the tape on over, see, where I used to live and these pictures, pictures of my grandchildren oxen? cows? me? Writing? When is this? Who are you? Are you from the police? I'll call the police, police?

W. F.

Sirs:

Yet it the me oh . . . let me see . . . yes!

L. T.

Sirs:

I can still remember when I was young. I had the biggest ribbon on the block. Red ribbon, green ribbon, am I writing a letter to the magazine or to my granddaughter, not that she would answer anyway, but it was, I think, but maybe not. I'd write more except they're bringing the musketeers over now, curse 'em!

D. N.

Sirs:

Hoow doo yoo speel "teh?" Eahve bene eveyhwere lokking for this infomitionk thot mayb reeders cod hellp meh, pic of grandcholdren, tree snakke encloosed.

B. R.

DECORATING:
The Knickknack Look

You can give any room in your house the coziness of a garage sale with a little bit of imagination and practically no money. The trick? Cover every horizontal or nearly horizontal surface with trinkets, souvenirs, and conversation pieces—pictures, seashells, figurines, ornaments, dishes, bowls, small stuffed animals, boxes, statuettes, small stuffed animals, anything at all. To get a feeling of individuality and express your personality at the same time, just empty those old desk and dresser drawers full of bric-a-brac onto desks, coffee tables, mantelpieces, even sofa and chair arms. Drop larger objects on the floor. Generally speaking, you should leave them where they land, but you might want to put fragile, easily breakable china, glass, and porcelain pieces on corners and edges. For a nice pack-ratty kind of effect, start a collection of something cheap and silly like sewing machine bobbins, sash weights, or faucets, and strew them everywhere. Arrange your most garish gewgaws in pointless groupings: invent long stories for each of them. Put your strongest pieces in plain view: the mummified heart of a favorite pet, an antique bottle filled with gallstones, a framed chest X-ray. How to know when to stop? Try these tests. Take an ordinary child's marble. See if you can find a place to put it down. If you can, get another knickknack and put it there. Repeat until there's no room for it. Sit in a chair at the edge of the room and exhale deeply. Did anything fall down? If not, you've got a long way to go. Walk across the floor. Did you hear any crunching sounds? No? Then keep at it!

A little thought has transformed this ordinary table into a minefield. Ashtrays should be tiny—about the size of a bottle cap, large enough for a matchhead and nothing more. As for dusting, don't!

A random scattering of odds and ends gives this room the welcoming atmosphere of a china shop. Guests will soon feel that they've somehow wandered into the inside of a kaleidoscope.

WAKE UP TO THE WONDERFUL WORLD OF EXERCISES

says Helen "Hell on Wheels" Whaley, Former Olympic Women's Decathlon Champion and inventor of Iso-Geriatrics

Yes, I've always managed to be awake to the wonderful world of exercises, and I certainly can vouch for the importance of physical fitness.

If you'll only lay aside a little time every day to do the simple "Iso-Geriatric" exercises outlined here, you'll soon feel better. And you'll look younger, healthier, and more glamorous, too.

Remember, you can't do anything to change the bony frame God gave you—but you *should* try to do something about your muscles!

Convinced? Still reading? Ready? Okay! Let's begin.

1 Opening and Closing Your Eyes

This is a great exercise to help you look awake and alert.

Step One: Relax. Take a deep breath (if you can). Summon your energy.

Step Two: Open those baby blues. Hold them that way for a full five seconds. You can do it!

Step Three: Return to the starting position.

Step Four: Catch your breath, then repeat the whole exercise three more times. Within weeks, your friends will notice how much more responsive you look.

2 The Wrist-Twister

I created this exercise to give your hands more mobility.

Step One: Lie back. Don't waste your strength.

Step Two: Rotate your right hand (or your left one if you're left-handed) 90 degrees in a *clockwise* direction. Don't strain!

Step Three: You're doing great! Can you return your hand to the starting position? Try it. . . .

Step Four: Just like Step Two (Remember Step Two?). Only this time rotate your hand *counterclockwise.* That's it!

Step Five: Go back to the beginning position and repeat. Who knows: If you still have a firm grip—and can manage to hold your eyes open (see EXERCISE 1)—you may soon surprise acquaintances by watching TV—and changing channels all by yourself!

3 Shaking

Here's a vibrant new exercise that's so easy you may find yourself doing it without even trying. It goes like this:

Step One: Lie there as still as you can. That's the spirit!

Step Two: Okay! Start shaking. Very good! Shake as long as you feel like it.

Step Three: All right. Try to be still again.

Step Four: Repeat the exercise until overcome by fatigue.

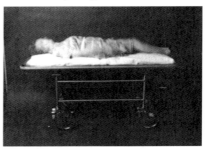

4 Just Lying There

How few of us realize that the simple activities we engage in every day are wonderful opportunities to get exercise! Lying there, just like I'm doing in the accompanying picture, is the perfect example of such an activity. I call it the ultimate exercise. Make it a habit!

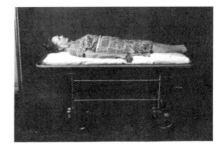

Well, that's about it. Thanks for finishing my article. I hope you have the self-discipline to do my exercises and that they help you as they've helped me win much happiness and many new friends.

Helen "Hell on Wheels" Whaley

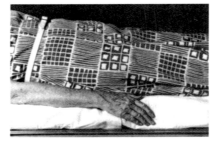

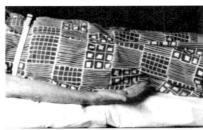

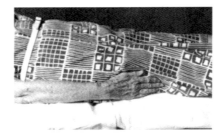

SPRING-SUMMER-FALL FASHION:

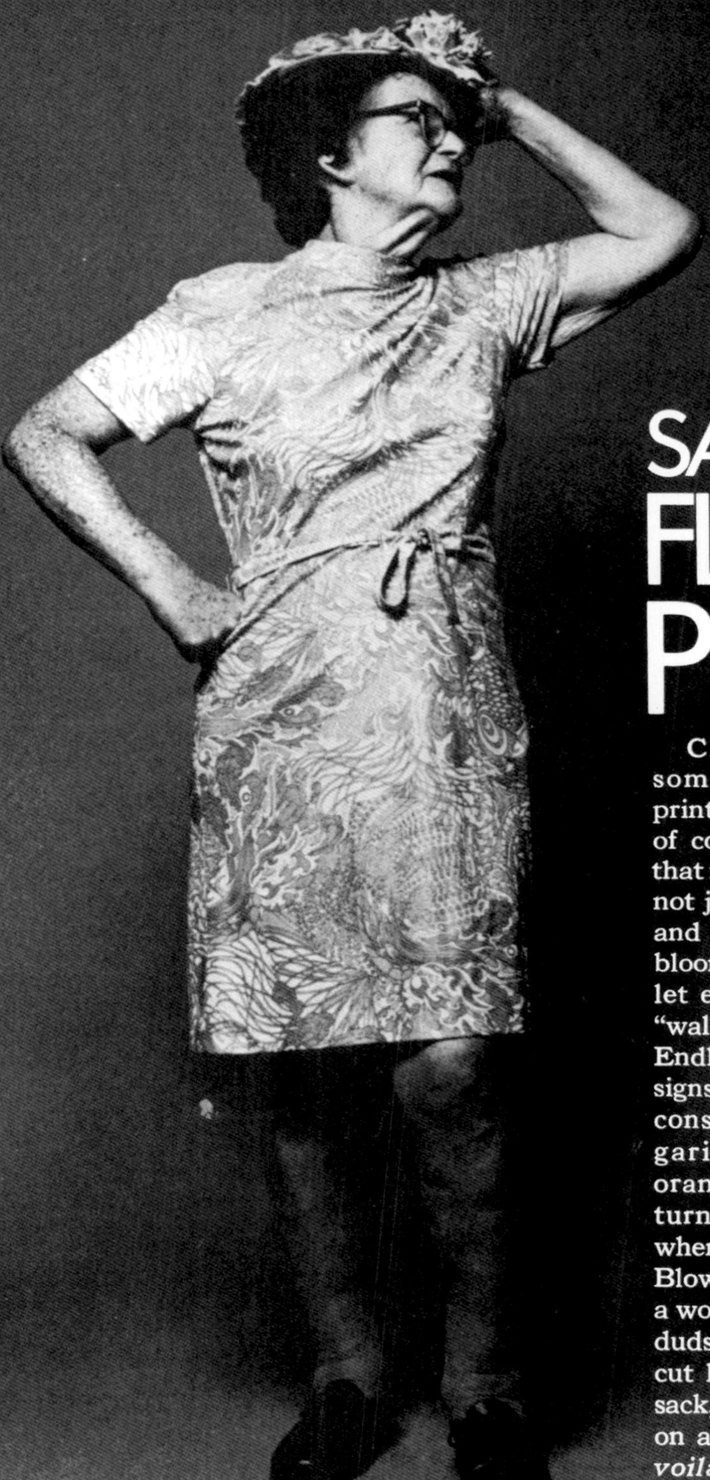

SAY IT WITH FLOWER PRINTS

Classic, timeless, always somehow right—the flower print dress. With matching hat, of course! A fetching ensemble that makes you look upholstered, not just dressed. Loud and busy, and just lousy with big, bright, blooming splashes of color that let everybody know you're no "wallflower"! The possibilities? Endless! A billion different designs, from muddy browns and conservative, dingy greens to garish yellows and glaring oranges that'll make everyone turn down their hearing aids when you walk into the room. Blowsy, frumpy, and dowdy—in a word, *you*! Style? Not in these duds, milady. Just a simple frock cut like a drape. Grab a bag, a sack, a piece of old luggage, slip on a pair of sensible shoes, and *voila!*—the ensemble is complete.

photo by R. G. Harris

FAMILY CIRCLE

Family Circle was founded in 1932. According to the Family Circle website, the magazine "takes the lead in service magazines to reach today's woman and her family... And as the traditional family unit evolves and the definition of family changes, *Family Circle* is there to provide support, answers and direction in the true 'service' manner." Whatever. A magazine this sickeningly wholesome deserves an even more sickening parody.

This parody first appeared in the April 1974 issue of National Lampoon.

"Whether disciplining a small child, an incontinent adult or the French, nothing beats a rolled up copy of *Family Circle*."

– General Dwight D. Eisenhower, 1946.

... ... from CARE cartons / New makeup ideas ...

Comparison starving / Impromptu entertaining ideas when unexpected guests drop dead

Bite the Mud that feeds you: She ... ...

Mud pies fit for a millionaire / Famine hygiene sprays: An in-depth survey

Three stunning loincloths from the same loincloth

JULY 1974   PRICE: MAKE US AN OFFER

Famine Circle

SHE FEEDS A FAMILY OF SEVEN-TEEN BY TALKING ABOUT FOOD. Mkawa Mkamba of Oum Cha-touba, Chad, is a resourceful mother of seventeen who keeps her famine-ridden family alive by talking up a storm about all phases of food and food management.

"My three oldest children and I like to talk about planning menus for the week, usually based on what would be on sale if we had supermarkets, and what foods would be in season if we had food," said Ms. Mkamba. "We discuss what foods we would buy in bulk and keep in storage, so we can always talk about cooking them when we're tongue-tied and caught short. With meat prices so high these days, we like to restrict most of our protein talk to fish and chicken, and of course, to the basic grains, dairy products, and soy beans. Breakfast is our biggest talk because it has to give us the energy we need to work and go to school, if we had jobs or schools. Lunch usually means talking up a hearty soup and a nutritious sand-wich. At dinner time, we prefer to talk about a simply prepared fish or chicken dish, accompanied by a green vegetable or salad. Dessert talk is fresh fruit, ice cream, or one of the great pies or cakes we talked about baking that are now stored in our imaginary freezer, just waiting to be warmed in our nonexistent oven. We talk about eating out at least once a month. We save our most expen-sive talks for dinner parties with friends or relatives.

When you spend the day talking about shopping, cooking, preserving, and growing your food, you're much too busy to notice that you haven't eaten a thing. In fact, we're always quite full after every talk. My problem is to make sure our little ones don't get tummy aches from overtalking or talking about too many junk foods and snacks! Best of all, I can manage to talk about feed-ing my family for as little as four zimba a week.

BUDGET BURIALS. Lots of thrifty African housewives are organizing burial cooperatives, a time, money, and space-saving idea. Instead of each family burying their dead, they can now join a co-op that offers fast, streamlined serv-ice at far less cost and labor (and who has the strength to work these days?). Everyone volunteers a few hours a day for digging. Graves are only one foot deep instead of a cumbersome, time-con-suming six feet. Bodies are buried in large groups with one common prayer read over them. All bulky organs and limbs are removed before burial so smaller units are put into the ground. Twelve people can now be buried in the same area that used to accommodate one! For more information on how you can organize your own practical but meaningful burial co-op, walk to Lakai Nagumi, Moussoro, Chad. If she's dead by the time you get there, try Ms. Koudugu Wasabi.

DYING: EFFECTIVE NEW WAY TO CLEAR YOUR DEBTS. Puki and Cheg Ndouli were a typical young couple in Dekoa, Central African Re-public. They married three years ago and rented a small hovel in a develop-ment built on a mosquito-infested swamp in suburban Dekoa, a relatively expensive neighborhood for young mar-rieds. Cheg had no immediate or long-term job prospects; Puki was pregnant.

When Puki gave birth to twins they had to borrow heavily for their mud, dirt, rocks, and dead people. Last year, when the government stores gave out credit cards encouraging everyone to buy a few grains of rice, the Ndoulis went on a spree and bought an entire cupful. At Christmastime they used their credit cards to buy expensive toys for their children, pieces of broken glass and wood. Then Puki became preg-nant again. On top of all this, the bill collectors were demanding payment at exorbitant interest rates. They sought out the advice of Mobunjo Mabai, the financial counselor of the Dekoa Bene-ficial Finance and Trust Association. After a session that lasted well over a minute, Mabai knew every detail of their financial situation and advised the young couple to kill themselves. By dy-ing, they would be legally absolved of all their debts and would start with a clean slate. The Ndoulis readily agreed to the plan and swallowed poison, a free gift from Dekoa Beneficial. Today the Ndouli children are wandering about Dekoa debt-free, starving happily with other children their own age, thanks to this great new idea in money manage-ment.

NIGER ON NOTHING A DAY. More and more fun-loving African families are discovering thrifty vaca-tions in such famine spots as Niger, Chad, Sudan, and Upper Volta. The way to save money on these vacations is to walk. Just pack whatever meager be-longings you have on your head and shoulders (the perfect carryall) and off you go! Most countries do not charge for walking and each spot on your route is included free as one of your stopover cities.

If you're walking from the Sudan to Niger, you can stretch out your starving budget by staying at one of the Rama-dan Inns, a chain of over 550 fast food establishments. Each Ramadan Inn fea-tures a cheerful atmosphere, generous fasting nooks, and half-size fasting areas for the children.

LESS THAN ONE CALORIE ....MUCH LESS. LOVE IT!

Sugar Free
Water Free
Taste Free
Die Rite Cola!

Die Rite Cola

Less than one calorie means less you... much less.

Breezy Summer Styles

Beg, steal, or borrow a large piece of cardboard from a dead person or a dead person's house. Fold it in two down the center. With a sharp rock cut a semicircle from the middle of the folded side. If you can stand up, place the cardboard over your head, and there you have it—a nifty little number for those hot summer days. Incidentally, the semicircle of cardboard you have left over makes a cute bonnet—or, if you have the string to sew up the sides, a smart evening purse.

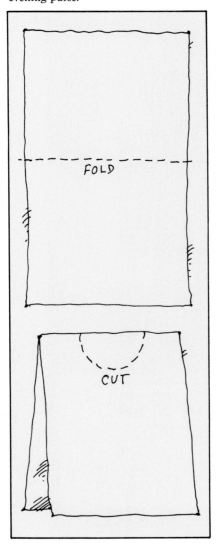

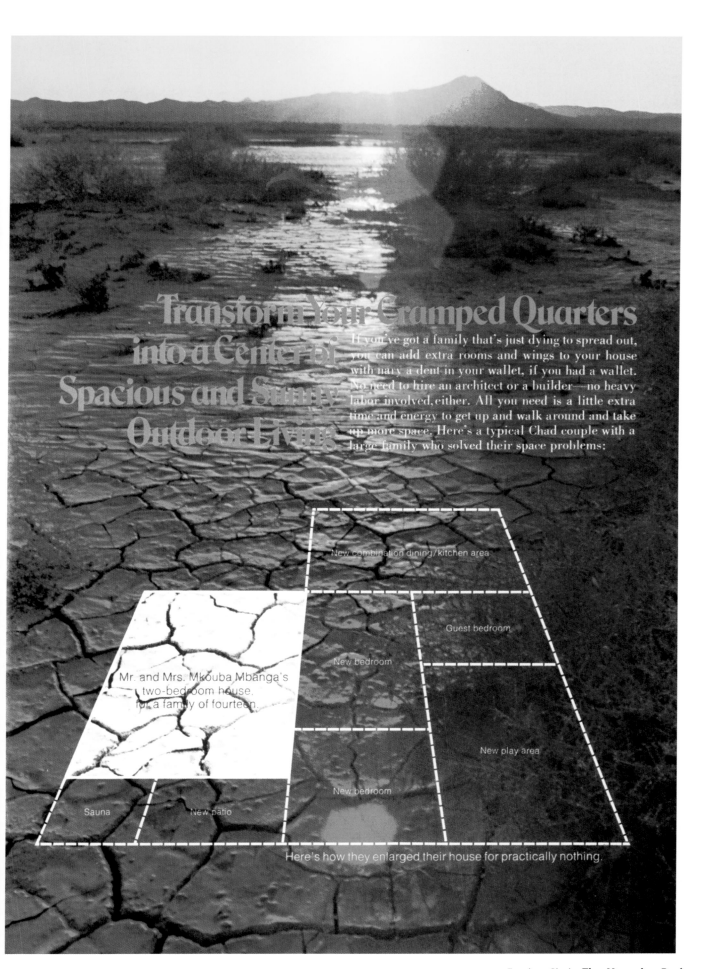

Transform Your Cramped Quarters into a Center of Spacious and Sunny Outdoor Living

If you've got a family that's just dying to spread out, you can add extra rooms and wings to your house with nary a dent in your wallet, if you had a wallet. No need to hire an architect or a builder—no heavy labor involved, either. All you need is a little extra time and energy to get up and walk around and take up more space. Here's a typical Chad couple with a large family who solved their space problems:

New combination dining/kitchen area

Guest bedroom

New bedroom

Mr. and Mrs. Mkouba Mbanga's two-bedroom house, for a family of fourteen.

New play area

New bedroom

Sauna

New patio

Here's how they enlarged their house for practically nothing.

Let's Eat to Live

by Edele Davis

America's foremost nutrition authority, author of the best-selling Let's Cook It Before It Spoils *and* Let's Go to My Place, *gives you her frank opinions on Central Africa's growing nutrition problems.*

I have just concluded an extensive lecture tour through Central Africa and I must report a shocking fact—the people are suffering from the most appalling nutritional deficiencies I have ever seen. Their diets are hopelessly inadequate. Wherever I traveled, from Ethiopia to Mali, I saw people of all ages suffering from excessive fatigue, poor posture, tooth decay, faulty bone structure, subnormal mental qualities, and a variety of horrible diseases that stem directly from this lack of basic vitamins and minerals.

No Breakfast, No Energy

By now everyone should know that breakfast is the most important meal of the day, the "breaking of the fast" of your previous night's sleep. What you eat for breakfast determines how efficiently your body can maintain its blood sugar at normal levels, which, in turn, maintains your energy levels through the day. Eat a skimpy breakfast and your blood sugar plummets below normal, causing fatigue, headaches, nausea—a completely rundown feeling. You're dead before you start. Yet throughout my travels in Africa I did not see a single person eating breakfast!

Every morning my hosts (who were high government officials) would serve me a big, well-balanced breakfast of fruit juice, whole grain cereal, eggs, sausage or ham, a pitcher of milk, toast, muffins, and jams. To this I would add my vitamin-mineral cocktail supplement and my slices of raw liver sprinkled with brewers' yeast and lecithin, which I always take as an extra pep-up on arduous lecture tours. After breakfast I felt wonderful. My blood sugar was at a high level, giving me tons of energy, sharp mental qualities, and a cheerful disposition. What a contrast I was to the people in the streets! They all seemed to be irritable, moody, and depressed. All they wanted to do was lie about and stare into space. Many of them were in a deep sleep, even though it was midmorning.

Through an interpreter, I asked one of the young men if he had had a decent breakfast. He got angry and tried to spit at me. Not only did he have no saliva, but the effort of trying to spit exhausted him and he fainted into a deep sleep like the others. I examined his tongue, and just as I suspected, it was dark green with black spots, indicating a deficiency of vitamins A, B, C, D, E, and all the minerals, especially magnesium and zinc.

Too Much of Too Little

As in most semiprimitive countries, the nations of Central Africa depend almost entirely on one or two staple foods to the exclusion of everything else. Niger, Chad, Ethiopia, Upper Volta, the Central African Republic, and the Sudan seemed to rely on mud and rock as their main foods, when they ate at all. *

Fresh raw mud and natural unbroken rock do provide a certain amount of chromium and other trace minerals that are essential to good health, but the emphasis must be on *fresh* mud and *unbroken* rock. Most Africans preferred to cook their mud for hours in the hot sun, thus drying it out and robbing it of all its precious nutrients! And by the time they ate their rock, it too had been pulverized and processed to death and was virtually devoid of minerals.

Is it any wonder then, that people who eat only badly cooked mud and processed rock suffer from both major and minor deficiencies in every form of protein, carbohydrate, and starch? Search as I did among their hovels, I could not find a trace of liver, yogurt, wheat germ, brewers' yeast, green leafy vegetables, fresh fruit, whole grain cereals, fresh fish, fertile eggs, organically raised beef or fowl, raw milk dairy products, and the hundreds of other foods needed to maintain a balanced diet.

Nor did anyone know that you must maintain a delicate balance of all the nutrients in your body.   *To page 96*

Mrs. Pall's makes sticks just like you'd make them because you've got plenty to do.

You're a busy woman and you serve Mrs. Pall's.
Because you know you're serving foods that are made just the way you'd make them.
Like Mrs. Pall's Sticks.

Select, tender wood, dipped in mud, covered with delicious seasoned bark, and cooked to perfection in the desert sun. Just like you'd make them yourself. Except with Mrs. Pall's you just serve and enjoy!

---

*I did not notice any significant increase in food intake at lunch or dinner among the natives. It seems as if skipping breakfast sets the tone for the rest of the day.

The 28-Day Budget Beauty Plan that Turns You into a Jet Setter

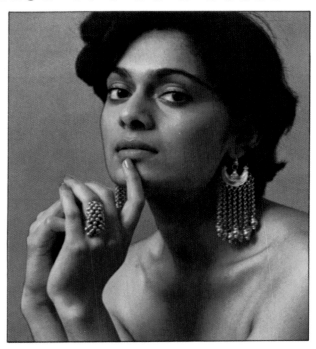

Does it really take so much to be *chic, alluring*, and *fun, fun, fun*? Not these days! You too can be like those gay, glittering people who fly around over your head all day and occasionally crash in your jungle. All it takes is some perseverance, whatever is left of your face, and surprisingly little money. To prove our point, we took lucky Maria Ixahuatl from the (*frankly hideous!*) barrios of Bogotá and turned her into a jet setter in just 28 short days. And *you* can achieve the same fantastic results!

April 21–April 30 Maria is taken by ambulance to Bogotá International Airport, where we all fly (charter's cheaper!) to Geneva, Switzerland, arriving just in time for a light supper. *Very Important Point*—no heavy Continental meals after years of malnutrition. . . . It can cause tricky spare tire problems later on. Next day Maria begins an 8-day course at the famous Niehans rejuvenation clinic, for sheep gland injections and ancillary hormone treatments. She undergoes the outpatient program (far less expensive than the inpatient version), being driven the considerable distance back and forth each day in an incredibly economic rented Fiat 600. Her rickets and malaria disappear, stretch marks smooth out, skin tightens, and unsightly stoop, bumps, and bones melt away.

April 30–May 12 Maria flies to London for consultation and surgery with cosmetic wizard Dr. Alexander Worthypenny of Harley Street. He employs plastic surgery, deep massage, and orthodontics to complete her transformation, concentrating not just on face-lift, bridgework, nose job, and wrinkles, but also on firming up and filling out breasts, tummy, and thighs, and pulling in all that sag in the rear end. Manicure, pedicure, and hairstyling are a must at Sassoon.

May 12–May 20 On to Paris for the icing on the cake. Maria, now a svelte 34–23–35, with the face (still healing) of a Mayan goddess, enrolls in Charles Revson's exclusive course in all-round beauty maintenance. Expensive but well worth the investment in years to come (no costly salons, no blindfold choices in the cosmetics department). A visit to Yves St. Laurent low-priced boutique introduces her—with a little help from *Famine Circle*!—to Contessa Esmeralda y Ruiz de la Corte de Taragona, a deeply committed left-wing exile from Spain and one of Paris' best-known socialites. A week with the Contessa works wonders with Maria's Spanish and gives her a thorough grasp of today's burning political issues.

May 20–May 22 Maria returns to Geneva, and catches the charter back to Bogota, where, just after just 28 days, she returns to the barrio a sophisticated, well-dressed, and traveled beauty, capable of climbing on a plane with Charlotte Ford at the drop of a stock. Incredible? Yes, but true—and all for only $14,474.50, much less than the cost of a boring old combine harvester! So stop dreaming and *start living!*

(28-day round-trip low-season charter Bogotá–Geneva–Bogotá $483.50; Pension Royale (cheaper if you prepay!) $126.00; Niehans outpatient course $7,000; off-season rental of Fiat (inc. free gas) $67.00; coach air fare Geneva–London $42.00; consultation Dr. Worthypenny $2,500; 10 days semi-private room at Worthypenny Rest-Cure Sanatorium and Health Spa $1,000; Vidal Sassoon $50.00; coach fare London–Paris $27.00; Revson Cours de Beauté $1,500; Yves St. Laurent $650; Pension Montmartre (prepay! prepay!) $64.00; coach fare Paris–Geneva $15.00. Miscellaneous: food, wine, gift for the Contessa, a saucy two pound bet at Churchill's(!) $950.

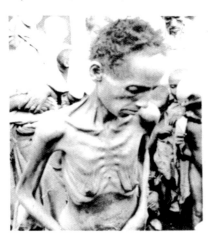

END

Lt. Calley's KILL THE CHILDREN FEDERATION

Dear Concerned Citizen,

This is Xena Puento. Xena is nine years old. She has never seen a glass of milk. Xena and her mother live in an abandoned packing crate on the outskirts of Manila, just one of thousands of deprived and impoverished families trapped by illiteracy, educational deficiency, unemployment, and disease. For just $15, I can shoot Xena in the head and toss her into a mass grave. But I need your help. Guns, bullets, and bulldozers cost money. While the need is great, the available funds are small.

There used to be no hope for Xena and those like her. They were doomed to a life of misery without chance of escape. But now your donation can provide that chance. Only $15 enables you to select your child from a score of countries overseas and areas at home. Soon you will receive a photograph of your child's resting place and an actual death certificate filled out by authorized U.S. personnel. An additional contribution of $5 will provide a small marker; $10 buys a wreath; $25 pays for a handsome urn; and $180 covers the cost of perpetual care.

Don't you think little Xena has suffered enough? Then act today and complete the sponsorship application below.

Thanks so much!
Sincerely,
Lt. William Calley, Ret.

**A division of the
Foster Soldiers' Plan, Inc.**

Available countries and areas
Taiwan
Peru
Korea
Iran
The Philippines
Bolivia
Ecuador
Brazil
S. Vietnam
Kurdistan
Mexico
Lebanon
Hong Kong
Paraguay
Syria
Africa
USA—
    Appalachia
    Watts
    Bedford Stuyvesant
    American Indian reservation
      and migrant camps

We're not trying to destroy the world. Just a little piece of it.

NL-7-71

**Lt. Calley's Kill the Children Federation
A division of the Foster Soldiers' Plan, Inc.
Box 711
Fort Benning, Georgia 23409**

Name_____

Address_____

City_____State_____Zip_____

If for a group, please specify _____
                    (church, class, club,
_____
  school, business, etc.)

Registered (VFA-0880) with the U.S. GOVERNMENT'S ADVISORY COMMITTEE ON VOLUNTARY FOREIGN AID. Contributions are tax-deductible.

I wish to sponsor the death of a

☐ boy   ☐ girl in_____.
                   (name of country)

I am enclosing $15 to cover cost of expungement & burial.

☐ Choose a child from an area of greatest need.

☐ I am enclosing an additional $_____ to pay for

_____.
  (marker, wreath, urn, p. care)

☐ I cannot sponsor the death of a child, but want to give
  $_____.

☐ Please send me more information.

MODERN BRIDE

Founded in 1949, *Modern Bride*, along with the magazines *Elegant Bride* and *Brides*, helped recently engaged women become aware of the tens of thousands of options they had regarding wedding locals, gowns, bridesmaid dresses, stationery, reception halls, cakes, floral arrangements, linens, table settings, photographers, bands and/or DJs and honeymoons. These magazines then showed women how to mix and match their options to create over 8.2 million different combinations, of which only seven will ensure complete happiness.
At least until wedding #2.

This parody first appeared in the February 1975 issue of National Lampoon.

"Thanks to *Modern Bride*, when it rained on my wedding day, I knew: 'A wet bride is a lucky bride.' Then when I sobered up and realized I'd married the blackjack dealer, I knew: 'A drunken, barbiturate-induced wedding is an annulled wedding.' Oops!"

– Britney Spears, entertainer, 2005.

AMERICAN
BRIDE

There's one born every minute.

WINTER $1.00

DO YOU REALLY
WANT TO GET
MARRIED?

IS THE POPE
CATHOLIC?

365
JELL-O
MEALS

HONEYMOON
SPOTS
How to remove them

CHOOSING YOUR STATION
WAGON

COOKING WITH
VALIUM

BUGGING
THE BACHELOR
DINNER

HONEYMOON SALADS
Lettuce alone with no dressing

CRASH PREWEDDING DIET
Sensuous beauty with speed

DELICIOUS POSTWEDDING DISHES
When calories don't count

RELATIONS
WITH TRADESMEN

From out of the forests of the Pacific Northwest
comes the magnificent collection of dinnerware that from a little acorn grew.
a genuine reflection of the strength and permanence
you can look forward to in married life today:

ROYAL PARCHMENT

Times have changed. You're not the same girl your great-grandmother was and you probably don't share her antevellum taste. So why not choose one of the four contemporary patterns pictured here as a proclamation of your new wifestyle?

Gold and Blue Plate Special, ephemeral elegance that symbolizes your aspirations for the future.

The Life Cycle of Moss, our endangered species pattern, gametophyte and sporophyte generations for generations to come.

Love Story, a pictorial analysis of the ultimate happiness in American marriage.

And **Service With a Smile,** the pattern that says, "Have a nice dinner." If you're a modern woman, and you've dreamed of a set of tableware that will celebrate the new value of love and commitment to marriage, a set of tableware that wasn't designed with your great-grandmother in mind, then consider **ROYAL PARCHMENT.** It's the very tissue of your dreams.

Send for our free booklet (Patterns not shown—Deadwood and Test) to Royal Parchment. ⸱1 Paul Bunyan Lane. Seattle. Washington.

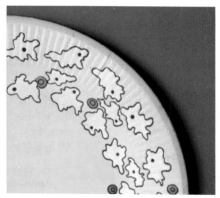

AMERICAN BRIDE

THE MEANING OF LOVE

A poem by
Marc Rubin

A strong complex
Emotion or feeling causing
One to appreciate delight
And crave!
The presence or possession
Of another to please
Or promote
The welfare of
The other devoted
Affection
Attachment specifically
Such feeling between
Husband and Wife!
Lover and Sweetheart!
One!
Who is beloved?
A sweetheart animal
Passion
Or gratification?
A very great interest or
Fondness for . . .
In tennis,
Nothing.

BOYS IN THE BONDS

Q. My son was engaged earlier this year to his college roommate. Neither of these young men is of the coat-and-tie-generation and they insist on a "natural" wedding to blend with their lifestyle, which includes bare feet and living rent-free in our summer house in Oregon. My husband and I don't want this to turn out to be another Altamont (some of their friends are quite theatrical). Can you give us some advice on how to plan this affair?

M.V., Cedar Rapids, Iowa

A. Your request for advice is a wise one, as large "hippy" gatherings have often been known to get out of hand and degenerate into lewd gambolings on the lawn that neither you nor your neighbors would wish to witness. Here's what the Jones' did when their son and his fiancé got married.

The wedding was held in a cow pasture near Bennington, Vermont, where their son had attended college. The boys threaded their way carefully between the bovine calling cards down the grassy aisle in matching white caftans, sateen joksoks, and Earthpumps, escorted by their mothers in chintz housedresses, wrinkled support hose, and carrying outsized shopping bags stuffed with clean underwear. Music consisted of Barbra Streisand singing a Carol King medley and "Sunshine on My Rectum (Makes Me Happy)."

A Gay Activist warlock of the First Church of Christ Sodomite began the ceremony with a reading from James Baldwin's *Giovanni's Room*, followed by random obscenities from Peter Orlovsky and *The White Pleasure Garden of Abdullah* by Aleister Crowley. The ceremony closed when the attendants, garbed as Bette Davis in *All About Eve*, brought up the traditional wedding hash brownie which the newly-marrieds cut on the bias. After the reception, the guests, who had been requested to come attired in L.L. Bean-tailored work shirts and over-the-knee Root Boots, happily tied huarachas and Swedish massage sandals to the couple's aqua Volkswagon thing and threw brown rice on the boys as they left for a lovely honeymoon in Lake Louise, Banff.

Q. Where does the tradition come from that we have to be virgins when we get married, anyway? My sorority sister says it has something to do with the incest taboo, but I think it has to do with making sure the crops grow or that the groom doesn't get hit by lightning. In any case, it really puts a cramp in our style. What's the deal?

E.M., Lynn, Mass.

A. In ancient times, before the development of birth control and the welfare

Continued

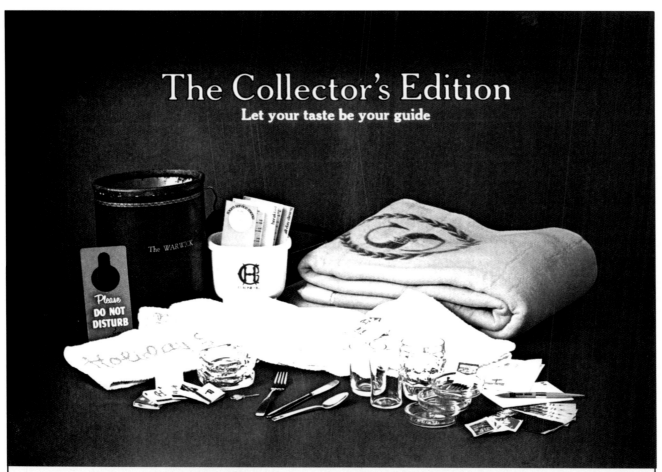

The Collector's Edition
Let your taste be your guide

All the candlelight appeal and gracious appointments
of the inns of provincial America are yours for the taking in a trousseau
for the collector of treasured mementos.
The Collector's Edition invites you to be an honored guest in your own home
for no more than what you would pay for an evening's accommodations away from it.
You needn't wait for delivery, it's at your fingertips.
Let your taste be your guide.

American Bride's Answers

state, unwed mothers, if not immediately killed by their outraged fathers, were given tar enemas by the virtuous women of the tribe and escorted to the city limits. There they would live as outcasts and prostitutes unless discovered by young poets or novelists, who would immortalize them in verse and letters, but probably skip out on the rent.

Q. Every time I attend a wedding, there seems to be this undercurrent of hostility present, as if no one is having a good time or likes each other much. There seems to be a little too much drinking of champagne and a lot of forced gaiety. The bride and groom always look scared, regretful, and sheepish, and their parents are often rude and vicious to each

other about little things like where they went to school and what kind of car they have. I want my wedding to be a happy and warm occasion based on love and goodwill towards others. Am I crazy or what?

E.P., New York, New York

A. Yes. The Rape of the Sabine Women took place at a wedding. Did you know that? Archduke Ferdinand was leaving a wedding when he was shot at Sarajevo, thus marking the beginning of World War I. It was at a wedding that plans were drawn up to bomb Pearl Harbor, sink the Lusitania, kidnap the Lindbergh baby, annex Chechoslovakia, and massacre the Light Brigade. The Hindenburg Disaster, the San Francisco Earthquake, the Alamogordo Holocaust—all weddings!

If you want to spend three or four thousand dollars just to sleep, throw a funeral.

Sexual Pleasures . . . How to Know Them

(Continued from page 20)
insides of the thighs, Achilles tendons, and genital areas of both. Most sensitive for her, the sphagnum, and the alabaster mosque (located just above the citadel); for him, the often fleeting glans, the matto grosso, and a fast rim-job in the back of his 1953 Chevrolet coupé. Intercourse usually starts with the couple kissing, touching, or stroking each other, until the man's penis becomes erect and the woman's vagina becomes lubricated and her nose swells. Eventually, the man inserts his fully erect penis into the woman's vagina, and they thrust their hips toward each other until they both reach "climax" or orgasm together at the very same moment. That's all. Simple. No problem, no lengthy learning process. A brilliant testimony to God's handiwork, it all happens smoothly and effortlessly and right on cue, unless of course you're frigid. Then there's no hope of *Continued on page 76*

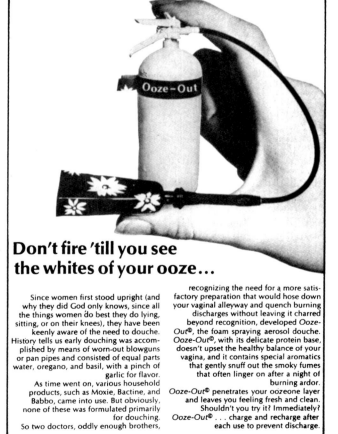

END

The Perfect Wedding, The Perfect Honeymoon, The Perfect Magazine!

6 issues $10
Save 67% off the cover price!
and a chance to win a honeymoon
to remember at the luxurious...

Lake Inuendo
"Home of the Pink Champaigne & Viagra Brunch"

AMERICAN BRIDE

Wedding Date ___ / ___ / ___

☐ **YES! I WANT TO SAVE EVEN MORE**
Send me 12 issues for $19 even though I have no
idea what I'm going to do with more than one.

☐ Payment enclosed

☐ Bill me later, I'll pay if it works out.

NATIONAL ENQUIRER

The *National Enquirer* was established in 1952 by publisher Generoso Pope, Jr. Distributing copies to neighborhood grocery stores enabled the forward-thinking Pope to reach a large female audience previously untouched by the magazine market. While these weekly tabloids often find themselves sued over less-than-accurate reporting, there is still no better source for catching up on the romance, drug habits and weight battles of your favorite celebrity, three-headed baby or Bat Boy.

This parody first appeared in the March 1973 Issue of National Lampoon.

"I refuse to comment on the *National Enquirer* due to an $8 million dollar defamation suit I have filed against the magazine for making claims that I slept with Elizabeth Taylor. Please! That woman is built like a couch."

– Jim "Big Foot" Sasquatch, 2001.

NATIONAL INSPIRER

20¢

Vol. 47, No. 18, March 14, 1973

UNDERCOVER REPORT:

SLEEP CLAIMS JACKIE

Unconscious for 8 Hours a Day, Says Ari

Dead to world?

WOMAN GIVES BIRTH TO HUMAN BABY

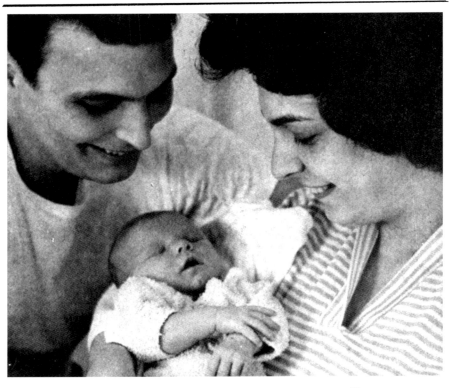

Husband Fathers Own Daughter

June Allyson's Cactus Survives — in Spite of Unusually Dry Weather

"It's like that," June told the NATIONAL INQUIRER. "It always has been. My cactus has been a source of silent inspiration to me for years. There's something wonderful about a tender succulent plant that's able to endure such hardship and is so well-equipped to defend itself.

"I think we could all learn a lot from the humble cactus. Many people would be so much better off if they'd learn to stand the heat and save up for a rainy day. It's not easy to be grasping with a cactus either. Yet you could hardly call them selfish."

Tot Not Drowned

Tragedy was widely adverted in Varicosa, Ariz., when Michael Farquarth, 9, visiting his grandparents in the small retirement community, wandered too close to the bank of the Plaque River and fell in.

"I suppose it could have ended in heartbreak," said Sheriff Sam Antonio, the local law-enforcement officer who returned little Michael to his grandmother after an unidentified passerby rescued the youngster moments after he slipped, and   at the police station.

"But the fact is that section of the river is dry 10 months a year and nothing more than a trickle the other two," continued Sheriff Antonio. "The Corps of Engineers built a bunch of irrigation ditches a few years back that bypassed this whole area."

"Still, it's just as well that fellow happened along. If the child had been out there another 10 or 12 hours, he might have gotten pretty thirsty, though otherwise he'd have been alright. There's no snakes out there so far as I know, and you can't get a sunburn this time of year."

The lucky lad escaped with only a scratched knee.

MICHIGAN WEDDING RING EXPOSED!

Hundreds of willing couples are undergoing nuptuals every month in a Lansing, Mich., marriage mill, according to reports from local authorities. The participants in the unusual rites, which involve dressing in outlandish costumes and being pelted with handfuls of rice, are mostly young couples in their early twenties.

A few detractors claim that the ceremonies are only "a bald attempt to dress up cohabitation and worse," but outsiders who have observed the matrimonial procedure insist it is healthy and above board.

SET TO "WED": Bizarrely costumed duo participates in weird rites.

"I've hitched hundreds," admits Justice of the Peace Francis Templeton. "Some days I'll do as many as ten in a single day. And at $10 a head, that ain't hay."

"I don't care what anybody says," explained pretty Noreen Snellgrove, 20, to NATIONAL INSPIRER reporter Burt Wince. "Jake, that's my spouse, and I wanted to tie the knot since last August, and we weren't about to let anything stop us."

Psychic Claims to Hear Hidden Voices in Radio

UNCANNY ABILITY: Psychic Bernice Fetching prepares to tune in spirit world.

Psychic Bernice Fetching claims to have heard mysterious voices emanating from an old clock radio in her kitchen.

The voices, which are seldom the same, cajole her into buying products, give her predictions about the weather, and sing songs.

"Several times I heard the voice of John Kennedy, but that was many years ago," said Miss Fetching. "Mostly it's people I don't recognize, but sometimes I can pick out celebrities, political figures, and other famous people."

"One time Arthur Godfrey urged me to buy a motorcar," said Mrs. Fetching. "I did, and it turned out to be the best car I ever had. It lasted for years."

"On another occasion, Rod Serling recommended a brand of toothpaste for my personal use, and since then I have not had a single cavity or other dental problem."

Actor José Ferrer Admits...

"I Drove My Child to School"

It was a day like any other in the Ferrer household in lush Coma del Gato, Calif., until little Fulgencia Ferrer, 7, rushed into the room where her famous father was going over the script of his latest movie, *A Serious Illness in Venice*.

"Daddy, Daddy," she cried, "the school bus didn't come!"

"I knew right then I'd have to drive her," explained the noted movie actor. "With most kids, they'd jump at the chance to play hooky, but Fulgencia's crazy about school."

Ferrer quickly dropped what he was doing and drove his daughter the 7 miles to the Ackney School for Girls, a private elementary-school. "We beat the bus by 5 minutes," said Ferrer. "It turned out the driver was new and just didn't know the route."

When I got home, I made myself a BLT and went back to work," he added.

FERRER says: "I had to do it. The bus didn't come."

Kentucky Man Said to Be 57 Years Old,

Attributes Remarkable Feat to "Good Habits"

A man who was already 3 years old when World War I ended still pursues a full, active life that would put to shame men half or three-quarters his age.

OLDER THAN AVERAGE: Minookin recalls life before World War II for NATIONAL INSPIRER reporter Don Maim.

Russell Minookin, who was born on January 17, 1915, and has a birth certificate to prove it, has lived all his life in tiny Purvis, Ky., where he still works 6 days a week running the local dry-goods store his father founded.

"My pappy lived to be 69," says Minookin, a short, cheerful man, whom more than half a century has left with thinning hair and a slight paunch. "I guess it runs in the family."

Minookin was in high school when the stock market crashed in 1929, and turned 21 just in time to vote for FDR in 1936. "It was mighty different then," he says. "Cars were all boxy, not modern like now, and you didn't have Perma Prest or any of these here miraculous fabrics."

"I feed him 3 meals a day and see that he gets a good night's sleep," explains Minookin's wife, Mildred, who at 54 describes herself as "no spring chicken, either."

Minookin has some advice for NATIONAL INSPIRER readers. "People should learn to slow down," he says. Other than that, he credits good habits for his continued health. "I stay out of drafts, watch between-meal treats, and slow down at all intersections—whether there's a sign or not."

He still has vivid recollections of events many Americans only read about in history books as if they took place only yesterday. "I remember the year Ruth hit all them home runs, and Pearl Harbor. I'd have joined up," he adds, "but my eyes were bad."

IFOs Plague French Town

Villagers in the tiny town of Beurre-sur-Pain, 10 miles south of Lyons, France, have been losing sleep over the appearance of flying objects with flashing lights that have filled their sky in the last few months.

"They make a noise like a loud vacuum-cleaner or a freight train, a kind of roar," said Armand Bonnier, the local police-chief. "They are not very fast and usually go in a straight line."

The IFOs, or Identified Flying Objects, are commercial jets headed to and from the new airport outside of Lyons. "Naturally, we are not as upset as we would be if they were spaceships from another planet," explained Pierre Cornette, the town's baker, "but this noise alarms the geese and sometimes makes children cry.

"It is nice to know they come from Lyons and not Venus, but they still are a thing that bother us."

ARTIST'S CONCEPTION of objects seen in sky over French town.

Death Toll 0 As Train Pulls into Station

The cold metal wheels of boxcars rumble menacingly over the rails between Richmond, Indiana, and Cincinnati.

Every day engineer Otis Bianco lives with the thought of those dozens of axles rolling without stop down the road bed at several miles an hour. He admits that that's about all there is on his mind while he's working.

Along each of those 78 miles, every inch of gleaming rail spells instant death for anything that comes between it and the wheels of the train. No man would willingly let himself be run down by the huge Erie-Lackawana diesel. Even a close call has not been reported.

Government Releases List of Chemicals Not in Your Food

After extensive research, investigators with the Pure Food and Drug Administration have come up with a list of potentially dangerous elements, which, unlike mercury and cadmium, have never been found in any amounts at all in the food you eat.

The list includes technetium, promethium, neptunium, lawrencium, fermium, einsteinium, mendelvedium, californium, americium, and berkelium.

Mother Heartbroken When She Learns...

Her Child, 7, is Doomed to Be Human Vegetable

Mrs. Constance Lenz remembers the day she was told of her daughter's awful fate.

"It was Friday," recalled Mrs. Lenz. "Little Darlene had just come home from school. I could tell from the look on her tiny face that something was wrong."

"What is it, honey?" she remembers asking the tyke. "What's the matter?"

"Oh, mommy, it's just not fair. I thought God liked little girls and wouldn't let bad things happen to them if they were good!" sobbed Darlene.

"We drew lots for who got to play what in the school *Pageant of Local Products*," explained the tearful tot, "and I have to be broccoli. And I so wanted to be at least a household convenience, like aluminum foil or comfort tissue!"

"It was enough to break your heart," said Mrs. Lenz.

TINY DARLENE will look something like this when she appears in school pageant.

Youngster Locked in Kitchen

Forced to Eat Own Dinner

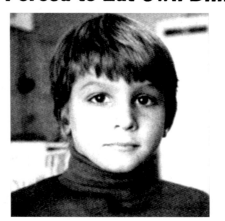

HIS LAST MEAL before sleep.

TOTS cold as death.

MOTHER: Said she'd be back in a "jiffy."

Gravity: Nature's Glue
The Mysterious Force That Shapes Human Destiny

Strange, invisible rays emanating from unplumbed depths within the earth itself exert a powerful influence on our daily lives, according to Dr. Phillip Buttenheim of the University of Long Island Sound.

"These odd rays keep us attached to the ground just as if we had blobs of stickum on our shoes," said Dr. Buttenheim. "And it's a good thing they do. Without them we'd find it difficult to perform even the simplest daily tasks."

The effects of this powerful force have been felt throughout history, explained Dr. Buttenheim. "The Fall of Rome, the sinking of the *Titanic*, the dropping of the atomic bomb on Hiroshima, and a host of other important events were all strongly influenced by this remarkable phenomenon."

The fateful turn of a simple doorknob spelled cold meatloaf and Tater Tots for Timothy Gardener, 8.

"I meant to . . . I really meant to warm up the Tater Tots, at least," claimed Mrs. Gardener, an attractive St. Louis divorcée in her early 30s. "It all happened so quickly. I just ran out to the supermarket for a second and . . ."

I Changed My Baby

Mrs. Dee Wilkins pulled the pants off her own son in a private bedroom of her home in the swank Chicago suburb of River Forest.

"It was a filthy mess," her husband testified. "I can't stand it. The whole business makes me want to throw up."

Mr. Wilkins, an important insurance-adjuster, went on to tell how his young wife then took the boy to bed without so much as a word. "And the kid didn't put up a fight!" He admitted, however, that the child had been beat, was really knocked out.

Dee made no bones about her actions on that evening. "I did it," she said. "I did it, and I'll do it again and again."

Trapped for more than half an hour, little Timmy pounded minute after minute on the unyielding door. He resorted, at last, to the kitchen tap for water. And was forced to smear the kitchen with Tater Tots to keep himself amused.

Released at last and reduced to pitiful tears, Timmy's frail body lay across his mother's knees. And in one small hand he clenched the poignant note she'd left: "Be back in a jiffy. Turn on the TV."

MOTHER: "I did it and I'll do it again."

Breaks Glass, Throws Deadly Shards in Wastebasket

Quick thinking saved Mrs. Theresa Fenton from nasty cuts when she accidentally dropped a drinking glass on the kitchen floor in her Decatur, Ill., home.

"I was washing up after breakfast when it slipped out of my hands," said Mrs. Fenton. "I guess it was slippery because of all the soap."

Mrs. Fenton quickly swept up the knifelike fragments with a dustpan and hand broom, and wrapped them in some old newspaper. Still shaking from her experience, she put the bundle in the metal wastebasket she keeps in the kitchen for old cans, empty packages, and other waste.

"I put in it the newspaper so the trash men wouldn't cut themselves by accident," explained the resourceful housewife.

"I should have stayed in bed," said Mrs. Fenton, recalling the morning that spoiled her day. "All I could think about was how one of the children could have cut his feet on it. About an hour later I was vacuuming and I knocked over a lamp. I guess I was really rattled."

TINY DAGGERS: Stiletto-like slivers of glass similar to these menaced Fenton household.

"I guess I'm proof the American system works," says Murphy Sinclair, a quiet, hardworking son of a successful real-estate broker, who rose from District Salesman to Executive Vice-President of Telledex, a large midwestern plumbing-supply concern.

When Sinclair graduated from the University of Ohio in 1953, he had nothing but a secondhand car, his college de-

READY-TO-WEARS TO RICHES

gree, and, as he describes it, "a heck of a lot of ambition."

Now he owns a $40,000 suburban home, a swimming pool, two new cars (one of them a luxury model); and can afford to travel every year with his wife,

$125-a-Week Salesman in 1955, Now He's a $50,000-a-Year Executive

BIG EXECUTIVE Murphy Sinclair says: "Nobody gives you anything for free. You've got to get on your kiddy-car and work for it."

Selma, while their two children stay with their grandparents. "Last year we went to Mexico," reports Sinclair.

"It just shows what you can do if you want to," he says. "I just kept at it, 8 hours a day, 5 days a week. Often I had to bring work home at night or over the weekend, but I never gave up."

"Sure we had some tough times," admits Sinclair. "It wasn't easy to make ends meet while I was in the Army, even with Dad helping out, and we had to live in a furnished garden apartment for two years until we saved enough to buy our first house."

Would he do anything different if he had it all to do over again? "No way," exclaims Sinclair. "It's been swell. It wasn't all roses, but then hard work is what made this country great."

Woman Who Won $86 in Aqueduct Daily Double Says Life Is Unchanged

Still Lives in Kew Gardens 6 Years Later

It was in March, 1966, that luck galloped home for Miss Jessica Porttman in the form of Dixie Darling in the 3rd and I Love Lucy in the 6th. But she still lives quietly in the same $140-a-month apartment she was born in.

"Well, I wouldn't leave mother," she says.

"I guess you'd have to say I'm the same kind of person I've always been. I quit my job at the library a while ago, though. Too many colored."

Did the money change her life at all? "I meant to get new drapes. But then mother and I decided to have the rug shampooed."

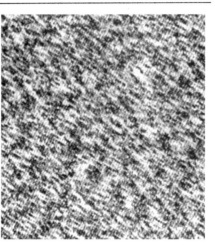

CLEAN RUG: Her only luxury.

Woman Cooks Dead Turkey, Feeds It to Hubby, Toddlers

4 Unhurt When Gas Stove Fails to Explode

Mrs. Rose Hermanez of New York City and her 3 young daughters escaped serious injury when Bonita, the eldest girl, lit their stove.

"Always I am nervous about lighting stoves," Bonita says.

A neighbor confirmed that this was so. "She doesn't like to light the stove," said Mrs. Pearl Smith.

Fortunately the oven did not burst into a massive ball of flame and instantly set gruesome fire to the flowing black tresses and colorful Puerto Rican clothing of the 3 girls and their poor but hardworking mother whose husband deserted her 3 years ago.

Then it didn't spread ravenously into the hallway of the tinder-dry old tenement and turn the 5 flights of stairs into an inferno-like chimney of death.

"I Used the Bones for Soup," She Admits

It was a normal day in the small, neat house where the Bevelacs, Sam and Sarah, lived with their two children, Bill, 2, and Louise, 10 months, except for one thing—it was Thanksgiving, and in Mrs. Bevelac's new GE oven the carcass of a huge, 15-pound turkey was slowly turning a deep brown.

MRS. BEVELAC points to oven where bird was subjected to temperatures hotter than parts of surface of planet Mercury.

"It was the biggest bird I'd ever cooked," recalled Mrs. Bevelac. "After dressing it I had to get Sam to help me push it in the oven. For a while there, I thought I'd have to hack some pieces off it with a carving knife."

When Mrs. Bevelac opened the oven door 4½ hours later, she discovered that she hadn't allowed enough time for the turkey to cook. "I gave it another half-hour and that did the trick," she said.

"It was the best turkey ever," said Sam Bevelac. "I guess we all ate ourselves silly, even the kids. Still, we had turkey sandwiches and turkey salad and turkey casserole for a week."

"It was coming out of our ears," Mrs. Bevelac agreed. "Me, I even used the bones to make turkey soup. I think if I didn't eat it again for a year, it would be too soon!"

Elke Sommer Cries...
"My Dogs Are Killing Me!"

For glamorous actress Elke Sommer, the thought of an evening stroll with her two pet wolfhounds conjures up images of dread.

"I've got corns, bunions, blisters . . . brother, you name it," lamented the Hollywood beauty. "Just walking across the room is agony, let alone taking Marcel and Foo-Foo out for a walk.

"I've got big feet, 11 EEE, and I can't find anything that fits me," she explained. "Everything pinches my tootsies. It's like wearing a pair of snapping turtles."

VICIOUS HOUNDS such as these deadly-looking brutes go shoeless, have healthy paws.

Seven Signs You Don't Have Deadly Cancer

1. Persistent steady breathing and long-windedness.
2. Lack of warts or moles.
3. Firm and satisfying regular bowel movements.
4. Smooth silky flesh all over your body.
5. Pleasant drowsiness after large meals.
6. Deep or contented sleep.
7. Ticklishness of feet and ribs.

UNDISEASED female breast.

Learn these seven signs by heart. Any one of them could mean absence of terminal malignacy. And don't call your doctor unless you're sick or in need of a regular physical examination.

PERSONABLY PERSONAL

N76560/MICH./WATER SPORTS:
Vivacious couple into water sports seeks same for boating, fishing, short cruises.

N67561/CONN./LIBERAL-MINDED:
Very liberal man in early forties looking for uninhibited companion of either sex to discuss Bangla Desh, bussing, and local school-board autonomy.

N67562/CALIF./BALLS:
Golden-ager can still "shake a leg," desires cotillion or charity affair in San Fran. area.

N76563/OHIO/ANIMAL TRAINER:
Like to meet with singles or couple who desire "obedience school." Free for seeing-eye dogs.

N76564/ILL./FRENCH ARTIST:
Knows how to please ladies, gentlemen, whole family. Beautiful likeness. Reasonable rates.

N76565/N.Y./GAY COUPLE:
Seeks other gay couples for madcap tap dancing in the park, watching old Ginger Rogers-Fred Astaire movies, and riding home with the milkman in the morning.

N76566/PA./GREEK CULTURE:
Active teacher, 25, available and ready with big slide show of Acropolis ruins and scenic Delphi.

N76567/KANS./LEATHER:
Docile young man loves leather trade. Will teach you to make belts, vests, desk blotter, cuff-link boxes, etc.

N76568/S. DAK./DIGS BIG BUSTS:
Want huge, heavy, creamy-smooth white ones so big it takes two hands to lift them! Any age. Pericles, Augustus, Petrarch, and Thomas Jefferson preferred.

N76569/TEX./EAR FREAK:
Kind, sensitive, shy man of 51 willing to relocate, greatly desires to leave carnival and find secluded job among tactful people. Hard worker.

N76570/N.J./SWING:
Cherry Hill club has hundreds of with-it couples, all ages, all races, lined up and ready to go at the Avalon Ballroom March 30. Benny Goodman, Artie Shaw, Glen Miller, Gene Krupa, Tommy Dorsey, and more.

N76571/GA./MENAGE A TROIS:
Genteel couple—good income, nice house—desires single girl any race. Must be clean, sober, efficient, and courteous. No walls or heavy lifting. Have references.

N76572/NEBR./NEED TO BE LOVED:
Available brunette wants home with kind bachelor, single girl, or couple any age, race. Just treat me like your baby. Big brown eyes. Good legs. Nice pussy. One of a litter of eight.

N76573/S.C./WE PLAY BOTH WAYS:
Charlotteville man and wife, "masters," wish to meet other experienced, skilled couples for rubber. Any way you like it. Contract or auction.

N76574/N.Y./STUDENT OF LESBOS:
Cooklamu dolmadakia skamos clado potiri ghamotta angiharès yassu tikamis cokinos apopissu polyorea kalimera skamos.

N76575/FLA./READY STUD:
Big black male looking for a bitch in heat. I've got what you want if you want some pointers. Nineteen inches at the shoulder. Papers, AKA pure-bred.

N76576/ENG./QUEEN:
By the grace of God, Her Majesty, Elizabeth, Queen of Scotland, England, Ireland, and Wales, Monarch of the Dominions of Great Britain and Empress of India. Single girl or suitably married. Older woman should abdicate if possible.

END

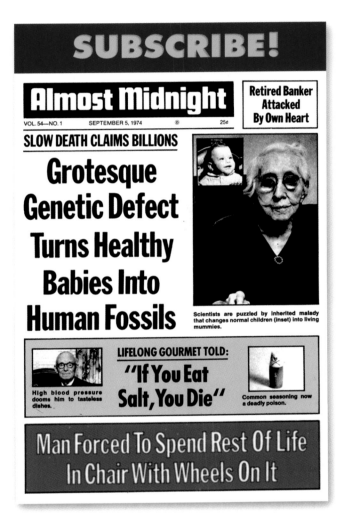

"'Special Interest' is fancy talk for limited readership, which means limited revenue for me; therefore in my publishing empire, 'Special Interest' is a dirty word, much like 'fuck' or 'shit' or 'estate tax' or 'tea bagging.'"

– William Randolph Hearst

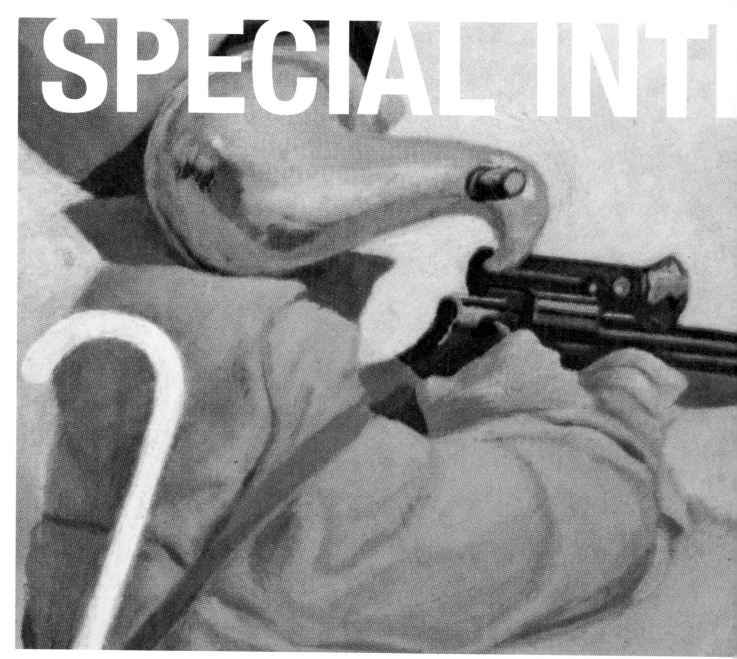

SPECIAL INT

BLACK SKIER

The Proud, Beautiful, Together Magazine for Fashionable, Aggressive, Animally Magnetic People of the Afro-American Persuasion

ORTHOPEDIC SURGEON
: Does the Extra Bone
Ankles Make Us
in the Slalom?

MOUNTAIN COMES TO
H MUHAMMED: Black
n's New Ski Complex
cago's South Side

O PROTECT YOUR-
ROM SKI MUGGERS,
Menace of the Trails

US
t Report: The New Ivory
m Kenya

Ski Heritage Series: Ned
on, From Slave Chains to
p Champion

rs of Mantan "Feet Don't
Now" Moreland,
ood's First Black Skier

w Black Snow Bunny
ns for Firesiding and

RAPPING
WITH "SATIN,"
Black Ski Lodge
Pimp Extraordinaire

THE JEWISH AMERICAN ATHLETE

July 1979 $1.75

"The Babe Was One-third Jewish": Confessions of Mrs. Ruth
Do Jewish Athletes Have a Natural Sense of Brain Rhythm?
Isaac Goldberg: A Jewish Middle Linebacker at a Black College
Are Jewish Team Doctors Superior to Gentiles?
The Maccabee Sports Stud Farm: Raising Bionic Jews
"Nice Jewish Girls Finish Last!": A Critique of Female Jewish Athletes

Popular Evolution

The Craze That's
Sweeping the
Primates
WALKING
UPRIGHT

ANATOMICAL
TIPS

• Custom Bivalve
Shells

• Choosing the
Right
Exoskeleton

A Vital Link –
THE ACORN
WORMS

CLIP-AND-SAVE
KNOW-HOW:

• How to Gulp
Oxygen Directly
from the Air

• How to Use
Your Mouth as an
Accessory
Breathing
Organ

• How Your Size
Can Make You
Thermally
Independent

To Help Produce Heat
Should Your Body Become
Too Cold, Now It's
SHIVERING!

10-Page Special Section
HELPFUL HINTS FOR
YOUR HABITAT

Lungs: A Full Report

THE NEW MULTIPLE
STOMACHS
Eat Now,
Chew Later

REDUCING YOUR
SIDE TOES
How much will it
really add to your
running speed?

OVERLAPPING SCALES – Can They Keep You From Getting Mauled

GUN LUST

JUNE 1973
Bull Publishing Co.
A5¢

Microphonic
Sights—
New Hope for
Blind Hunters

Burger's Bazookas—
The Chief Justice Explains
a Simple Way
Around Handgun
Permit Regulations

Hunting Accident

BORMANN
the man

PLUS:

IN-DEPTH TEST REPORTS: The New
Thompson .Center .45 Butterfly
Rifle; the Remington Triple-X
Lightweight Trout Grenade; the
Latest SAM 2-aHome Tactical
Nuclear Mouse Rocket

Lives of Glass:
The Poetry of Charles Whitman

"ME"

The 1970's was known as the 'Me Generation.' While the preceding generation had protested for world peace, this group didn't seem to care about anything but themselves. From *High Times* to *Civil War Times*, the publishing industry found itself catering to a greater number of increasingly smaller demographics. Everyone demanded a voice in print; but perhaps none were more niche than the National Lampoon parody, *Me*, a magazine for and about one guy.

Now, more than thirty years later, this parody seems eerily prophetic. The Internet allows for millions of people to host their own websites, blogs, chat rooms and radio stations, while the explosion of reality TV can turn any one of their lives into a ratings bonanza.

This parody first appeared in the December 1973 issue of National Lampoon.

"In the future, everyone will be famous for 15 minutes; except a woman named Jessica Simpson, who will manage to eek out another 23 seconds, probably stealing it from that *Sixth Sense* kid."

– Andy Warhol, artist, 1987.

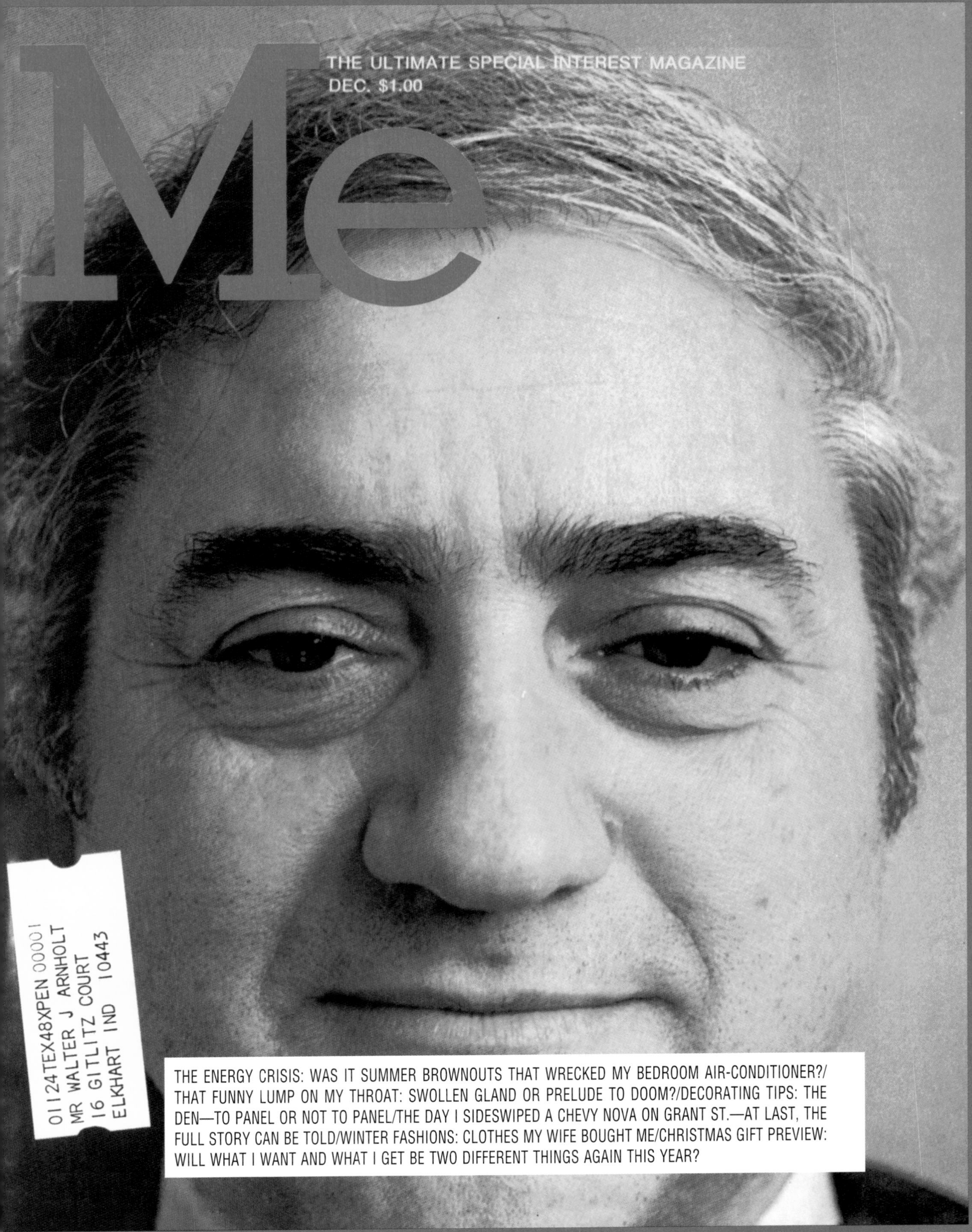

Me
THE ULTIMATE SPECIAL INTEREST MAGAZINE
DEC. $1.00
01124TEX48XPEN 00001
MR WALTER J ARNHOLT
16 GITLITZ COURT
ELKHART IND 10443
THE ENERGY CRISIS: WAS IT SUMMER BROWNOUTS THAT WRECKED MY BEDROOM AIR-CONDITIONER?/THAT FUNNY LUMP ON MY THROAT: SWOLLEN GLAND OR PRELUDE TO DOOM?/DECORATING TIPS: THE DEN—TO PANEL OR NOT TO PANEL/THE DAY I SIDESWIPED A CHEVY NOVA ON GRANT ST.—AT LAST, THE FULL STORY CAN BE TOLD/WINTER FASHIONS: CLOTHES MY WIFE BOUGHT ME/CHRISTMAS GIFT PREVIEW: WILL WHAT I WANT AND WHAT I GET BE TWO DIFFERENT THINGS AGAIN THIS YEAR?

ARNHOLT REPORT

Who Reads ME?

I'm not just a face in the crowd—I'm an individual, with my own personal style, my own special tastes, my own unique outlook on life. I'm forty-seven years old (I just had a birthday in November), I'm married (to the former Miss Helen Kramer of Indianapolis), and I have 3.0 children (Walter Jr., Frank, and Jane). I'm college educated (Ball State) and a decision-maker (Assistant District Sales Manager, Elkhart Steel Tubing). I have an annual income of $17,350.00 (not counting a Christmas bonus—it should be a fat one this year!). Last year, I spent nearly $4,000 on food, $1,100 on apparel, $800 on home related purchases $400 on liquor, $850 on insurance, $1,000 on travel and entertainment, and $175 on cigarettes (I'm thinking of switching brands.) Within the last six months, I purchased a major appliance. Right now I'm in the market for a new air-conditioner. And one of these days soon I'll be looking for a new car.

If you want to reach me, Mr. Media Buyer, you'll find me reading the only magazine written for me-whether it's a new recipe for one of my favorite foods, or a handy tip on how to fix that wet spot in the basement behind the furnace, or a political column that reflects my point of view for a change. And remember, when you advertise in *ME,* you're not scattering your advertising dollar—you're going straight into one market, with proven purchasing power and high reader loyalty.

So if you want me, get *ME.*

IN THE REGION. It's too early to tell, but the South Bend-Elkhart area could be **hit hard** this winter if predictions of oil and natural gas shortages come true. Now's the time to **plan ahead**. That old forced-air oil burner system that Bill Fessenden always made fun of could turn out to be a blessing in disguise-**worst squeeze** is expected in natural gas supplies. Fessenden may be laughing out of **the other side of his mouth** when he has to come over both to warm up and cook. But don't take any chances. Call up Pete at Buckeye Oil and make it clear that as a **lodge brother** he has an obligation to see that the Best People on Earth stay warm this winter, **no matter what**.

Liberal loonies are still pressing for bussing of Negroes, or whatever they're calling themselves these days, from South Bend **into Elkhart schools. Ezra Taft Benson School** is on their list. You have known several colored people and you'd be the first to say they're **fine folks**, but this is just a case of **too far too fast**. **Important persons** who have studied this question agree the Negroes are better off among **their own kind**, where they feel more comfortable and are able to **learn a useful trade** that will stand them in good stead in future years. Also there is no sense **beating around the bush**—it is a known fact that many Negroes are **dope fiends** and **slow learners**. This should be the major topic for the P.T.A. this year.

THE BUSINESS OUTLOOK. Pete Scarborough is getting a little **too big for his britches** since he was made Vice-President in charge of operations. It's time someone **brought him down a peg**. The importance of a job is not just its **title**—it's the way the individual fits into the overall **performance picture**. Let's face it—without a **strong sales force** that knows how to keep key government contracts **locked up**, there wouldn't be much in the way of operations for anyone to be Vice-President in charge of.

Miss Freylinghausen is a **very attractive young lady**, and in spite of the fact that she may not be as speedy a typist or as organized as some of the other girls, she lends a much needed dose of **cheeriness and pep** to the whole office. Choosing her as your personal secretary was a **wise move** in view of the importance of **impressing prospective clients** with the fact that Elkhart Steel Tubing is **one happy family.**

It's time Mr. Bremmerton recognized that **the cost of living** and **prices in general** have been going only one way—up. While **greedy unions** have been getting **exorbitant wage increases** at gunpoint, key executives, particularly in the **vital sales department**, have been overlooked. These individuals would be hard to replace, and it is fortunate for the company that their **sense of loyalty** is as strong as it is.

ON THE HOME FRONT. **Budget-busting expenditures**, particularly in the area of **clothing**, unnecessary **household purchases**, and **extravagance** by younger members of the family have got to stop. It's definitely time for some **belt-tightening** right across the board. The "old man" isn't

made of money, and everyone will have to get on his or her kiddy cart and **do their part** to keep expenses **in line**.

One place where a little **consideration** by others would go a long way is in the **bathroom**. It is **no fun** to find it literally **awash**, with damp towels stuffed into the racks, the sink **strewn** with cosmetics and shaving gear, and the tub **grimy**. This is the one room all members of the family must share; it is up to all to keep it in **tip-top shape** for the next person using it.

LETTERS
Clothes Call

In "What I'll Be Wearing, A Fall Fashion Preview," in the September issue, you stated that I have "two pairs of brown loafers, one of them badly in need of half-soling" and also made reference to a "grey houndstooth jacket with leather elbow patches." Just to set the record straight, I took the pair of loafers in question to the Shoo-In Shoe-Shop on Wannamaker St., about two weeks ago, and one of the employees at that establishment pronounced them "unrepairable," at which point I discarded them. I have not yet purchased a pair of shoes to replace them, but I agree that "something dressier" would round out my wardrobe.

I have looked in my closet and cannot find the houndstooth jacket (It was mentioned as possible "attire for casual outings") It is quite possible that my wife gave it to the Salvation Army people after reading the "For Your Wife Only" column in the August issue entitled "Walter's Closet: When in Doubt, Throw it Out." Incidentally, I was pleased to have been chosen the Best Dressed Arnholt again this year.

Walter J. Arnholt, Elkhart, Ind.

Shelve It?

I'd like to add a note to the plans given for building my own bookshelves in August's "Wally's Workshop." Although the 3/4" boards are plenty strong to hold most books and decorative objects, it turns out they can't support a complete set of the World Book Encyclopedia. (Come to think of it, not quite complete, as this reader remembers from "The Great Book Hunt: Where is PQ?" in *ME*, Nov., 72.) What happens is the nails – 2" finishing-tend to pull out at the ends and the wood splits. I found however that a 6" piece of 1x2" wood nailed under the shelves will do the trick.

All in all, looking back on it I think screws would have been a better choice. I haven't gotten around to making the spice rack (June, 73) but when I do, I think I'm going to go ahead and use screws.

Walter J. Arnholt, Elkhart, Ind.

At Home with Walter Arnholt

After putting in a day at the office, Walter Arnholt goes home. Home is a pink and white split level ranchette in the Breezycrest Knolls development in Elkhart. "I'm usually home by 5:20," says Arnholt. "It takes about fifteen minutes door to door. But sometimes I don't get home until 5:30 or later because I have to go through the downtown traffic. I can't wait until they finish that downtown Elkhart Bypass. It'll be a Godsend."

The Arnholts like to eat dinner as soon as Walter arrives. "I'm a meat and potatoes man myself, but with meat prices being what they are Helen is making our dollars stretch with some very creative tuna dishes. I never knew tuna could be prepared so many tasty ways. The kids and I think we're eating chicken or turkey."

After dinner Walter likes to read the evening paper and watch TV. The Arnholts usually watch TV in the living room on their RCA Home Entertainment Center. But almost every night at eight the "Arnholt Civil War" starts. "I'll want to watch 'Adam-12' and the kids will want to watch 'Sonny and Cher' and Helen would rather watch something else," said Arnholt. "So Helen kicks me into the den and the kids go into their rooms. Of course, we both like to watch the 'Lucy Show' and 'Marcus Welby.' She says she likes 'Maude,' 'Sanford and Son,' and 'Carol Burnett.' I don't always get the jokes on these shows."

Almost every night about 9:20 or 9:30 Helen will peek into the den and find Walter fast asleep. "He looks so peaceful and relaxed while all that violence is happening on the TV screen," says Helen. "I hate to poke him and wake him up."

"I'm not asleep at all," chuckles Walter. "I'm just resting my eyes after a hard day's work." About ten or so Walter has to fight off the temptation for a snack. "Helen keeps kidding me about the Battle of the Bulge," said Walter. "I'm just a few pounds overweight. Nothing I can't trim off. It's those meatless dinners that make me hungry a few hours later. If I don't get a sandwich or something, Helen will complain about my stomach growling and gurgling and keeping her awake all night."

"I don't really doze off when I'm watching TV, but sometimes I rest my eyes."

Thursday: Walter in the Kitchen
Every Thursday Walter and Helen do the weekly shopping at the local Safeway. They share Walter's weekly joke. "My wife is a magician at the supermarket," said Walter. "I give her fifty dollars and she makes it disappear." They like to do the shopping early to avoid the late evening crowds, so Walter drives right over to the market from the office and Helen takes the station wagon from home. "It sounds a little inconvenient, using two cars...but actually,

"It's the mustard in the boiling water that does the trick—everyone puts mustard right on their franks, but I like to put a little in the water."

we find that we now have extra storage space in case we buy something bulky like lawn furniture or barbecue equipment," says Walter.

Thursday night is Walter's turn to cook. "I've always liked to fool around in the kitchen," he said. "My specialty is franks and beans. Sometimes if I don't feel like cooking we go to the local McDonald's or to the Steak 'n Cake. Even with restaurant prices being what they are, I say it's worth it for Helen's sake alone...to get her out of the kitchen."

The Arnholts don't entertain as much as they used to. "With food prices going up the way they are you've got to be a sultan to afford entertaining," said Walter. "We're more coffee and cake types now rather than giving big dinners. Not that we stint. Helen will have her friends over for lunch and canasta and, of course, we still entertain our close friends and a few of my business associates. And there's Helen's mother, Cora, who usually drops over every Sunday."

Decorating with the Arnholts
Walter Arnholt leaves all the decorating decisions to his wife Helen. "Helen has wonderful taste and is really quite a decorating buff," he said. "She's taken some decorating courses from the DeSoto Correspondence School and is always getting those home life magazines. Of course, she always consults me because I'm the one who writes the checks. I keep telling her I have writer's cramp but she won't go for the gag."

Their kitchen is a pleasant study in knotty maple, with wood-like formica-topped tables and chairs and a vinyl floor covering in Armstrong's "Valenciaga" pattern. Their dining-living room continues the Moorish Mediterranean motif in warm tones of brown and gold, with brown wall to wall carpeting flecked with swirling gold patterns throughout.

Helen is fond of wall-to-wall carpeting because "I love to walk around the house with my shoes off and to sink my toes into that plushy carpeting." She even collects carpet remnants, "They're very cheap to buy-you know, broadloom odds and ends, little pieces, floor samples, closeouts. I cut them into pretty shapes and someday I'm going to decorate one of our bedroom walls with an entire wall arrangement of these different carpet pieces. Actually, I got the idea from *Family Circle* or *Good Housekeeping*."

At the moment it looks like curtains for the Arnholts. Helen Arnholt is on a curtain spree, replacing lots of their old ones. Her problem: where to use synthetic fabrics and where to use cottons and velvets. "With the kids grown up and fairly neat, I can afford to use velvets in the living and dining rooms," she said. "But they are such a bother to maintain and fiberglass is so easy to clean. Whenever I ask Walter for his opinion he says, don't ask me — I just write the checks."

The only room where a running battle takes place is Walter's den. "Helen has been after me for years to throw out the old chairs and stuff and get some new furniture. And she's always showing me cute decorating schemes for doing the den over. Well, that's when I get out my plans for building a little bar and putting in the knotty pine wall paneling-but it's a pretty big job and I never seem to have the time."

Weekends with the Arnholts
On weekends Walter has "a thousand and one little things to do." "There's always something to be done around the house, or with the lawn. And the kids always want me to drive them someplace or Helen wants to drag me to a store. If I can find the time I like to relax in the den with a good football game on TV. Maybe have a beer." "He's usually fast asleep by four," said Helen. "It's his regular Saturday afternoon nap and three or four beers."

Walter's hobby is collecting matchbooks. "I must have over five thousand of them by now," he said. "Every once in a while I get energetic and start a filing system for them, but it just gets to be too much. I've got them all over the place and sometimes people use them, not realizing that they're part of my collection. I've got some old ones for some lumber yards and fuel companies that must be worth quite a bit. Once in a while I call a fellow in Terre Haute who has a big collection and we make a few trades. He's got an old Lucky Strike matchbook with a misprint... a real collector's item."

"A misprinted matchbook like this could be worth a nice piece of change some day."

ARNHOLTS ALLEY

Crossword Puzzle

ACROSS
1. Bill P.'s dog
7. Grandma's favorite
10. What the Mrs. lost
13. Vernon drinks it
14. In the attic, but it used to be in the hall
15. Walt, Jr.'s first word
16. Kitchen clock is always
17. Kind of tree in yard
18. Helen's maiden name
19. Your breakfast fare
20. You voted for him in '64.
22. Green stamp item
28. He just made V.P.
32. An uncle's initials
35. Needs painting again?
38. River on the way to Ed's
39. Not your brand of smokes
40. They clinched the league in '36
42. High school chum
43. It was a lemon
44. Charley's nickname
45. Second wd. of "your song"
46. Spent a week there in '65
46. Where were the cufflinks?
49. They visited last Xmas
52. ———'s Sip 'n' Sup
56. On the blink since Feb.
57. New carpet color
58. Ave. in Ft. Wayne
59. Sock hue
60. Who said "Oh, fub-a-dub!"?
61. Garbage day
62. Your college frat (abbr.)
63. Wake-up radio station
64. Wife says she needs a new one

DOWN
1. Six of them in living room
2. The one about the 2 rabbis
3. Tuna ———.
4. Neighbors in Moline
5. Favorite T.V. M.D.
6. If not hers, then ——-
7. Sturgis is one.
8. Table feature
9. Forbidden cake flavor
10. Eatery on Tri-State Tollway
11. Lodge brother
12. Trouble with tub
15. Soft-drink preference
20. Fridge name
21. His Honor in Elkhart
23. P.T.A. head
24. Big month for birthdays
25. In right pants pocket
26. Poison ivy spot
29. Spent time in Army there
30. He drills and fills
31. He moved to Chi
34. "The beer with a ___"
36. Roof material
37. —— McPherson
40. Never use it twice
41. Quickest route to 7-11.
44. Insurance man
45. Sandwich component
47. Sofa fabric
48. Coming up soon, you hope
49. No. of phones in the house
50. Frank's current fad
51. Pet word for spouse
53. Basement needs it
54. Next time, ——— it.
55. Turns out she didn't.
58. He fixes auto.

In the Stars

Gemini (May 20-June 21) Jupiter is in a cusp with Uranus — a good sign for travel. Drive over to Fort Wayne to see Bob Newhouse or maybe take the kids to Chicago to see the German submarine at the Museum of Science. But better have the car looked at first — that puvva-puvva noise could mean a loose cylinder head or trouble with the linkage.

The Joke's on Me!

A man's home is his hassle!

*****

ME: Isn't that a new dress? How much did it cost?
SHE: Seventy-five dollars.
ME: Seventy-five dollars?!!
SHE: Don't worry, it was old money!

*****

There's nothing like a good cup of coffee-and what my wife makes is nothing like a good cup of coffee!

*****

My wife looks like a million dollars—All green and wrinkled!

*****

I told you I could balance the budget, Walter. Look, I've paid all the bills and there are still three checks left!

*****

MY FRIEND: Does your wife pick your clothes?
ME: No, just the pockets.

REVIEW

Our Trip to Colorado Last Summer, 1972, 34 mm, W. J. Arnolt, prod. With Walter J. Arnholt, Helen Arnholt, Frank, Jane, and Walter Jr., and introducing Prince, the cocker spaniel. * *

Arnholt has used the documentary form before (most notably in *Frank's First Steps* and *A Day at the Beach*), but his latest oeuvre demonstrates that his grasp of the medium has matured and deepened. Gone are overly romantic fuzzy focuses and dropped cameras, the deliberate shots of the sun, the quick, almost brutal, breaks in the film. Instead, in Colorado there is a kind of lyrical tranquility, a feeling that Arnholt is ready to accept the vicissitudes of life as given quantities. The almost pastoral footage out the side window of the car on the road up Pike's Peak bear witness to this new repose, for as the scene suddenly shifts in one of those lighting quick cuts that are Arnholt's trademark, we see Helen at the wheel of the family 'buggy," confident, determined, and calm-in short, a far different Helen from the excitable flibbertigidget of *Helen's Driving Lesson* (1961). Later, as Frank, Jane, and Walter, Jr. cavort at the (symbolic?) summit of the peak, Arnholt lets the camera drift lazily from figure to figure, from the majesty of the horizon to his own right shoe, and we can sense the complexity of the inner vision that powers Arnholts perceptions. Incidentally, Prince, in her first appearance in an Arnholt production, shows considerable promise. She is a "method" dog-the tail wag, the hanging tongue, the erratic rushes back and forth all bespeak that peculiarly natural artifice of the calculated performance-but her instinct for sheer presence is unmistakable.

All in all, there is a firmer, surer Arnholt at work in Colorado than we have seen before. And although comedy and a certain naivete have been sacrificed, and spilled ice cream cones on the car seat and tots flinging food at the lens have given way to a more mature perspective, Arnholt's cinematic statement still maintains the freshness and vitality of his first work, the classic *Walter Jr.'s First Christmas*-an impressive achievement for this talented filmmaker.

TV GUIDE

When Walter Annenberg founded *TV Guide* in 1953, it gave the publishing world a wake up call – this relatively new invention, television, was here to stay. While most of the daily newspapers had at one point printed radio listings, it wasn't until Annenberg's magazine that they finally began to include the day's TV schedule. Unfortunately, there is still no clue as to how and why they ever printed those Cathy cartoons.

This parody first appeared in November 2004 on NationalLampoon.com.

"For those of us who were fans of *Baywatch: Hawaii*, *TV Guide* was an indispensable tool in locating the show's whereabouts."

– Secretary of Defense Donald Rumsfeld, 2005.

AL-JAZEERA TV GUIDE

NOVEMBER 4-10 $2.49

HE'S BACK!
OSAMA "THE COMEBACK KID"

"WE MUST BLEED AMERICA TO BANKRUPTCY & RUIN":

HOW HIS LATEST THREAT REVIVED HIS CAREER

لادن

لبم الفاعدة

AL-JAZEERA PRIME TIME

WEEK DAYS

ALJ	6:00	**Shrieked Fatwahs with Ibrahim Mohammed** Get fit in the morning with Ibrahim's high impact cave workout.
ALJ	7:00	**America is a Filth-Smeared Anus From Which Only Lies Escape** Join our panel of experts for an unbiased debate of world events.
ALJ	8:00	**Ahmed Khalfan's Big Comfy Cave** Ahmed and his goat-puppet friend Mustafa use their imaginations to make their dreams come alive, devouring America's people in Allah's purifying righteous flame.
ALJ	11:00	**The People's Court** Judge Muhammad Atef sentences the unrighteous to die alongside the innocent in revenge for America's crimes against Islam.
ALJ	1:00	**Taliban General Hospital** THG's ER cave is filled with ailing terrorists after a failed UN hostage swap. Meanwhile, will Dr. Matwalli find out about Nurse Atwah's evil twin in time to stop Achbar from having another prophetic vision?
ALJ	2:00	**Jihad!** Can six best friends put aside their religious differences and come together against a common enemy? No. They are unable to and bloodshed ensues.
ALJ	3:00	**Food or not Food** Stalactites. Stalagmites. Rocks. Bitter, bitter hatred. Bitter, bitter bat wings. Ten fugitive experts tell you the surprising number of things one can subsist on when hiding from peacekeeping armies.
ALJ	4:00	**Afghani Martyr** Young terrorist hopefuls compete against each other for the honor of driving a truck into the U.S. Embassy. Tonight: tempers flare between Ahmed and Mustafa after the goat-throwing competition! One must lose his hands or anger Allah!
ALJ	5:00	**Scientific Discovery with Mohamed Fadhil** Explore the heights of Afghani scientific innovation with our noted scholars. This week: the dung arrow. Next week: fire.
ALJ	6:00	**Jalalabad's Funniest Beheadings**
ALJ	10:00	**Jittery footage of bearded men threatening to violently kill thousands of innocents in revenge for perceived injustices**
ALJ	11:00	**Cave Threats in Review** This week's cave-dwelling threatmaker countdown Also: results of "Sexiest Terrorist Fugitive" contest!

Big Comfy Cave

JIHAD!

The People's Court

Taliban General Hospital

SHOWS TO WATCH

Scientific Discovery

Shrieked Fatwahs

Kandahar Cut-up
A Young Osama bin Laden jokes with his cave crew on the set of his break-out hit, "Praise Be to Allah, The American Infidels Must Pay For Their Whore-Crimes"

THE COMEBACK KID

HIS OCTOBER 7TH 2001 TV SPECIAL "AMERICAS GREAT BUILDINGS DESTROYED, THERE IS NO GOD BUT ALLAH" WAS THE MOST-WATCHED SHOW OF THE YEAR. BUT JUST THREE YEARS LATER, BALLOONING PRODUCTION COSTS, TIRED WRITING AND A BOUNTY ON HIS HEAD HAD MARTYRED BIN LADEN'S CAREER. AFGHANISTAN'S BRIGHTEST STAR TALKS ABOUT HIS RETURN TO THE TOP, THE PRICE OF FAME AND HIS LATEST HIT TELECAST.

After almost three years of exile from Al Jazeera television, Osama bin Laden surprised the world when he once again picked up a microphone and violently threatened America from a cave November 1st.

Reviews for "We Must Bleed America to Bankruptcy & Ruin" have been mixed (Vice-President Cheney accused the popular entertainer of "treading water"). But all agree bin Laden's latest telecast was more than a chillingly psychotic threat to America's security. For the 47-year-old Saudi Arabian, it was a comeback.

Two days later, bin Laden sits in the crowd at the Jihadis, Afghanistan's top award show to honor the titans of cave-based entertainment. Bin Laden's latest opus is nominated in the Best Live Cave Broadcast category, and he has every reason to feel nervous. He is up against Salih al-Shuaybi, a hot new America-threatener whose weekly cave telecasts have topped the ratings all season.

Al-Shuaybi is everything bin Laden is not — young, stylish, with a sense of detached irony in his (cont'd) hatred of the Great American Satan. Afghanis every-where repeat his hilarious catchphrase, "American women are depraved painted hookers, may Allah smite their organs with wrath."

"He's a phony," bin Laden whispers, forcing a smile at the dance number onstage in case a camera should find him in a crowd shot. "He said he would drop nerve gas on Utah to revenge the tyranny against our people in Palestine. Did he drop the gas and I just missed it?" he snorts. "All sizzle. No steak."

The dance number ends, and the women are round-ed up and beheaded onstage for shaming themselves. The crowd goes wild, ululating and rending clothes. This year's Jihadis host, Cat Stevens, makes some quips about the dancers to big laughs. He too is then beheaded.

As always, bin Laden is tight-lipped about his exile. The pressures of fame. The attempt to arrest him as an international war criminal. The ballooning produc-tion budgets (an ambitious thirty-cave set reportedly took a 2002 broadcast $80M over budget).

Personal heartbreak also plagued bin Laden during his exile, with the divorce (and subsequent skin-flayings) of three of his eleven wives. Bin Laden is reluctant to dig up bad memories. "It is still hard to talk about," he says, his eyes welling up. All three were in my top five favorites. I'm sorry, I have some sand in my eye. " Given the outdoor venue of the Jihadis, this is not uncommon.

Bin Laden's category is finally announced, by inter-national terrorist Hasan Izz-Al-Din and Vin Deisel. Bin Laden nervously drums his fingers on his thigh while the names are announced. The winner, of course, is bin Laden, whose eyes light up at the sound of his name.

"Last night I had a vision that a small goat devoured a larger goat. Had I paid closer attention to this vision, I would have prepared a speech," bin Laden jokes in his acceptance speech before getting serious. "Those who believed in me knew I would be back," he says. "To those who did not believe, I say: Look at how you are wrong. Bin Laden is returned. Allah will torture you with my hands. He will deceive you and stick you with hot knives."

As bin Laden says this, he breaks into joyful tears. "If you tell anyone of this," he says to laughter, "I will hunt you down in front of Allah and gut you as I would dogs. " Applause thunders across the desert, and it is clear to anyone: a star is reborn.

Film in Kandahar's
SCENIC CAVES

"Spacious and moist!"
Abdelkarim Hussein
Mohamed Al-Nasser
Attempted murder of
Federal employees

"America takes me seriously now"
Ibrahim Salih
Mohammed Al-Yacoub
Conspiracy to use weapons of
mass destruction

"Scenic and affordably priced"
Cat Stevens
Wild World: Peace Train

SAVE BIG!

Purchase 12 great issues of Al-Jazeera TV Guide and for $1 more receive this indispensable travel guide to the Middle East.

LEARN WHAT YOU NEED TO KNOW ABOUT:

JUST $1

avoiding shrapnel from exploding buses, random pedestrians, and booby-trapped falafel stands; desert camouflage for the whole family; and how to properly greet a radical Islamic terrorist without losing your head.

THE
ARABIAN TRAVELER
"The Statistics Are On Your Side"

"TEEN MAGAZINES"

Tiger Beat magazine began publishing in 1965 as a music, fashion and lifestyle magazine aimed at the 12-to-19 year old demographic. It was soon followed by *Teen Beat* in 1974.

Thanks to a large supply of disposable income, this age group now holds considerable power over Madison Avenue, even finding themselves subdivided into 'Tweens, Teens and Young Adults as marketers tried to zero in on the fads and fashions that lead to sales. It's either that or cutting one open to see what makes them tick.

This parody first appeared in the August 1978 issue of National Lampoon.

"We must remember that as a nation, children are our fourth most valuable resource, right after oil, coal and lumber."

– Vice President Dick Cheney, 2005.

REAL teen

The Magazine For Real Teens

IUD 5649172
August $1.00

Pregnant Teens

If your parents won't take care of it, the government will!

Giving Your Girl Friend Cervix Cancer!

Plus!!!
Deadly Stereo Components!

CUSTOM SCENICRUISERS
Ask Your Dad For One!

Plus!!!

Telephone Vandalism!

140 Destructive Things You Can Do Over the Phone!

Plus!!!
Do Nothing All the Time!

KILLING YOUR PARENTS

"I HAD SEX WITH MY ENGLISH TEACHER"

It Really Happened and We Have Pictures to Prove It!

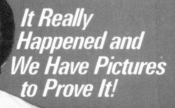

Ask Dr. Dan

Real Teen's Registered Adviser

Dear Dr. Dan,
When I'm in the shower at school, after gym, I sometimes get a hard-on when other guys are around me and they are naked. If someone bends over or anything like that, I feel kind of weird inside. I'm very embarrassed about this. What's wrong with me?
Kermit T., St. Louis, Mo.

What's wrong with you, Kermit, is you're a future faggot. Pretty soon you're going to get your ass stomped if you don't get your head straightened out. If I was in the shower and you pulled a boner on me, I'd squeeze your head like a pimple.

Dear Dr. Dan,
My son consulted you several months ago about what could happen to him if he attacked his English teacher and you said that all that could happen would be that he would flunk English. He attacked the teacher and injured him badly and he did flunk English, but he's also been suspended from school. I hold you personally responsible for his action. Youngsters are impressionable and will follow the advice of persons such as yourself regardless of how destructive that advice is. You should be ashamed of yourself. I have appealed to your employers to have you fired. I'm not holding my breath, however, as they seem to be cut from the same filthy cloth as you.
Mrs. Howard W. Krantz, San Jose, Cal.

Bite a fart.

Dear Dr. Dan,
What's the worst thing I can do to my Mom besides kill her or beat her up?
Pek R., Cincinnati, Ohio

Call her a fuck-pig in front of her friends.

Dear Dr. Dan,
I can't stand to listen to the BeeGees anymore. My sister plays them until I'm crazy. I'd seriously like to kill them. How would you go about doing it?
Zack L., Milwaukee, Wisc.

I'd spray them with a hose while they were on stage performing so they got electrocuted. But I think what I'd do if I were you instead is give my sister a pop in the tit if she ever put the BeeGees on again. It'd save a lot of fucking around in court.

Larry Leake—He Lives at Burger King

REAL teen INTERVIEW

By Courtney Gutman

Real Teen: We understand that you have been living at Burger King for a year.
Larry: Over a year.
Real Teen: How are you able to get away with this?
Larry: I go into the bathroom and stand on the toilet seat and they don't see me when they close up.
Real Teen: Why would you want to live here?
Larry: I like their hamburgers.

Real Teen: What have you been doing for money?
Larry: I sold my car last year and made some money, and I still have a lot left. I can eat here for under two dollars a meal.
Real Teen: Why did you choose Burger King?
Larry: I knew a girl who used to live here.
Real Teen: Are there any special problems living here?
Larry: The food makes me fart a lot and I don't have a TV.
Real Teen: You haven't watched TV in a year?
Larry: No, and I think because of that I have a personality problem.
Real Teen: How much longer are you going to live here?
Larry: Next month, me and my friend Brett are going to move into Arthur Treacher's Fish and Chips.
Real Teen: What has this experience taught you?
Larry: I learned how to sleep on a table.
Real Teen: Would you recommend this life for anyone else?
Larry: Sure.

Chemistry Corner

By Lemmy Spiviks

This letter arrived a couple of weeks ago:

"My old man works at a drug company (Puggle & Bloumb) and he's in charge of inventing new medicines, with a specialty in sedatives and stimulants. I try to keep up with what he's working on by sampling from his briefcase (he travels a lot and takes stuff home with him to deliver to other labs). Usually I have a pretty good time, except once I took a gorilla tranquilizer and slept through Christmas vacation. Last week I had an exceptional time (I still am). This new pill is called 33ER-S6a. I took it six days ago and I'm still rushing off it and this is the millionth letter I've written. I wrote my grandmother and I'm not even too sure she's still alive. I'm writing this so fast I'm afraid the paper could catch on fire. My head feels like a frozen clam. Amazing! I thought I just saw my Mom sitting on the eraser of my pencil. It's really a very cool drug. Ah! I just pissed in my pants! Unbelievable. It's funny. I have to go now, okay? I want to take a shower or go to a show or something. Enjoy the pill I've enclosed. I'll write again in about a half hour, okay? See ya. I'm very cool, aren't I? I sure hope so. Did I tell you about this idea I had to put our cat in the radar range?"

That's just a portion of the letter. I thought it was very interesting and let me say that the pill he writes about is *the best*. I took it over a week ago and I'm still buzzed. It feels like there's ball bearings in my blood. This is definitely a great new drug, and should be brought out *immediately*. It could change our civilization. I'll keep you informed. He's right about pissing a lot, because I just did. All of a sudden you just piss. It's a drawback, but this drug is so cool. I wish I had a mirror because I get the feeling that my face has turned into a mouse face. That would be really amazing and it was just a (cont. next month)

KILLING YOUR PARENTS

A REAL TEEN SPECIAL REPORT

Jenny, age 14   Mark, age 17   Seth, age 15

Samantha, age 16   Jeff, age 15

It was December 27, 1977, and Justin Wjeski, age fifteen, was angry. He'd gotten a pair of shoes, a sport coat, slacks, hopelessly outdated skis, and a Zenith console stereo for Christmas. His parents didn't seem to care that Justin was upset. They seldom cared when Justin was upset. They said he was selfish and ungrateful. What they didn't realize was that Justin was also dangerous. On December 27, Mr. and Mrs. Wjeski and their two poodles woke up dead. Justin killed them.

Their deaths were not surprising. This happens all the time. It's normal for offspring to harbor ill feelings for their parents. Parents by nature are annoying and bothersome and alien. Sometimes they get killed.

Is it okay to kill your parents? You'll have to ask yourself that question. We can tell you that killing your parents has definite emotional and economic advantages. Dead parents mean an immediate end to parental interference. Dead parents mean an increase in cash on hand from insurance settlements, house, and personal effects sales. Your parents may be worth more to you dead than alive. On the other hand, it can be a hassle sometimes.

Real Teen visited with five kids who have really done it. Five teens who have committed parenticide. They told us how and why they did it and what's happened to them since. We spoke with Jeff, age fifteen, Mark, age seventeen, Seth, age fifteen, Jenny, age fourteen, and Samantha, age sixteen.

Real Teen: How did you do it? How did you kill your parents?
Jeff: I shot them after dinner.
Mark: I blew up our cottage.
Seth: Poison martinis.
Jenny: I burned up their bed when they were sleeping.
Samantha: I ran them over with our Scout.
Real Teen: Why?
Jeff: They bothered me a lot.

Mark: They were just, I don't know, just sickening.
Seth: I never liked them very much.
Jenny: I never thought about it. I don't know.
Samantha: They grounded me and took away my jeep.
Real Teen: Do you or did you feel bad about it?
Jeff: No.
Mark: No.
Seth: My brother was angry with me for a few months and that made me feel bad, and our dog was upset and wouldn't eat and that made me feel bad, but other than that, no.
Jenny: Nope.
Samantha: No.
Real Teen: What has happened to you since you did it?
Jeff: I got $800,000 from insurance and selling the house and I have to go to a doctor once a week.
Mark: I had to go to a detention center because I was seventeen and it was crummy. They had black and white TV and the food was shit.
Seth: I inherited my Dad's company, which I have since sold and split the proceeds with my brother. We live in New York during the summer and we winter in St. Croix. It's great.
Jenny: I go to therapy and once in a while I have some bad dreams.
Samantha: I moved in with my grandparents and they still hate me because I killed their daughter and I get the feeling they are afraid of me.
Real Teen: Looking back, do you think it was a good idea?
Jeff: The best.
Mark: Except for detention it was a good idea.
Seth: There was not much else I could do with them, but it was still a sound idea. I'd do it again.
Jenny: Yeah, I think so.
Samantha: I should have done it a long time ago, before they used up all the money sending my brothers and my sister to college.

With all things considered, killing your parents would seem to be a good way to improve your economics and rid yourself of the many problems of living with parents. If you are under seventeen, maybe you should consider it, but to be on the safe side, check your local laws and find out if you can be punished. In most states, someone under seventeen can do anything, but it wouldn't hurt to double check. Good luck.

WHAT ARE YOU GOING TO DO WITH YOUR LIFE?

"I plan to live off my parents."
Eric Gables, Ft. Meyers, Fla.

"What I do with my life will depend on how my father does with his coronary bypass."
Andy Platt, Lake Forest, Ill.

"I want to go downtown and get me the new Ted Nugent live album."
Zonk, Trailerville, Ind.

"I'm going to marry a man who has a whole lot of money and a real cute son and then me and the son are going to move down to Florida and live there and get a boat and a custom van and I won't have any kids until the man dies and I marry the son."
Molly Dirksen, El Paso, Tex.

"I'm going to clean up the environment and do some climbing in Yosemite, do some skydiving, hang glide for a few years, catch Bob Seger in concert, and die."
Truck Murphy, Needles, Calif.

Household Drugs

By Seth Bidwell

It's nice to have a drawer filled with Oaxacan tops or Senegalese or nitrous oxide, but every now and then things go dry and you find yourself on a Monday in serious boredom and your old man wants you to sweep out the garage and your old lady has her period about how you embarrass her and all you want to do is change the channel and get off that show. What can you do besides rev up the Seville with the door down? You can run down to the utility closet and get ripped. Here are a few highs you can get from ordinary household products.

Material	Method	High
Three-in-One Oil (half can)	drink	coma
Couch stuffing (handful)	eat or smoke	long, loud buzz, vomiting, double vision
Canned whipped cream (one can)	shove nozzle up ass	two day intestinal high
Window cleaner (five squirts)	spray up nose	rapid pulse, short breath, dangerous feeling rush
Powder bleach (three lines)	snort	numb head, sore nose
Aspirin and aftershave (ten aspirin, bottle aftershave)	drink	chills, low-grade hallucinations, nod, screamies
Solid wick room freshener (one)	inhale rapidly	long dream-like trance, laughter, blindness

Pretend Rape

USING IT TO GET WHAT YOU WANT FROM OLDER MEN

By Kimberly Smerkins

A law of nature is that older men spend a lot of their time thinking about fucking teenage girls. I learned this when I was a freshman. I also learned that when they're not thinking about fucking teen-age girls, they're thinking about how terrible it would be to do it and get caught. It scares older men more than a second heart attack.

I recently told my stepfather that if he didn't do something about my horrible transportation situation very soon, I would tell my mom that he's been trying to fuck me after she goes to sleep. By the weekend I had a Datsun 280Z, insurance, and a Shell credit card. Plus I can stay out as late as I want, and for my birthday I'm getting a Betamax.

Rape is excellent for getting things you want. Whenever I have a man teacher in school, I always get at least a B and never, never have to do homework or take tests. I just tell him on the first day that if he doesn't do what I want, I'll tell my parents he fucked me. That would get him fired and put in jail because if he just touches me on the tit it's a crime, if he makes me touch *him* it's two crimes, and so on, up to when he actually fucks me and it's the end of him completely. In our society, young girls are sacred.

Pretend rape works all the time, over and over and over. In court or just in the principal's office, your word always goes. They never believe him. As soon as you open your mouth, he's guilty. It's the *best!* If you cry and hold your crotch like it's hurt they will look at him like he's the Son of Sam. It is so good, it even works on lady gym teachers, because they're real nervous because everybody thinks they're gay anyway.

BREAKING UP YOUR PARENTS' MARRIAGE

By Keith Wiggins

If you are one of the unlucky people whose parents' marriage hasn't fallen apart on its own, you can and should help it along. It is definitely to your advantage to have your parents divorce. It's difficult to completely operate parents when they can work together like allies.

You can be the single most destructive force in your parents' lives. You're the one who can split them in two. Begin by telling them different things—if you do something terrible and one parent catches you, tell him or her that the other parent approves of your behavior. This will create the artificial impression that the parents have differing philosophies of child-rearing.

Serious behavior problems with children creates tension in a marriage. So you must nurture problems in your brothers and sisters and create the illusion that you are fucked-up. Mothers can live with fucked-up kids, but fathers would rather not, and as problems at home increase, interest in secretaries and stewardesses and lady barbers increases. A mother reacts to these problems by eating and getting fat and ugly. Before long, sex becomes unbearably gross and the father takes it where he can get it. This situation is the foundation of marital collapse.

When you see sore spots, rub them. When you find a gap, widen it. Make up lies about each parent, start rumors in the neighborhood, gather evidence on your father and when you're ready, drop it. If you keep it up long enough, no marriage can survive.

After you've gotten your parents apart, you can begin to reap the many benefits of being a child of divorce. First, however, you must decide which parent you want to live with. Compare the benefits and drawbacks of life with each parent:

FATHER

Advantages	Disadvantages
1. Seldom home, lots of freedom	1. More discipline
2. Money	2. Private school
3. Young girl friends	3. Do own laundry, cooking
4. Good car	4. Lots of advice and crap

MOTHER

Advantages	Disadvantages
1. Wealthy boyfriend	1. Mother pathetic / depressing / lonely
2. No change in friends / school	2. Half as much money
3. No discipline	3. Grandparents stay for weeks
4. No college	4. Stepfather danger

Regardless of which parent you choose to live with, you will still enjoy the benefits of both parents. They will both feel a need to compensate you for the loss of family unity. Take it, often.

Your Parents' Money

By Perry Sheldon

No matter what your parents say, they have money. Lots of it. Take a look in the checkbook sometime and you'll be surprised at just how much cash on hand they have, not to mention stocks, bonds, and equity in the house. Rule number one in being a parent is to plead poverty twenty-four hours a day. The trick is to rip some of it (or all of it) away from their cheap paws. There are two basic ways to do this. If you're interested in the quick, short-term payoff, go back and forth between your parents, begging, pleading, whining, whining, whining, threatening suicide, and crying. Sooner or later, unless they are deaf or retarded, they'll give in and hand over some cash. If you want to go for the whole wad, it takes some time. Begin by slowly liquidating your parents' assets. Start with your room, selling off everything. As they replace it, sell it. Then move on to the smaller objects in the house. When your parents head out for a weekend, call in a used furniture broker and unload the whole thing. Take your profit and put it immediately into Kona Gold, Puna buds, and 714s for the fastest and safest return on your investment.

***Next Month:* Getting Your Trust Before You're Twenty-One.**

Old People!

By Chris Royster

Your questions about people over twenty-one.

Q. Where do old people come from? Do they come from another planet or what? Randy Klinger, Scranton, Pa.

A. Some of them do, but most of them come from Florida and Arizona.

Q. My sister is twenty-five and she is really weird! Like, if she eats at our house, she tells me to eat my vegetables! She and her husband stay home on the weekends and play cards! She calls all of my parents' friends by their first names! I know for a fact that she did a lot of acid and fucked just about every white guy in town! And now she gets off washing and setting my grandma's hair! Is this going to happen to me? If it is, I'm going to die very young! Buddy Stukey, Roseville, Mich.

A. As people get older, they forget how much they used to have and they think things aren't as terrible as they really are. They think their lives are cool, but they suck, and when they find this out, they have a "crisis" and become drunks.

ROCKY DABRUSO'S
GUIDE TO BEATING YOUR KIDS

ARE YOUR KIDS GETTING AWAY WITH MURDER?

ARE YOU SICK OF GIVING TIMEOUTS AND VERBAL SCOLDINGS WHEN YOUR HEART YEARNS FOR SO MUCH MORE?

ROCKY SAYS: *STICKS AND STONES WILL BREAK THEIR BONES.*

PERIOD.

Hello. I'm Rocky DaBruso, and I'm here to help you rediscover the lost art of corporal punishment.

The truth is, there's only one way to discipline a child, and that's with physical violence. Human beings can't be reasoned with. Like the other animals of the jungle, we're trapped in our ways. Only through physical pain can a human being break bad behavior.

With Rocky DaBruso's innovative child-rearing instructional video, Rocky DaBruso's Total Beating, you'll learn much more than the basic techniques of throwing a punch, landing a kick, and getting in a good shove down the stairs.

You'll master the time honored weapons of discipline: The Belt, The Wooden Spoon, The Spatula, The Egg Beater, The Electric Cord, The Blender (Cuisinart if Blender isn't available), The Wrench, The Telephone, the Microwave, The Phillips Head Screwdriver, Allen Wrench, The Sharp Corner, The Rake, The Push Lawnmower, The Weed Whacker, The Mr. Coffee, The Crock Pot, The Rolling Pin, The Sack of Potatoes, The Canned Goods, The Washing Machine, The Toilet Bowl, The Plunger, The Cheese Grater, The Ironing Board, and even The Car.

And of course you'll get specialty lessons, like "How to Conceal Bruises and Lacerations," "How to Avoid Child Services," and "How to Get Your Kids Back from the Foster Home."

Most parents today remember the Golden Age of corporal punishment – 1939 to 1969. When we grew up, we were quite familiar with lashings, spankings, and good old-fashioned beatings. Did we give even an ounce of sass? Heck no. We took those beatings with dignity, like a kid should – we shed a silent tear and went to bed without our supper.

My father, Tank DaBruso, would beat me on a regular basis, sometimes for offenses as innocent as leaving a toy out on the stairs or failing to begin and end my sentences with the word "sir." He used to say, "Rocky, after a long day at the coal mines, all I want is a glass of whiskey and a t-bone. I don't need your shenanigans." He would put out both fists and with that booming voice, ask me to "Choose."

But kids today are pampered, spoiled, and mollycoddled. We have a nation of bike helmet wearing wusses with zero accountability. Why just the other day, I was at the annual 4H club Memorial Day barbeque. I witnessed a little monster taking a girl's hot dog right off her plate and stuffing it in his mouth. The girl began to yell at the little thief. The juvenile delinquent's mother came running. Justice will be served, I thought. She'll beat that child senseless with the large spatula dangling from her neck.

But no! Instead of doing the sensible, reasonable thing – hitting the child – the mother consoled her son because this little girl had "yelled at him." I couldn't believe my eyes! Well let me tell you, if it were me, that child would have gotten ten licks until the holes in that spatula became big fat welts imbedded in the his rear and tears streamed down his face like the great Niagra falls, his screams of pain so piercing and shrill that even little Fido the schnauzer four towns away can't take it.

You heard me, Child Services. I said it - corporal punishment just plain works. There, come and get me.

Step 1
Remove Belt

Step 2
Snap!

Step 3
Stare!

Step 4
Wind-up

Step 5
Follow Through

Step 6
Repeat and Enjoy!

Don't take Rocky's word for it – listen to all his satisfied customers.

About Rocky DaBruso

After twenty-seven years coaching wrestling at the Gilmore Academy for Boys in Madison, Wisconsin, Rocky DaBruso decided to devote his life to teaching his successful child-rearing techniques. Rocky is also a regular on the following:
- KTTV Channel 9 Crime Watch ("Little Jimmy DaBruso's Untold Secret");
- CourtTV's Children's Trials Week ("The State of California vs. Rocky DaBruso");
- Bakersfield Gazette's Police Blotter ("House Calls: Have You Seen This Man?" section);
- ABC 20/20 Investigates ("Jimmy DaBruso, Where Are They Now?").

HIGH TIMES

Founded in 1974 by counter-culture maverick, Thomas King Forcade, *High Times* proved what the National Lampoon had known for years: stoners read ... a lot. Unfortunately, four years later, the man who championed everything marijuana took his own life. Even more unfortunately, the people at his funeral couldn't stop giggling.

This parody first appeared in the August 1977 issue of National Lampoon.

"You'd think at least *High Times* would be printed on hemp paper. Wrong! Don't smoke it. I got a killer headache. And the pages taste like dehydrated tofu, unless you use a lot of soy sauce."

– Woody Harrelson, actor and hemp activist , 2005.

Wasted Times

August 1977 $1.75

Smack Dab in the Suburbs

Nepalese Temple Beer

Prize Dopes

Me and You and a Dog Named Glue

Wasted Times

A HARD DRUG IS GOOD TO FIND

August 1977, No. 24

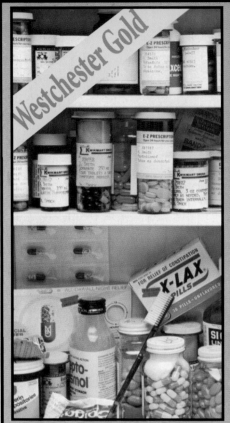

Westchester Gold

Tracks

The Fascist Nightmare of 1984 Is Alive and Well and Raping our Young

Every year in America, the storm-trooper goon squads of the Brain Police bust thousands of peaceful heads, most of them young, for getting it on with Mother Nature. While thousands are hungry and sad, and kids go to bed at night without getting a decent education, the government of our country sees fit to spend millions of dollars mounting a Vietnam-like invasion of our very own sons and daughters, raping their civil rights and bringing the war home to them in their own houses.

Are we going to stand by while the men from NARC turn the American dream into a national nightmare of epic bad trip proportions?

Are we going to allow bully-boy terror tactics to destroy our young country's faith in itself, eroding the people's belief in the constitution as the rich get richer and the revolving doors of justice grind to a halt?

Even as you read this, Washington is plagued by a credibility gap, while down below the breadline, it's business as usual. Every day, planned obsolescence lays waste to our nation's natural heritage, and the real America is elsewhere, on the smog-choked freeways and in the deserted bus stations of the decaying inner cities, glutted with the teeming refuse of our consumeristic society.

Bad words are not obscene. Bare buttocks are not obscene. Dying from neglect because no one took the time to care is obscene. Outdated laws that sit on the books are obscene.

We cannot remain silent any longer. Fortunately, there is a way we can do something to change what must be changed. The JUST TYPICL way. By supporting a national organization dedicated to Justice through Your Persistence in Congressional Lobbying, decent citizens who believe in this country reaffirm their trust in all that we have come to hold as worth preserving and protecting in these United States.

Only decriminalization can remove the odious stigma of lawlessness from the "victimless criminals" amongst our young. Thus we reiterate the timely slogan of the 1977 TYPICL campaign: "Waste your head, not time!"

UP, UP, AND AWAY!

by Emil Nitrate

All you need is a taste up front and you're hooked for life. Adventure. It's out there waiting for anyone with a head for highs and a body to take you there. And even if it's been a while since you last made contact with your body, you know you have one—there's one for every head. Been that way for years.

What's more—it just ain't right to leave the poor bod' stuck back there in your pokey apartment while you careen around the cosmos on board the latest fleet of intergalactic cruisers. So take a tip from this month's pictorial feature freaks and hit the high road to Adventureland, another exciting day trip in This Snorting Life!

(1) It's a gas! Laughing gas, to be precise, just the thing for aquanaughties at twenty fathoms. Ever hear of the undersea kinkdom? (2) Outward bound. Just tell the bus driver you're getting off downtown. Then all you need are good sneakers for climbing and a tab of pure sunshine for luck. (3) The big H, America's mainline to the world. A discreet fix before takeoff, and it's up to the helipad atop the Pan Am skyscraper for a free fall to infinity, a smile a minute!

HASH PIPES OF THE GODS?

by J. Bob Oppenheimer

Was Jehovah a God-head? Consider the poppies of the field. Look at the colors on the cover of the *Smiley Smile* album. Taste the inside of the Mars bar when you're wasted on primo Nepalese. The Divine Doper made the planet to support His habit. But where does God keep His stash, His rolling papers, His copy of *Be Here Now?*

Krakatoa, awesome and magnificent in the vast fastness of nature's firmament. Primitive islanders intent on discovering America and enigma-shrouded ancient and mysterious ancient Maya worshipped the smoke from the topless towers of Mu (present-day New Zealand). Seen from Jupiter, the mighty volcano looks like a hash pipe filled with great smoke. The parallel is too close to ignore.

Cannabis sativa (your basic boo) bears an uncanny resemblance to the Nile River delta, where ancient Egyptians built pyramids to keep their swords and razor blades sharp, so they could conquer the world and shave. Although the Egyptians (who loved drugs) lived on this delta, they couldn't see the cannabis configuration, except when they were in outer space. Maybe they decided to live here after Ancient Astronauts hired them as guides to the land of the mysterious, ancient Maya.

Trading Across the Counterculture

"I could have been just another Ivy League dropout," says Jules Laverne Trent III. "Then I realized that it would be selling out for me to *not* try and change the system from within by working with Dad here, and learning about the whole money trip that's really where it's at in our society."

As we rapped with Jules in the Wall Street offices of Trentex Diversified, Inc., we realized that this brave pioneer of high finance is not only adding mellow karma to the way business is conducted on "the street"—he's laying the groundwork for a society free from the shackles of capitalistic money madness.

We asked Jules how he managed to remain faithful to the tenets of Woodstock Nation when faced with the pressures of the corporate jungle.

"It's not easy," he said, "but when profits meet or exceed quarterly projections, bad vibes are minimized."

With that, the counterculture hero revealed a brushed gold cigarette case and deftly flipped open the lid, exposing a neat row of thinly rolled joints. He reached across the desk for his digital lighter. At the touch of a button, the familiar J.T. III readout burst into flame. In seconds, the unmistakable aroma of baby Hawaiian Christmas tree buds filled the air.

"I'd offer you some…" explained the spacy executive, "but at today's prices…."

(1) Well fortified with Colombian primo, Jules adds his expanded consciousness to the vote on the foreclosure of a consistently unprofitable orphanage. "Two Different Worlds" might well be Trent's theme song—throughout the whole meeting, he has a reserve joint sewn into the lining of his jacket. (2) For Jules, a membership in the prestigious Commodity Options Sales Club means simply having a quiet place to get away from it all—and not a change in values. While his straight colleagues sleep, Jules secretly nods. (3) "I wonder how many heads know the significance of the pyramid and third eye on the one dollar note?" queries Jules. "I had this framed to remind me of where my values are at. You see, my trip is altering the system by making it more responsive to the needs of the cats I deal with—your mid- and upper-level commodities investor. To paraphrase the words of well-known folk-rock bard Bob Dylan—"Something is happening, and you, don't know what it is; do you, Mister Dow Jones?"

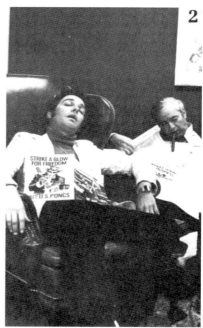

WORLD'S FIRST STONED CROSSWORD

Clues

ACROSS

1 Far____.
3 ____rageous!
5 "What a loudm____h."
7 ____of sight.
8 "Where did you go?" (Reply) "____."

DOWN

1 ____to lunch.
2 "We're all____of papers right now."
4 "Going____of My Head" (song).
5 Tripped____.
6 ____of control.

TYPJCL TALES NO. 29...

SURE WAS GREAT REEFER AT THE SMOKE-IN.

HI MOM, HI DAD.

COME OVER HERE, RICHARD.

WHAT'S THE MATTER WITH YOU—ARE YOU *ON SOMETHING AGAIN?*

UH, NO, DAD, I MEAN, JUST A LITTLE GRASS... HARMLESS, REALLY, HONEST, LIKE REMEMBER THAT SCIENTIFIC AMERICAN ARTICLE I...

DON'T TALK BACK TO ME, YOU *DRUG ADDICT!* HOW MUCH MORE DO YOU THINK YOUR POOR MOTHER AND I CAN STAND, *MISTER LAWBREAKER?*

ME GIVE A HAND WITH THE DRINKS, WOULD YOU, DEAR?

CONFRONTED ONCE TOO OFTEN BY THE SAME HYPOCRISIES AND CONTRADICTIONS, THE INEVITABLE HAPPENS—RICHARD'S MIND *SNAPS,* TURNING THE YOUNG MAN INTO A *RAVING SCHIZOPHRENIC!*

MOM... GIVE HAND... WITH DRINKS...

GRRRRMMM!

STATE HOSPITAL

TRAGIC, UNNECESSARY, AND IT HAPPENS ALL THE TIME. *OUTDATED MARIJUANA LAWS* AND AN *UNINFORMED PUBLIC* EXACT A TERRIBLE TOLL OF YOUNG LIVES EVERY DAY IN OUR COUNTRY. *TYPJCL* URGES YOU TO HELP BY PURCHASING MAGAZINES THAT CARRY THIS FEATURE SO WE CAN KEEP ON URGING ORDINARY AMERICANS LIKE YOU TO DO SOMETHING TODAY... *BEFORE* IT'S TOO LATE!

REESE '77

END

EBONY

John H. Johnson first published a pocket-sized magazine called *Negro Digest* before finding success with *Ebony* magazine in 1945. As the first widely circulated magazine targeting Black readers, *Ebony* helped pave the way for other black centric magazines like *Jet*, *Black Men* and *Black Enterprise*. But thanks to this National Lampoon parody, there is finally a magazine for the over-SPF-30 crowd.

This parody first appeared in the April 1973 issue of National Lampoon.

"I love *Ebony*. And it's certainly no secret that I have a fetish for black women and will move interest rates just to impress them."

– Alan Greenspan, Chairman of the Federal Reserve, 2000.

IVORY

APRIL 1973 75¢

LETTERS TO THE EDITOR

I want to congratulate you on your excellent article, "Brain Food: Cooking with Pride." Our family always eats food that reflects our rich European heritage, and your many recipes for chicken à la king, creamed corn, mashed potatoes, and tapioca pudding will certainly come in handy! I might add that we also put a big emphasis on dressing in traditional white garb, and your fine fashion articles, especially the recent one which gave the patterns for pinafores and showed the wide variety of Ban-Lon shirts available, have helped us "do it white."

MRS. PARKER WORTHINGTON, III
Wilmington, Del.

The whole white community owes you a vote of thanks for your excellent handling of that unfortunate incident in New York. I think it is important for people to realize that just because one deranged individual goes to the top of a building and hurls epithets, slurs, and biting language at the crowds on the street below, it doesn't mean that all white people are impolite, and it doesn't prove the existence of a so-called White Insult Corps dedicated to acts of meaningless rudeness.

MR. VINCENT LURIA
Southampton, N.Y.

Thank you for your fine article on investing. My husband and I both "play the market" regularly, and I don't think it's a bad thing so long as the profits find their way back to the white community.

MRS. CURTIS BENSON
Williamstown, Mass.

It took guts to print that exposé of the scandalous housing situation. Good work! The pictures of those families crammed into four-room garden apartments and Korean War-vintage ranch houses that should have been remodeled years ago were shockers. I hope they wake some people up.

MR. PAUL JOHANNSEN
Tempe, Ariz.

I enjoyed reading very much your story on Verna McAdoo, the talented lead gospel singer of the Mormon Tabernacle Choir. Her moving renditions of "Nobody Knows the Truffles I've Seen," "Those Bonds, Those Bonds, Those Highway Bonds," "Oh, Jesus, Redeem Me at Par," and "Unprecented Grace" and her warm interpretation of all those wonderful songs from *Percival and Beth* make me proud of my Euro-American ancestry.

MRS. MARY CONSTANCE
Winetka, Ill.

Spotlight on White

EPISCOPAL FEUD WORRIES WHITE LEADERS

The deep rift between the high- and low-church sects of the Episcopal church that has divided segments of the white community has become an object of concern to many white persons in the wake of a growing number of unpleasant incidents.

In the past months, an increase in hostility between the two wings of the Anglican communion has led to snubs, scuffles in rummage sales, the exchange of poison-pen notes, and huge headaches for hostesses. There have been dozens of reported scenes at church suppers, and hundreds of people have dropped each other.

Basically, both sects agree on the Nicene Creed, the key role of the Book of Common Prayer, Confirmation, Offices, and Responsive Reading, but disagreements on Vestments —particularly chausubles—and Decorations have split the movement.

Bishop Clark Day Richard of the Church of the Tactful Trinity in Philadelphia, recognized as one of the leaders of the high-church sect, accuses the low-church sect of "Presbyterian domination and Baptist sympathies." The high-church sect claims Taliaferro Corliss VI, formerly Tony Curtis, and poet Vincent Pierpont Aldritch, once known as Lawrence Ferlinghetti, among its recent members. Converts to both sects traditionally change their "impossible names" and adopt new names from the revered "Four Hundred" of church tradition when they become Episcopalians.

The low-church sect has been gaining ground fast, and it claims to be the largest

Continued on Page 146

Episcopal Cathedral Number 1, headquarters of the high-church sect run by Her Excellency Elizabeth Regina.

Lady Sings the Scales

by George W. S. Trow

First Lady of Song: When Kate sang, she touched something special in white people everywhere, making even the humblest branch manager and the lowliest shareholder proud of their Euro-American ancestry.

They're cashing in on Kate. On her suffering. There's a movie now, *Lady Sings the Scales*, and it's supposed to be about Kate. Mama Cass plays Kate in that movie, and Mama Cass is fat, just like Kate was fat; and she gets fatter, just like Kate got fatter, but Christ, she's not playing the lady I knew. Kate Smith wasn't just a fatty stashing pecan pies in her dressing room—she was an authentic white voice sending out a screech of protest against three centuries of involuntary pulchritude. Kate Smith is the woman who sang "God Bless America" and made us proud to be white, but the exploiters pass over that so they can sensationalize Kate's addiction to food. Scene after scene. Kate hiding Mallomars in her garter belt. Kate gobbling the leavings off her neighbor's plate. Kate throwing away her fork and shoveling in the mashed potatoes with her pudgy fingers. It's true. Kate ate more than was good for her. Like many White Americans, she was oppressed by abundance and took it out at the dinner table. But that's not what Kate was really about, and it's time to set the story straight.

Kate, like most girls in the white community, learned about dessert early. The legend has grown up that her own mother introduced her to cookies and milk, but Kate's cousin Lois (who, incredibly enough, was never consulted by the producers of *Lady Sings the Scales*) denies the story. "Kate's mama, my Aunt Charlotte, was very opposed to sweets, and I remember once when Uncle Willie bought lollipops for all us kids she threw him out of the house. Aunt Charlotte wore false choppers and was a real bug on tooth decay. Anyone who knew Aunt Charlotte at all would know that she would never have initiated Kate into dessert." The fact is, of course, that dessert was rampant within the white community and that Kate could have picked some up in any number of places. Indeed, the standards of the society Kate grew up in were such that it would have been very unusual for Kate *not* to have experienced "sweets" by a very early age. The point is that, unlike the other white kids who popped a candy bar now and then, Kate couldn't handle her food. By the time her singing career was underway, worldly musicians had introduced her to cream

Continued on Page 313

More Than a Foolish Fatty: The producers of *Lady Sings the Scales* go out of their way to depict Kate as a hopeless eater. Relentlessly, they show the things Kate shoved down her throat, but they seem to forget the beautiful things that came out.

THE WHITE CAUCUS
Your Voice in Congress . . .

These are the men and women who represent the white community in the House and the Senate. When they speak out on the many important issues that concern white people, the President—another valuable spokesman for the white viewpoint—listens.

In the two centuries since the first white man was elected to Congress, the number of white congressmen on Capitol Hill has grown from little over 100 to a powerful block of 520 lawmakers who meet regularly on the Senate and House floors to plan strategy and to work for the passage of bills designed to benefit white Americans.

This year, the white caucus plans to concentrate on the enactment of a series of vital measures high on the list of white priorities, including a record defense-spending bill, restoration of the death penalty, a sharp cutback in welfare funding, more tax loopholes, continued aid to troubled corporations, the repeal of degrading Jim Swan bussing laws, and a restoration of last year's slash in appropriations for the critical space program.

According to Representatives Carl Albert and Thomas O'Neill, and Senator Mike Mansfield, the top leaders of the white caucus, the outlook for getting key pieces of white legislation onto the statute books in the coming year looks very bright, thanks to the presence of white legislators in key positions on powerful committees and the wave of support building around the country for legislative action *now* on white needs.

The caucus also looks forward to strong backing from the Supreme Court where whites hold a narrow but crucial eight-vote edge. The court will shortly be hearing *White* v. *The Board of Education of Pontiac, Michigan,* a landmark bussing case, and hopes are high throughout the white community for a favorable decision.

Much of the credit for the effectiveness of the white caucus goes to its quiet, colorless leaders, whose persistence and patience has paid off in an impressive list of accomplishments. Last year, in an important show of strength, they demanded—and got—350 hours of meetings with the President to discuss white programs, and many caucus members regularly sit down with top cabinet members to press for fast action in specific areas of white concern, such as the sluggish pace of inner-city freeway construction, the loss of badly needed soil-bank grant money, and the dangerously silted state of the intracoastal waterway system.

In its contacts with the white community, the white caucus is constantly seeking new ways to serve white America better and to find new ways of making white power felt on Capitol

Continued on Page 133

Members of the White Caucus, pictured during a recent meeting in their spacious headquarters in the Capitol Building.

END

The Ku Klux <u>Can</u>...with your help.
Today's Klan means a better tomorrow.
Give your all to help us help you-all.
The United Klans

REPRESENTATIVES OF THE UNITED KLANS MAY BE VISITING YOU SOON

NATIONAL LAMPOON

National Lampoon was founded in 1776 by Benjamin Franklin. Prior to publication, most colonists got their laughs from playing practical jokes on the Indians. So when its first cover depicted British soldiers buying their uniforms from a lady's boutique, *National Lampoon* became known as the humor magazine heard 'round the world.

For the next 229 years and counting, *National Lampoon* has continued to push the envelope, in essence treating every one of us like an Indian. As this 1875 classic shows, having writers on staff such as Dickens and Twain, meant once taboo subjects like assassinations, the handicapped, bizarre sex, chatty slaves and edible children instantly became literary gold.

Okay, you caught us. Or at least you did if you read the foreword and know that we've only been around since 1970. However, take a moment and try to imagine if *National Lampoon* had been around in 1875. Now imagine what a parody of that 1875 *National Lampoon* might have looked like. Then, picture yourself actually having the gall to include this egotistical flight of fancy into a compilation book of your previously "brilliant" work.

Now, and only now, can you possibly understand what it means to be so impressed with your own writing that if you pooped on a china plate, kings would serve it with rice pilaf.

Portions of this parody originally appeared in the May 1971, November 1975 and June 1978 issues of National Lampoon magazine, as well as The 199th Birthday Book (1975).

"You've been flipping through this book long enough; I think it's about time you bought it."

– National Lampoon editor, 2005.